BEHIND THE FOOTLIGHTS

BEHIND THE FOOTLIGHTS

MRS. ALEC-TWEEDIE

ISBN: 978-93-5420-751-8

Published: 1904

LECTOR HOUSE LLP
E-MAIL: lectorpublishing@gmail.com

Miss Constance Collier as Pallas Athene in "Ulysses."

From a Sketch by Percy Anderson.

Frontispiece.

BEHIND THE FOOTLIGHTS

BY

MRS. ALEC-TWEEDIE

AUTHOR OF
"MEXICO AS I SAW IT," "GEORGE HARLEY, F.R.S.," ETC.

WITH TWENTY ILLUSTRATIONS

1904

CONTENTS

CHAPTER IV
PLAYS AND PLAYWRIGHTS

CHAPTER V
THE ARMY AND THE STAGE

CHAPTER VI
DESIGNING THE DRESSES

CHAPTER VII
SUPPER ON THE STAGE

CHAPTER VIII

MADAME SARAH BERNHARDT

CHAPTER IX

AN HISTORICAL FIRST NIGHT

CHAPTER X

OPERA COMIC

CHAPTER XI

THE FIRST PANTOMIME REHEARSAL

CHAPTER XII

SIR HENRY IRVING AND STAGE LIGHTING

CHAPTER XIII

WHY A NOVELIST BECOMES A DRAMATIST

CHAPTER XIV

SCENE-PAINTING AND CHOOSING A PLAY

CHAPTER XV

THEATRICAL DRESSING-ROOMS

CHAPTER XVI

HOW DOES A MAN GET ON THE STAGE?

CHAPTER XVII

A GIRL IN THE PROVINCES

CHAPTER XVIII

PERILS OF THE STAGE

CHAPTER XIX

"CHORUS GIRL NUMBER II. ON THE LEFT"

A Fantasy Founded on Fact

LIST OF ILLUSTRATIONS

BEHIND THE FOOTLIGHTS

CHAPTER I

THE GLAMOUR OF THE STAGE

Girlish Dreams of Success—Golden Glitter—Overcrowding—Few successful—Weedon Grossmith—Beerbohm Tree—How Mrs. Tree made Thousands for the War Fund—The Stage Door reached—Glamour fades—The Divorce Court and the Theatre— Childish Enthusiasm—Old Scotch Body's Horror—Love Letters—Temptations—Emotions—How Women began to Act under Charles I.—Influence of the Theatre for Good or Ill.

"I WANT to go on the stage," declared a girl as she sat one day opposite her father, a London physician, in his consulting-room.

The doctor looked up, amazed, deliberately put down his pen, cast a scrutinising glance at his daughter, then said tentatively:

"Want to go on the stage, eh?"

"Yes, I wish to be an actress. I have had an offer—oh, such a delightful offer— to play a girl's part in the forthcoming production at one of our best theatres."

Her father made no comment, only looked again steadily at the girl in order to satisfy himself that she was speaking seriously. Then he took the letter she held out, read it most carefully, folded it up—in what the would-be actress thought an exasperatingly slow fashion—and after a pause observed:

"So this is the result of allowing you to play in private theatricals. What folly!"

The girl started up—fire flashed from her eyes, and her lips trembled as she retorted passionately:

"I don't see any folly, I only see a great career opening before me. I want to go on the stage and make a name."

The doctor looked more grave than ever, but replied calmly:

"You are very young—you have only just been to your first ball; you know nothing whatever about the world or work."

"But I can learn, and intend to do so."

"Ah yes, that is all very well; but what you really see at this moment is only the prospect of so many guineas a week, of applause and admiration, of notices in the papers, when at one jump you expect to gain the position already attained by some great actress. What you do *not* see, however, is the hard work, the dreary months, nay years, of waiting, the many disappointments that precede success—you do not realise the struggle of it all, or the many, many failures."

She looked amazed. What possible struggle could there be on the stage? she wondered.

"Is this to be the end of my having worked for you," he asked pathetically, "planned for you, given you the best education I could, done everything possible to make your surroundings happy, that at the moment when I hoped you were going to prove a companion and a comfort, you announce the fact that you wish to choose a career for yourself, to throw off the ties—I will not call them the pleasures—of home, and seek work which it is not necessary for you to undertake?"

"Yes," murmured the girl, by this time almost sobbing, for the glamour seemed to be rolling away like mist before her eyes, while glorious visions of tragedy queens and comic soubrettes faded into space.

"I will not forbid you," he went on sadly but firmly—"I will not forbid you, after you are twenty-one, for then you can do as you like; but nearly four years stretch between now and then, and during those four years I shall withhold my sanction."

Tears welled up into her eyes. Moments come in the lives of all of us when our nearest and dearest appear to understand us least. Even in our youth we experience unreasoning sadness.

"I do not wish," he continued, rising and patting her kindly on the back, "to see my daughter worn to a skeleton, working when she should be enjoying herself, taking upon her shoulders cares and worries which I have striven for years to avert—therefore I must save you from yourself. During the next four years I will try to show you what going on the stage really means, and the labour it entails."

She did not answer, exultation had given place to indignation, indignation to emotion, and the aspirant to histrionic fame felt sick at heart.

That girl was the present writer—her father the late Dr. George Harley, F.R.S., of Harley Street.

During those four years he showed me the work and anxiety connection with the stage involves, and as it was not necessary for me to earn my living at that time, I waited his pleasure, and, finally, of my own free will abandoned the girlish determination of becoming an actress. Wild dreams of glory and success eventually gave place to more rational ideas. The glamour of the footlights ceased to shine so alluringly—as I realised that the actor's art, like the musician's, is ephemeral, while the work and anxiety are great in both.

The restlessness of youth was upon me when I mooted the project, and an injudicious word then would have sent me forth at a tangent, probably to fail as many another has done before and since.

There may still be a few youthful people in the world who believe the streets of London are paved with gold—and there are certainly numbers of boys and girls who think the stage is strewn with pearls and diamonds. All the traditions of the theatre are founded in mystery and exaggeration; perhaps it is as well, for too much realism destroys illusion.

Boys and girls dream great dreams—they fancy themselves leading actors and actresses, in imagination they dine off gold, wear jewels, laces, and furs, hear the applause of the multitude—and are happy. But all this, as said, is in their dreams, and dreams only last for seconds, while life lasts for years.

One in perhaps a thousand aspirants ever climbs to the top of the dramatic ladder, dozens remain struggling on the lower rung, while hundreds fall out weary and heart-sore before passing even the first step. Never has the theatrical profession been more overcrowded than at the present moment.

Many people with a wild desire to act prove failures on the stage, their inclinations are greater than their powers. Rarely is it the other way; nevertheless Fanny Kemble, in spite of her talent, hated the idea of going on the stage. At that time acting was considered barely respectable for a woman (1829). She was related to Sarah Siddons and John Kemble, a daughter of Charles and Fanny Kemble, and yet no dramatic fire burned in her veins. She was short and plain, with large feet and hands, her only charm her vivacity and expression. Ruin was imminent in the family when the girl was prevailed upon after much persuasion to play Juliet. Three weeks later she electrified London. Neither time nor success altered her repugnance for the stage, however. When dressed as Juliet her white satin train lying over the chair, she recalled the scene in the following words:

"There I sat, ready for execution, with the palms of my hands pressed convulsively together, and the tears I in vain endeavoured to repress welling up into my eyes, brimming slowly over, down my rouged cheeks."

There is a well-known actor upon the stage to-day who feels much as Fanny Kemble did.

"I hate it all," he once said to me. "Would to Heaven I had another profession at my back. But I never really completed any studies in my youth, and in these days of keen competition I dare not leave an income on the stage for an uncertainty elsewhere."

To some people the stage is an alluring goal, religion is a recreation, while to others money is a worship. The Church and the Stage cast their fascinating meshes around most folk some time during the course of their existences. It is scarcely strange that such should be the case, for both hold their mystery, both have their excitements, and man delights to rush into what he does not understand—this has been the case at all times and in all countries, and, like love and war, seems likely to continue to the end of time.

We all know the stage as seen from before the footlights—we have all sat breathless, waiting for the curtain to rise, and there are some who have longed for the "back cloth" to be lifted also, that they might peep behind. In these pages all hindrances shall be drawn away, and the theatre and its workings revealed from behind the footlights.

As every theatre has its own individuality, so every face has its own expression, therefore one can only generalise, for it is impossible to treat each theatrical house and its customs separately.

The strong personal interest I have always felt for the stage probably originated in the fact that from childhood I had heard stories of James Sheridan Knowles writing some of his plays, notably *The Hunchback*, at my grandfather's house, Seaforth Hall, in Lancashire. Charles Dickens often stayed there when acting for some charity in Liverpool. Samuel Lover was a constant visitor at the house, as also the great American tragedian, Charlotte Cushman. Her beautiful sister Susan (the Juliet of her Romeo) married my uncle, Sheridan Muspratt, author of the *Dictionary of Chemistry*. From all of which it will be seen that theatrical stories were constantly retailed at home; therefore when I was about to "come out," and my father asked if I would like a ball, I replied:

"No, I should prefer private theatricals."

This was a surprise to the London physician; but there being no particular sin in private theatricals, consent was given, "*provided*," as he said, "*you paint the scenery, make your own dresses, generally run the show, and do the thing properly.*"

A wise proviso, and one faithfully complied with. It gave an enormous amount of work but brought me a vast amount of pleasure.

Mr. L. F. Austin, a clever contributor to the *Illustrated London News*, wrote a most amusing account of those theatricals—in which he, Mr. Weedon Grossmith, and Mrs. Beerbohm Tree assisted—in his little volume *At Random*. Sir William Magnay, then a well-known amateur, and now a novelist, was one of our tiny company. *Sweethearts*, Mr. W. S. Gilbert's delightful little comedy, was chosen for the performance, but at the last moment the girl who should have played the maid was taken ill. Off to Queen's College, where I was then a pupil, I rushed, dragged Maud Holt—who became Mrs Tree a few weeks later—back with me, and that same night she made her first appearance on any stage. Very shortly afterwards Mrs. Beerbohm Tree adopted acting as a profession, and appeared first at the Court Theatre. Subsequently, when her husband became a manager, she joined his company for many years.

We all adored her at College: she was tall and graceful, with a beautiful figure: she sang charmingly, and read voraciously. In those days she was a great disciple of Browning, and so was Mr. Tree; in fact, the poet was the leading-string to love and matrimony.

Mrs. Beerbohm Tree considers that almost the happiest moments of her life were spent in reciting *The Absent-minded Beggar* for the War Fund. It came about in this wise. She had arranged to give a recitation at St. James's Hall on one particular Wednesday. On the Friday before that day she saw announced in the *Daily Mail* that a new poem by Rudyard Kipling on the Transvaal war theme would appear in the Tuesday issue. This she thought would be a splendid opportunity to declaim a topical song at the concert, so she wrote personally to the editor of the paper, and asked him if he could possibly let her have an advance copy of the poem, so that she might learn and recite it on Wednesday, as the Tuesday issue would be too late for her purpose.

Through the courtesy of Mr. Harmsworth she received the proof of *The Absent-minded Beggar* on Friday evening, and sitting in her dining-room in Sloane Street with her elbows on the table she read and re-read it several times. This, she thought, might bring grist to the war mill. Into a hansom she jumped, and off to the Palace Theatre she drove, boldly asking for the manager. Her name was sufficient, and she was ushered into the august presence.

"This is a remarkable poem," she said, "by Mr. Rudyard Kipling, so remarkable that I think if recited in your Hall nightly it would bring some money to the fund, and if you will give me £100 a week——"

Up went the manager's hand in horror.

"One hundred pounds a week, Mrs. Tree?"

"Yes, £100 a week, I will come and recite it every evening, and hand over the cheque intact to the War Fund."

It was a large sum, and the gentleman could not see his way to accepting the offer on his own responsibility, but said he would sound his directors in the morning.

Before lunch-time next day Mrs. Tree received a note requesting her to recite the poem nightly as suggested, and promising her £100 a week for herself or the fund in return. For ten weeks she stood alone every evening on that vast stage, and for ten minutes she recited "Pay, pay, pay." There never have been such record houses at the Palace either before or since, and at the end of ten weeks she handed over a cheque for £1,000 to the fund. Nor was this all, large sums were paid into the collecting boxes in the Palace Theatre. In addition Mrs. Tree made £1,700 at concerts, and £700 on one night at a Club. More than that, endless people followed her example, and the War Fund became some £20,000 richer for her inspiration in that dining-room in Sloane Street.

This was one of the plums of the theatrical cake; but how different is the performance and the gold and glitter as seen from the front of the curtain, to the real thing behind. How little the audience entering wide halls, proceeding up pile carpeted stairs, sweeping past stately palms, or pushing aside heavy plush curtains, realise the entrance to the playhouse on the other side of the footlights.

At the back of the theatre is the stage door. Generally up an alley, it is mean in appearance, more like an entrance to some cheap lodging-house than to fairyland. Rough men lounge about outside, those scene-shifters, carpenters, and that odd list of humanity who jostle each other "behind the scenes," work among "flies," and adjust "wings" in no ornithological sense, but merely as the side-pieces of the stage-setting.

Just inside this door is a little box-like office; nothing grand about it, oh dear no, whitewash is more often found there than mahogany, and stone stairs than Turkey carpets. Inside this little bureau sits that severe guardian of order, the stage door keeper. He is a Pope and a Czar in one. He is always busy, refuses to listen to explanations; even a card is not sent in unless that important gentleman feels assured its owner means business.

At that door, which is dark and dreary, the glamour of the stage begins to wane. It is no portal to a palace. The folk hanging about are not arrayed in velvets and satins; quite the contrary; torn cashmeres and shiny coats are more *en évidence*.

Strange people are to be found both behind and upon the stage, as in every other walk through life; but there are plenty of good men and women in the profession, men and women whose friendship it is an honour to possess. Men and women whose kindness of heart is unbounded, and whose intellectual attainments soar far above the average.

Every girl who goes upon the stage need not enjoy the privilege of marrying titled imbecility, nor obtain the notoriety of the Divorce Court, neither being creditable nor essential to her calling, although both are chronicled with unfailing regularity by the press.

The Divorce Court is a sad theatre where terrible tragedies of human misery are acted out to the bitter end. Between seven and eight hundred cases are tried in England every year—not many, perhaps, when compared with the population of the country, which is over forty millions. But then of course the Divorce Court is only the foam; the surging billows of discontent and unhappiness lie beneath, and about six thousand judicial separations, all spelling human tragedy, are granted yearly by magistrates, the greater number of such cases being undefended. They record the same sad story of disappointed, aching hearts year in year out.

Divorces are not more common amongst theatrical folk than any other class, so, whatever may be said for or against the morality of the stage, the Divorce Court does not prove theatrical life to be less virtuous than any other.

The fascination of the stage entraps all ages—all classes. Even children sometimes wax warm over theatrical folk. Once I chanced to be talking to a little girl concerning theatres.

"Do you know Mr. A. B. C.?" she asked excitedly, when the conversation turned on actors.

"Yes, he is a great friend of mine."

"Oh, do tell me all about him," she exclaimed, seizing my arm.

"Why do you want to know?"

"Because I adore him, and all the girls at school adore him, he is like a real prince; we save up our pocket-money to buy his photographs, and May Smith *has actually got his autograph!*"

"But tell me why you all adore him?" I asked.

"Because he is so lovely, so tall and handsome, has such a melodious voice, and oh! doesn't he look too beautiful in his velvet suit as— —? He is young and handsome, isn't he? Oh, do say he is young and handsome," implored the enthusiastic child.

"I am afraid I cannot, for it would not be true; Mr. A. B. C. is not tall—in fact, he is quite short." She looked crestfallen. "He has a sallow complexion."

"Sallow! Oh, not really sallow! but he *is* handsome and young, isn't he?"

"I should think he is about fifty-two."

"Fifty-two!" she almost shrieked. "*My* A. B. C. fifty-two. Oh no. You are chaffing me; he must be young and beautiful."

"And his hair is grey," I cruelly added.

"Grey?"—she sobbed. "Not grey? Oh, you hurt me."

"You asked questions and I have answered them truthfully," I replied. She stood silent for a moment, then in rather a subdued tone murmured:

"He is not married, is he?"

"Oh yes, he has been married for five-and-twenty years."

The child looked so crestfallen I felt I had been unkind.

"Oh dear, oh dear," she almost sobbed, "won't the girls at school be surprised! Are you quite, quite sure he is not young and beautiful? he looks so lovely on the stage."

"Quite, quite sure. You have only seen him from before the footlights. He is a good fellow, clever and charming, and he works hard, but he is no lover in velvet and jerkin, no hero of romance, and the less you worry your foolish little head about him the better, my dear."

How many men and women believe like this child that there are only princes and princesses on the stage.

There was an old Scotch body—an educated, puritanical person—who once informed me, "The the-a-ter is very bad, very wicked, ma'am."

"Why?" I asked, amazed yet interested.

"It's full of fire and lights like Hell. They just discuss emotions there, ma'am, and it's morbid to discuss emotions and just silly conceit to think about them. I like deeds, and not talk—I do!"

"You seem to think the theatre a hotbed of iniquity?"

"Aye, indeed I do, ma'am. They even make thunder. Fancy daring to make thunder for amusement as the good God does to show His wrath—thunder with a machine—it's just dreadful, it is."

The grosser the exaggeration the more readily it provokes conversation. I was dying to argue, but fearing to hurt her feelings, I merely smiled, wondering what the old lady would say if she knew even prayers were made by a machine in countries where the prayer-wheel is used.

"Have you ever been to a theatre?" I ventured to ask, not wishing to disturb the good dame's peace of mind.

"The Lord forbid!"

That settled the matter; but I subsequently found that the old body went to bazaars, and did not mind a little flutter over raffles, and on one occasion had even been to hear the inimitable George Grossmith in Inverness, when——

"He was not dressed-up-like, so it wasn't a regular the-a-ter, and he was just alone, ma'am, wi' a piano, so there was no harm in that," added the virtuous dame, complacently folding her hands across her portly form.

Wishing to change the subject, I asked her how her potatoes were doing.

"Bad, bad," she replied, "they're awfu' bad, the Lord's agin us the year; but we must jist make the best of it, ma'am."

She was a thoroughly good woman, and this was her philosophy. She would make the best of the lack of potatoes, as that was a punishment from above; but she could not sanction play-acting any more than riding a bicycle on the Sabbath.

Her horror of the wickedness of the stage was as amusing as the absurd adoration of the enthusiastic child.

Every good-looking man or woman who "play acts" is the recipient of foolish love-letters. Pretty girls receive them from sentimental youth or sensual old age, and handsome men are pestered with them from old maids, or unhappily married women. Some curious epistles are sent across the footlights, even the most self-respecting woman cannot escape their advent, although she can, and, does, ignore them.

Here is a sample of one:

"For *five* nights I have been to the theatre to see you play in——. I was so struck by your performance last week that I have been back every night since. Vainly I hoped you would notice me, for I always occupy the same seat, and last night I really thought you did smile at me" (she had done nothing of the kind, and had never even seen the man), "so I went home happy—oh so happy. I have sent you some roses the last two nights, and felt sorry you did not wear them. Is there any flower you like better? I hardly dare presume to ask you for a meeting, but if you only knew how much I admire you, perhaps you would grant me this great favour and make me the happiest man on earth. I cannot sleep for thinking of you. You are to me the embodiment of every womanly grace, and if you would take supper with me one night after the performance you would indeed confer a boon on a lonely man."

No answer does not mean the end of the matter. Some men—and, alas! some women—write again and again, send flowers and presents, and literally pester the object of their so-called adoration.

For weeks and weeks a man sent a girl violets; one night a diamond ring was tied up in the bunch—those glittering stones began her ruin—she wrote to acknowledge them, a correspondence ensued.

That man proved her curse. She, the once beautiful and virtuous girl, who was earning a good income before she met her evil genius, died lately in poverty and obscurity. The world had scoffed at her and turned aside, while it still smiled upon the man, although he was the villain; but can he get away from his own conscience?

Every vice carries with it a sting, every virtue a balm.

There are many perils on the stage, to which of course only the weak succumb; but the temptations are necessarily greater than in other professions. Its very publicity spells mischief. There is the horrid man in all audiences who tries to make love and ogle pretty women across the footlights, the class of creature who totally forgets that the best crown a man or woman can wear is a good reputation.

Temptations lie open on all sides for the actor and actress, and those who pass through the ordeal safely are doubly to be congratulated, for the man who meets temptation and holds aloof is surely a finer character than he who is merely "good" because he has never had a chance of being anything else.

Journalism, domestic service, and the stage probably require less knowledge and training for a beginning than any other occupations.

It costs money and time to learn to be a dressmaker, a doctor, an architect, even a shorthand writer; but given a certain amount of cleverness, experience is not necessary to do "scissor-and-paste" work in journalism, rough housework, or to "walk on" on the stage; but oh! what an amount of work and experience is necessary to ensure a satisfactory ending, more particularly upon the boards, where all is not gold that glitters. At best the crown is only brass, the shining silver merely tin, and in nine theatres out of every ten the regal ermine but a paltry rabbit-skin.

Glitter dazzles the eye. Nevertheless behind it beat good hearts and true; while hard work, patient endurance, and courage mark the path of the successful player.

Work does not degrade a man; but a man often degrades his work.

If, as the old body said, it be morbid to discuss emotions, and egotistical to feel them, it is still the actor's art, and that is probably why he is such a sensitive creature, why he is generally in the highest spirits or deepest depths of woe, why he is full of moods and as varying as a weathercock. Still he is charming, and so is his companion in stageland—the actress. Both entertain us, and amusement is absolutely essential to a healthy existence.

When one considers the wonderful success of women upon the stage to-day, and their splendid position socially, it seems almost impossible to believe that they never acted in England until the reign of Charles I., when a French Company which numbered women among its players crossed the Channel, and craved a hearing from Queen Henrietta Maria. One critic of the time called them "unwomanish and graceless"; another said, "Glad am I they were hissed and hooted"; but still they had come to stay, and slowly, very slowly, women were allowed to take part in theatrical performances. We all know the high position they hold to-day.

In 1660 there were only two theatres in London, the King's and the Duke of York's, the dearest seats were the boxes at four shillings, the cheapest the gallery at one shilling. Ladies wore masks at the play, probably because of the coarse nature of the performances, which gradually improved with the advent of actresses.

In days gone by the playhouse was not the orderly place it is nowadays, and the unfortunate "mummers" had to put up with every kind of nuisance until Colley Cibber protested, and Queen Anne issued a Proclamation (1704) against disturbances. In those days folk arrived in sedan chairs, and their noisy footmen were allowed free admission to the upper gallery to wait for their lords and ladies, added to which the orange girls called their wares and did a brisk trade in carrying love-missives from one part of the house to the other. Before the players could be heard they had to fight their way on to the boards, where gilded youth lolled in the wings and even crossed the stage during the rendering of a scene.

It was about this time that Queen Anne made a stand against the shocking immorality of the stage, and ordered the Master of the Revels (much the same post as the Lord Chamberlain now holds) to correct these abuses. All actors, mounte-banks, etc., had to submit their plays or entertainments to the Master of the Revels in Somerset House from that day, and nothing could be performed without his permission.

The stage has a curious effect on people. Many a person has gone to see a play, and some line has altered the whole course of his life. Some idea has been put forth, some tender note played upon which has opened his eyes to his own selfishness, his own greed of wealth, his harshness to a child, or indifference to a wife. There is no doubt about it, the stage is a great power, and that is why it is so important the influence should be used for good, and that illicit love and demor-alising thoughts should be kept out of the theatre with its mixed audiences and susceptible youth. According to a recent report:

"The Berne authorities, holding that the theatre is a powerful instrument for the education of the masses, have decided that on two days of the week the seats in the theatre, without exception, shall be sold at a uniform price of fivepence. 'Under the direction of the manager,' writes a correspondent, 'the tickets are enclosed in envelopes, and in this form are sold to the public. The scheme has proved a great success, especially among the working classes, whom it was meant to benefit. To prevent ticket speculators making a "corner," the principle of one ticket for one person has been adopted, and the playgoer only knows the location of his seat after he enters the theatre. No intoxicants are sold and no passes are given. The expenses exceed the receipts, but a reserve fund and voluntary contributions are more than sufficient to meet the deficit.'"

Constantly seeing vice portrayed tends to make one cease to think it horrible. Love of gain should not induce a manager to put on a piece that is public poison. Some queer plays teach splendid moral lessons—well and good; but some strange dramas drag their audience through mire for no wise end whatever. The manager who puts such upon his stage is a destroyer of public morality.

Mrs. Kendal as Mistress Ford in "Merry Wives of Windsor."

Photo by Window & Grove, Baker Street, W.

CHAPTER II

CRADLED IN THE THEATRE

Three Great Aristocracies—Born on the Stage—Inherited Talent—
Interview with Mrs. Kendal—Her Opinions and Warning to
Youthful Aspirants—Usual Salary—Starving in the Attempt to
Live—No Dress Rehearsal—Overdressing—A Peep at Harley
Street—Voice and Expression—American Friends—Mrs. Kend-
al's Marriage—Forbes Robertson's Romance—Why he deserted
Art for the Stage—Fine Elocutionist—Bad Enunciation and Noisy
Music—Ellen Terry—Gillette—Expressionless Faces—Long
Runs—Charles Warner—Abuse of Success.

L ONDON is a great world: it contains three aristocracies:

The aristocracy of blood, which is limited;

The aristocracy of brain, which is scattered;

And the aristocracy of wealth, which threatens to flood the other two.

The most powerful book in the world at the beginning of the twentieth century is the cheque-book. Foreigners are adored, vulgarity is sanctioned; indeed, all
are welcomed so long as gold hangs round their skirts and diamonds and pearls
adorn their bodies. Wealth, wealth, wealth, that is the modern cry, and there seems
nothing it cannot buy, even a transient position upon the stage.

Many of our well-known actors and actresses have, however, been "born on
the stage"—that is to say, they were the children of theatrical folk, and have themselves taken part in the drama almost from babyhood.

The most successful members of the profession are those possessed of inherited talent, or that have gone on the stage from necessity rather than choice, men
and women who since early life have had to fight for themselves and overcome
difficulties. It is pleasant to give a prominent example of the triumph which may
result from the blending of both influences in the person of one of our greatest
actresses, Mrs. Kendal, who has led a marvellously interesting life.

She was born early in the fifties, and her grandfather, father, uncles, and
brother (T. W. Robertson) were all intimately connected with the stage as actors
and playwrights. When quite a child she began her theatrical career, and made her
London *début* in 1865, when she appeared as Ophelia under her maiden name of
Madge Robertson, Walter Montgomery playing the part of *Hamlet*. Little Madge

was only three years old when she first trod the boards, whereon she was to portray a blind child, but when she espied her nurse in the distance, she rushed to the wings, exclaiming, "Oh, Nannie, look at my beautiful new shoes!"

Her bringing up was strict; she had no playfellows and never went to school, a governess and her father were her teachers. Every morning that father took her for a walk, explaining all sorts of things as they went along, or teaching her baby lips to repeat Shelley's "Ode to a Foxglove." On their return home, he would read Shakespeare with her, so that the works of the bard were known to her almost before she learnt nursery rhymes.

"I was grown up at ten," exclaimed Mrs. Kendal, "and first began to grow young at forty."

When about fourteen, she was living with her parents in South Crescent, off Tottenham Court Road. One Sunday—a dreary heavy, dull, rainy London day—her father and mother had been talking together for hours, and she wearily went to the window to look out, the mere fact of watching a passer-by seeming at the moment to afford relaxation. Tears rolled down the girl's cheeks—she was longing for companions of her own age, she was leaving the dolls of childhood behind and learning to be a woman. Her father noticed that she was crying, and exclaimed in surprise, "Why, Daisy, what's the matter?"

"I feel dull," she said.

"Dull, dear?—dull, with your mother and *me*?"

A pathetic little story, truly: the parents were so wrapped up in themselves, they never realised that sometimes the rising generation might feel lonely.

"My father and mother were then old," said Mrs. Kendal, "I was their youngest child. All the others were out in the world, trying to find a place."

Early struggles, hopes and fears, poverty and luxury, followed in quick succession in this remarkable woman's life, but any one who knows her must realise it was her indomitable will and pluck, coupled, of course, with good health and exceptional talent, which brought her the high position she holds to-day.

If Mrs. Kendal makes up her mind to do a thing, by hook or by crook that object is accomplished. She has great powers of organisation, and a capacity for choosing the right people to help her. "Never say die" is apparently her watchword.

She, like Miss Geneviève Ward, was originally intended for a singer, and songs were introduced into her parts in such plays as *The Palace of Truth*. Unfortunately she contracted diphtheria, which in those days was not controlled and arrested by antitoxin as it is now, and an operation had to be performed. All this tended to weaken her voice, which gradually left her. Consequently she gave up singing, or rather, singing gave her up, and she became a "play-actress." She so thoroughly realises the disappointments and struggles of her profession that one of Mrs. Kendal's pet hobbies is to try and counteract the evil arising from the wish of inexperienced girls to "go upon the stage."

"If only the stage-struck young woman could realise all that an actress' life means!" she said to me on one occasion. "To begin with, she is lucky if she gets a chance of 'walking on' at a pound a week. She has to attend rehearsals as numerous and as lengthy as the leading lady, who may be drawing £40 or £50 for the same period; though, mark you, there are very few leading ladies, while there are thousands and thousands of walkers-on who will never be anything else. This ill-paid girl has not the interest of a big part, which stimulates the 'star' to work; she has only the dreariness of it all. Unless she be in a ballet, chorus, or pantomime, the girl has to find herself in shoes, stockings, and petticoats for the stage—no light matter to accomplish out of twenty shillings a week. Of course, in a character-part the entire costume is found, but in an ordinary case the girl has to board, lodge, dress herself, pay for her washing, and get backwards and forwards to the theatre in all weathers and at all hours on one pound a week, besides supplying those stage necessaries. Thousands of women are starving in the attempt.

"A girl has to dress at the theatre in the same room with others, she is thrown intimately amongst all sorts of women, and the result is not always desirable. For instance, some years ago, a girl was playing with us, and, mentioning another member of the company, she remarked, 'She has real lace on her under-linen.'

"I said nothing, but sent for that lace-bedecked personage and had a little private talk with her, telling her that things must be different or she must go. I tried to show her the advantages of the straight path, but she preferred the other, and has since been lost in the sea of ultimate despair."

So spoke Mrs. Kendal, the famous actress, in 1903, standing at the top of her profession; later we will see what a girl struggling at the bottom has to say on the same subject.

"Remember," continued Mrs. Kendal, "patience, courage, and talent *may* bring one to the winning-post, but few ever reach that line; by far the greater number fall out soon after the start—they find the pay inadequate, the hours too long; the back of a stage proves to be no enchanted land, only a dark, dreary, dusty, bustling place; and, disheartened, they wisely turn aside. Many of them drift aimlessly into stupid marriages for bread and butter's sake, where discontent turns the bread sour and the butter rancid.

"The theatrical profession is not to blame—it is this terrible overcrowding. There are numbers of excellent men and women upon the stage who know that there is nothing so gross but what a good man or woman can elevate, nothing so lofty that vice cannot cause to totter.

"I entirely disapprove of a dress rehearsal," continued Mrs. Kendal. "It exhausts the actors and takes off the excitement and bloom. One must have one's real public, and play *for* them and *to* them, and not to empty benches. We rehearse in sections. Every one in turn in our company acts in costume, so that we know each individual get-up and make-up is right; but we never dress all the characters of the play at the same time until the night of production."

Mrs. Kendal is very severe on the subject of overdressing a part.

"Feathers and diamonds," she said "are not worn upon the river. Why, then, smother a woman with them when she is playing a boating scene? The dress should be entirely subservient to the character. If one is supposed to be old and dowdy, one should look old and dowdy. I believe in clothing the character in character, and not striving after effect. Overdressing is as bad as over-elaboration of stage-setting: it dwarfs the acting and handicaps the performers."

Mrs. Kendal is an abused, adored, and wonderful woman. Like all busy people, she finds time for everything, and has everything in its place. Her house is neatness exemplified, her table well arranged, the dishes dainty, and the attendance of spruce parlourmaids equally good. She believes in women and their work and employs them whenever possible.

There is an old-fashioned idea that women who earn their living are untidy in their dress and slovenly in their household arrangements, to say nothing of being unhappy in their home life. Those of us who know women workers can refute the charge: the busier they are, the more method they bring to bear; the more highly educated they are, the more capable in the management of their affairs. Mrs. Kendal is no exception to this rule, and in spite of her many labours, she lately encroached upon her time by undertaking another self-imposed task, namely, some charity work, which entailed endless correspondence, to say nothing of keeping books, and lists, and sorting cheques; but she managed all most successfully, and kept what she did out of the papers.

"Dissuade every one you know," Mrs. Kendal entreated me one day, "from going on the stage. There are so few successes and so many failures! So many lives are shattered and hearts broken by that everlasting *waiting for an opportunity* which only comes to a few. In no profession is harder work necessary, the pay in the early stages more insignificant or less secure. To be a good actress it is essential to have many qualifications: first of all, health and herculean strength; the sweetest temper and most patient temperament, although my remark once made about having 'the skin of a rhinoceros' was delivered in pure sarcasm, which, however, was unfortunately taken seriously.

"I really feel very strongly about this rush to go on the stage. In the disorganisation of this democratic period we have all struggled to ascend one step, and many of us have tumbled down several in the attempt. Domestic servants all want to be shop-girls, and shop-girls want to be actresses—stars, mind you! Everything is upside-down, for are not the aristocracy themselves selling wine, coals, tea-cakes, and millinery?"

"Why have you succeeded?" I asked.

"Because I was born to it, cradled in the profession, my family have been upon the stage for some hundred years. To make a first-class actress, talent, luck, temperament, and opportunity must combine; but, mark you, the position of the stage does not depend upon her. It is those on the second and third rungs of the ladder who do the hardest of the work, and most firmly uphold the dignity of the stage, just as it is the middle classes which rivet and hold together this vast Empire."

Although married to an actor-manager, Mrs. Kendal has nothing whatever to do with the arrangements of the theatre. She does not interfere with anything.

"I never signed an agreement in all my life, either for myself or for anyone else. I never engage or dismiss a soul. Once everything is signed, sealed, and delivered, and all is ready, then, but not till then, my work begins, and I become stage-manager. On the stage I supervise everything, and attend to all the smallest details myself. To be stage-manager is not an enviable position, for one is held responsible for every fault."

The Kendals lived for years in Harley Street, which is chiefly noted for its length, and being the home of doctors. Their house was at the end farthest from Cavendish Square, at the top on the left. I know the street well, for I was born in the house where Baroness Burdett-Coutts spent her girlhood, and have described in my father's memoirs how, when he settled in Harley Street in 1860 as a young man, there was scarcely a doctor's plate in that thoroughfare, or, indeed, in the whole neighbourhood. Sir William Jenner, Sir John Williams, Sir Alfred Garrod, Sir Richard Quain, and Sir Andrew Clark became his neighbours; and later Sir Francis Jeune, Lord Russell of Killowen, the present Speaker of the House of Commons (Mr. Gully), Sir William McCormac, Sir William Church, and Mr. Gladstone settled quite near. Mr. Sothern (the original impersonator of Lord Dundreary and David Garrick) lived for some time in the street; but, so far as I know, he and the Kendals were the only representatives of the stage. A few years ago, not being able to add to the house they then occupied as they wished, the Kendals migrated to Portland Place, which is now their London residence, while Filey claims them for sea air and rest.

The Kendals spent five years in the United States. It was during those long and tedious journeys in Pullman-cars that Mrs. Kendal organised her "Unselfish Club." It was an excellent idea for keeping every one in a good temper. At one end of the car the women used to meet to mend, make, and darn every afternoon, while one male member of the company was admitted to read aloud, each taking this duty in turn. Many pleasant and useful hours were spent in speeding over the dreary prairie in this manner. Only those who have traversed thousands of miles of desert can have any idea of the weariness of those days passed on the cars. The railway system is excellent, everything possible is done for one's comfort, but the monotony is appalling.

Two things are particularly interesting about this great actress—her keen sense of humour and her love of soap. She is always merry and cheerful, has endless jokes to tell, has a quick appreciation of the ridiculous, and can be just as amusing off the stage as on it.

Her love of soap-and-water is apparent in all her surroundings; she is always most carefully groomed; there is nothing whatever artificial about her—anything of that sort which is necessary upon the boards is left behind at the theatre. That is one of her greatest charms. She uses no "make-up," and, consequently, she looks much younger off the stage than she does upon it.

Her expressions and her voice are probably Mrs. Kendal's greatest attractions. Speaking of the first, she laughingly remarked, "My face was made that way, I suppose; and as for my acting voice, I have taken a little trouble to train it. We all start in a high key, but as we get older our voices often grow two or three notes lower, and generally more melodious, so that, while we have to keep them down in our youth, we must learn to get them up in our old age, for the head voice of comedy becomes a throat voice if not properly produced, and tends to grow hard and rasping."

We had been discussing plays, good, bad, and indifferent.

"I have the greatest objection to the illicit love of the modern drama," she remarked. "It is quite unnecessary. Every family has its tragedy, and many of these tragedies are far more thrilling, far more heart-breaking, than the unfortunate love-scenes put upon the stage."

The charming impersonator of the "Elder Miss Blossom," one of the most delightful touches of comedy-acting on record, almost invariably dresses in black. A strong, healthy-looking woman, untouched by art, and gently dealt with by years, Mrs. Kendal wears her glorious auburn hair neatly parted in front and braided at the back. Fashion in this line does not disturb her; she has always worn it in the same way, and even upon the stage has rarely donned a wig. She tells a funny little story of how a dear friend teased and almost bullied her to be more fashionable about her head. Every one was wearing fringes at the time, and the lady begged her not to be so "odd," but to adopt the new and becoming mode. Just to try the effect, Mrs. Kendal went off to a grand shop, told the man to dress her hair in the very latest style, paid a guinea for the performance, and went home. Her family and servants were amazed; but when she arrived at her friend's house that evening her hostess failed to recognise her. So the fashionable hairdressing was never repeated.

"I worked the hardest," said Mrs. Kendal, in reply to a question, "in America. For months we gave nine performances a week. The booking was so heavy in the different towns, and our time so limited, that we actually had to put in a third *matinée*, and as occasionally rehearsals were necessary, and long railway journeys always essential, it was really great labour.

"As a rule I was dressed by ten, and managed to get in an hour's walk before the *matinée*. Back to the hotel after the performance for a six o'clock meal, generally composed of a cutlet and coffee, quickly followed by a return to the theatre and another performance. To change one's dress fourteen times a day, as I did when playing *The Ironmaster*, becomes a little wearisome when it continues for months."

"Did you not find that people in America were extraordinarily hospitable?" I inquired, remembering the great kindness I received in Canada and the States.

"Undoubtedly; but we had little time for anything of that sort, which has always been a great regret to me. It is hard lines to be in a place one wants to see, among people one wants to know, and never to have time for play, only everlasting work. We did make many friends on Sundays, however, and I have the happiest recollections of America."

Mr. W. H. Kendal.

Photo by Alfred Ellis, Upper Baker Street, W.

Pictures are a favourite hobby of the Kendals, and they have many beautiful canvases in their London home. Every corner is filled by something in the way of a picture, every one of which they love for itself, and for the memories of the way they came by it, more often than not as the result of some successful "run." They have built their home about them bit by bit. Hard work and good management have slowly and gradually attained their ends, and they laugh over the savings necessary to buy such and such a treasure, and love it all the more for the little sacrifices made for its attainment. How much more we all appreciate some end or some thing we have had difficulty in acquiring. That which falls at our feet seems of little value compared with those objects and aims secured by self-denial.

"There is no doubt about it," Mrs Kendal finished by saying, "theatrical life is hard; hard in the beginning, and hard in the end."

Such words from a woman in Mrs. Kendal's position are of vast import. She knows what she is talking about; she realises the work, the drudgery, the small pay, and weary hours, and when she says, "Dissuade girls from rushing upon the stage," those would-be aspirants for dramatic fame should listen to the advice of so experienced an actress and capable woman.

As said at the beginning of this chapter, Mrs. Kendal was cradled in the theatre: she was also married on the stage.

Madge Robertson and William Kendal Grimston were playing in Manchester when one fine day they were married by special licence. A friend of Mr. Kendal's had the Town Hall bells rung in honour of the event, and the young couple were ready to start off for their honeymoon, when Henry Compton, the great actor, who was "billed" for the following nights, was telegraphed for to his brother's deathbed.

At once the arrangements had to be altered. *As You Like It* was ordered, and Mr. and Mrs. Kendal were caught just as they were leaving the town, and bidden to play Orlando and Rosalind to the Touchstone of Buckstone. The honeymoon had to be postponed.

The young couple found the house unusually full on their wedding night, although they believed no one knew of their marriage until they came to the words, "Will you, Orlando, have to wife this Rosalind?" when the burst of applause and prolonged cheering assured them of the good wishes of their public friends.

Another little romance of the stage happened to the Forbes Robertsons. Just before I sailed for Canada, in August, 1900, Mr. Johnston Forbes Robertson came to dinner. He had been away in Italy for some months recruiting after a severe illness, and was just starting forth on an autumn tour of his own.

"Have you a good leading lady?" I inquired.

"I think so," he replied. "I met her for the first time this morning, and had never seen her before."

"How indiscreet," I exclaimed. "How do you know she can act?"

"While I was abroad I wrote to two separate friends in whose judgment I have much confidence, asking them to recommend me a leading lady. Both replied suggesting Miss Gertrude Elliott as suitable in every way. Their opinions being identical, and so strongly expressed, I considered she must be the lady for me, and telegraphed, offering her an engagement accordingly. She accepted by wire, and at our first rehearsal this morning promised very well."

I left England almost immediately afterwards, and eight or ten weeks later, while in Chicago, saw a big newspaper headline announcing the engagement of a pretty American actress to a well-known English actor. Naturally I bought the paper at once to see who the actor might be, and lo! it was Mr. Forbes Robertson. It seemed almost impossible: but impossible things have a curious knack of being true, and the signed photograph I had with me of Forbes Robertson, among those of other distinguished English friends, proved useful to the American press, who were glad of a copy for immediate reproduction. Almost as quickly as this handsome couple were engaged, they were married. Was not that a romance?

Mr. Forbes Robertson originally intended to be an artist, and his going on the stage came about by chance. He was a student at the Royal Academy, when his friend the late W. G. Wills was in need of an actor to play the part of Chastelard in his *Mary Stuart*, then being given at the Princess's Theatre. It was difficult to procure exactly the type of face he wanted, for well-chiselled features are not so common as one might suppose. Young Forbes Robertson possessed those features, his clear-cut profile being exactly suitable for Chastelard. Consequently, after much talk with the would-be artist, who was loth to give up his cherished profession, W. G. Wills introduced his friend to the beautiful Mrs. Rousby, with the result that young Forbes Robertson undertook the part at four days' notice.

Thus it was his face that decided his fate. From that moment the stage had been his profession and art his hobby; but a newer craze is rapidly driving paints and brushes out of the field, for, like many another, the actor has fallen a victim to golf.

There is no finer elocutionist on the stage than Forbes Robertson, and therefore it is interesting to know that he expresses it as his opinion that:

"Elocution can be taught."

Phelps was his master, and he attributes much of his success to that master's careful training. What a pity Phelps cannot live among us again, to teach some of the younger generation to speak more clearly than they do.

Bad enunciation and noisy music often combine to make the words from the stage inaudible to the audience. Why an old farmer should arrive down a country lane to a blare of trumpets is unintelligible: why a man should plot murder to a valse, or a woman die to slow music, is a conundrum, but such is the fashion on the stage. One sometimes sits through a performance without hearing any of what ought to be the most thrilling lines.

Johnston Forbes Robertson has lived from the age of twenty-one in Bloomsbury. His father was a well-known art critic until blindness overtook him, and then the responsibility of the home fell on the eldest son's shoulders. His father was born and bred in Aberdeen, and came as a young man to London, where he soon got work as a journalist, and wrote much on art for the *Sunday Times*, the *Art Journal*, etc. His most important work was *The Great Painters of Christendom*.

Mr. J. Forbes-Robertson.

From a painting by Hugh de T. Glazebrook.

The West Central district of London, with its splendid houses, its Adams ceilings and overmantels, went quite out of fashion for more than a quarter of a century. With the dawn, however, of 1900, people began to realise that South Kensington stood on clay, was low and damp, and consequently they gradually migrated back to the Regent's Park and those fine old squares in Bloomsbury. One after another the houses were taken, and among Mr. Forbes Robertson's neighbours are

George Grossmith and his brother Weedon, Mr. and Mrs. Seymour Hicks, Lady Monckton, "Anthony Hope," and many well-known judges, aldermen, solicitors, and architects.

In the old home in Bloomsbury the artistic family of Forbes Robertson was reared. Johnston, as we know, suddenly neglected his easel for the stage; his sister Frances took up literature as a profession; and his brothers, known as Ian Robertson and Norman Forbes, both adopted the theatrical profession. So the Robertsons may be classed among the theatrical families.

Who in the latter end of the nineteenth century did not weep with Miss Terry?—who did not laugh with her well-nigh to tears? A great personality, a wondrous charm of voice and manner, a magnetic influence on all her surroundings—all these are possessed by Ellen Terry.

In the days of their youth Mrs. Kendal and Miss Ellen Terry played together, but many years elapsed between then and the Coronation year of Edward VII., when they met again behind the footlights, in a remarkable performance which shall be duly chronicled in these pages.

Like Mrs. Kendal, Miss Ellen Terry began her theatrical life as a child. She was born in Coventry in 1848—not far from Shakespeare's home, which later in life became such an attractive spot for her. Her parents had theatrical engagements at Coventry at the time of her birth, so that verily she was cradled on the stage. She was one of four remarkable sisters, Kate, Ellen, Marion, and Florence, all clever actresses and sisters of Fred Terry; while another brother, although not himself an actor, was connected with the stage, Miss Minnie Terry being his daughter. Altogether ten or twelve members of the Terry family have been in the profession.

Ellen Terry, like Irving, Wyndham, Hare, Mrs. Kendal, and Lady Bancroft, learnt her art in stock companies.

Miss Ellen Terry has always had the greatest difficulty in learning her parts, and as years have gone on, even in remembering her lines in oft-acted plays; but every one knows how apt she is to be forgetful, and prompt her over her difficulties. Irving, on the other hand, is letter-perfect at the first rehearsal, and rarely wants help of any kind.

Ellen Terry is so clever that even when she has forgotten her words she knows how to "cover" herself by walking about the stage or some other pretty by-play until a friend comes to her aid. Theatrical people are extremely good to one another on these occasions. Somebody is always ready to come to the rescue. After the first week everything goes smoothly as a rule, until the strain of a long run begins to tell, and they all in turn forget their words, much to the discomfiture of the prompter.

Forgetting the words is a common thing during a long run. I remember Miss Geneviève Ward telling me that after playing *Forget-Me-Not* some five hundred times she became perfectly dazed, and that Jefferson had experienced the same with *Rip van Winkle*, which he has to continually re-study. Miss Gertrude Elliott suffered considerably in the same way during the long run of *Mice and Men*.

Much has been said for and against a long run; but surely the "against" ought to have it. No one can be fresh and natural in a part played night after night—played until the words become hazy, and that dreadful condition "forgetting the lines" arrives.

At a charming luncheon given by Mr. Pinero for the American Gillette, when the latter was creating such a *furore* in England with *Sherlock Holmes*, I ventured to ask that actor how long he had played the part of the famous detective.

"For three years," he replied.

"Then I wonder you are not insane."

"So do I, ma'am, I often wonder myself, for the strain is terrible, and sometimes I feel as if I could never walk on to the stage at all; but when the theatre is full, go I must, and go I do; though I literally shun the name of *Sherlock Holmes*."

We quickly turned to other subjects, and discussed the charm of American women, a theme on which it is easy for an English woman to wax eloquent.

If a man like Gillette, with all his success, all his monetary gain, and no anxiety—for he did not finance his own theatres—could feel like that about a long run, what horrors it must present to others less happily situated.

Long runs, which are now so much desired by managers in England and America, are unknown on the Continent. In other countries, where theatres are more or less under State control, they never occur. Of course the "long run" is the outcome of the vast sums expended on the production. Managers cannot recoup themselves for the outlay unless the play draws for a considerable while. But is this the real end and aim of acting? Does it give opportunity for any individual actor to excel?

But to return to Ellen Terry. She has played many parts and won the love of a large public by her wonderful personality, for there is something in her that charms. She is not really beautiful, yet she can look lovely. She has not a strong voice, yet she can sway audiences at will to laughter or tears. She has not a fine figure, yet she can look a royal queen or simple maiden. Once asked whether she preferred comedy or tragedy, she replied:

"I prefer comedy, but I should be very sorry if there were no sad plays. I think the feminine predilection for a really good cry is one that should not be discouraged, inasmuch as there are few things that yield us a truer or a deeper pleasure; but I like comedy as the foundation, coping-stone, and pillar of a theatre. Not comedies for the mere verbal display of wit, but comedies of humour with both music and dancing."

Miss Ellen Terry has a cheery disposition, invariably looks on the bright side of things, and not only knows how to work, but has actually done so almost continuously from the age of eight.

One of Miss Terry's greatest charms is her mastery over expression. It is really strange how little facial and physical expression are understood in England. We are the most undemonstrative people. It is much easier for a Frenchman to act than for an Englishman; the former is always acting; the little shrug of the shoulders, the movement of the hand and the head, or a wink of the eye, accompany every sentence that falls from his lips. He is full of movement, he speaks as much with his body as with his mouth, and therefore it is far less difficult for him to give expression to his thoughts upon the stage than it is for the stolid Britisher, whose public school training has taught him to avoid showing feeling, and squeezed him into the same mould of unemotional conventionality as all his other hundreds of schoolfellows. There is no doubt about it that everything on the stage must be exaggerated to be effective. It is a world of unreality, and the more pronounced the facial and physical expression brought to bear, the more effective the representation of the character.

To realise the truth of these remarks, one should visit a small theatre in France, a theatre in some little provincial town, where a quite unimportant company is playing. They all seem to act, to be thoroughly enamoured of their parts, and to play them with their whole heart and soul. It is quite wonderful, indeed, to see the extraordinary capacity of the average French actor and actress for expressing emotion upon the stage. Of course it is their characteristic; but on the other hand, the German nation is quite as stolid as our own, and yet the stage is held by them in high esteem, and the amount of drilling gone through is so wonderful that one is struck by the perfect playing of an ordinary provincial German. At home these Teutonic folk are hard and unemotional, but on the boards they expand. One has only to look at the German company that comes over to London every year to understand this remark. They play in a foreign tongue, the dresses are ordinary, one might say poor, the scenery is meagre, there is nothing, in fact, to help the acting in any way; and yet no one who goes to see one of their performances can fail to be impressed by the wonderful thoroughness and the general playing-in-unison of the entire company. Of course they do not aim so high as the Meiningen troupe, for they were a State company and the personal hobby of the Duke whose name they bore. We have no such band of players in England, although F. R. Benson has done much without State aid to accomplish the same result, and in many cases has succeeded admirably.

We have heard a great deal lately about the prospect of a State-Aided Theatre and Opera in London; and there is much to be said for and against the scheme. Municipal administration is often extravagant and not unknown to jobbery, neither of which would be advisable; but the present system leads to actor-managers and powerful syndicates, which likewise have their drawbacks. There is undoubtedly much to be said both for and against each system, and the British public has to decide. Meantime we learn that the six Imperial theatres in Russia (three in St. Petersburg and three in Moscow), with their schools attached, cost the Emperor some £400,000 a year. "It is possible to visit the opera for 5*d*., to see Russian pieces for 3*d*., French and German for 9*d*." These cheap seats are supposed to be a source of education to the populace, but there are expensive ones as well.

Some Englishmen understand the art of facial expression. A little piece was played for a short time by Mr. Charles Warner, under the management of Mrs. Beerbohm Tree. The chief scene took place in front of a telephone, through which instrument the actor heard his wife and child being murdered many miles away in the country, he being in Paris. It was a ghastly idea, but Charles Warner's face was a study from the first moment to the last. He grew positively pale, he had very little to say, and yet he carried off an entire scene of unspeakable horror merely by his facial and physical expression.

Some of our actors are amusingly fond of posing off the stage as well as on. One well-known man was met by a friend who went forward to shake his hand.

"Ah, how do you do?" gushed the Thespian, striking an attitude, "how do you do, old chap? Delighted to see you," then assuming a dramatic air, "but who the — — are you?"

And this was his usual form of greeting after an effusive handshake.

In a busy life it is of course impossible to remember every face, and the non-entities should surely forgive the celebrities, for it is so easy to recognise a well-known person owing to the constant recurrence of his name or portrait in the press, and so easy to forget a nonentity whom nothing recalls, and whose face resembles dozens more of the same type.

One often hears actors and actresses abused—that is the penalty of success. Mediocrity is left alone, but, once successful, out come the knives to flay the genius to pieces; in fact, the more abused a man is, the more sure he may feel of his achievements. Abuse follows success in proportion to merit, just as foolish hopes make the disappointments of life.

CHAPTER III

THEATRICAL FOLK

Miss Winifred Emery—Amusing Criticism—An Actress's Home
Life—Cyril Maude's first Theatrical Venture—First Perfor-
mance—A Luncheon Party—A Bride as Leading Lady—No
Games, no Holidays—A Party at the Haymarket—Miss Ellaline
Terriss and her First Appearance—Seymour Hicks—Ben Webster
and Montagu Williams—The Sothern Family—Edward Sothern
as a Fisherman—A Terrible Moment—Almost a Panic—Asleep as
Dundreary—Frohman at Daly's Theatre—English and American
Alliance—Mummers.

ANOTHER striking instance of hereditary theatrical talent is Miss Winifred
Emery, than whom there is no more popular actress in London. This pretty,
agreeable little lady—who, like Mrs. Kendal and Miss Terry, may be said to have
been born in the theatre—is the only daughter of Samuel Sanderson Emery, a well-
known actor, and grand-daughter of John Emery, who was well known upon the
stage. Her first appearance was at Liverpool, at the advanced age of eight.

The oldest theatrical names upon the stage to-day are William Farren and
Winifred Emery. Miss Emery's great-grandfather was also an actor, so she is really
the fourth generation to adopt that profession, but her grandmother and herself
are the only two women of the name of Emery who have appeared on playbills.

As is well known, Miss Emery is the wife of Mr. Cyril Maude, lessee with Mr.
Frederick Harrison—not the world-renowned Positivist writer—of the Haymarket Theatre.

Although Mrs. Maude finds her profession engrossing, she calls it a very hard
one, and the necessity of being always up to the mark at a certain hour every day
is, she owns, a great strain even when she is well, and quite impossible when she
is ill.

Some years ago, when she was even younger than she is now, and not over-
burdened with this world's gold, she was acting at the Vaudeville. It was her custom to go home every evening in an omnibus. One particularly cold night she
jumped into the two-horse vehicle and huddled herself up in the farthest corner,
thinking it would be warmer there than nearer the door in such bitter weather. She
pulled her fur about her neck, and sat motionless and quiet. Presently two women
at the other end arrested her attention; one was nudging the other, and saying:

"It is 'er, I tell yer; I know it's 'er."

"Nonsense, it ain't 'er at all; she couldn't have got out of the theayter so quick."

"It is 'er, I tell yer; just look at 'er again."

The other looked.

"No it ain't; she was all laughing and fun, and that 'ere one looks quite sulky."

The "sulky one," though thoroughly tired and weary, smiled to herself.

I asked Miss Emery one day if she had ever been placed in any awkward predicament on the stage.

"I always remember one occasion," she replied, "tragedy at the time, but a comedy now, perhaps. I was acting with Henry Irving in the States when I was about eighteen or nineteen, and felt very proud of the honour. We reached Chicago. *Louis XI.* was the play. In one act—I think it was the second—I went on as usual and did my part. Having finished, as I thought, I went to my room and began to wash my hands. It was a cold night, and my lovely white hands robbed of their paint were blue. The mixture was well off when the call boy shouted my name. Thinking he was having a joke I said:

"'All right, I'm here.'

"'But Mr. Irving is waiting for you.'

"'Waiting for me? Why, the act isn't half over.'

"'Come, Miss Emery, come quick,' gasped the boy, pushing open the door. 'Mr. Irving's on the stage and waiting for you.'

"Horrors! In a flash I remembered I had two small scenes as Marie in that act, and usually waited in the wing. Had I, could I have forgotten the second one?

"With wet red hands, dry white arms, my dress not properly fastened at the back, towel in hand, along the passage I flew. On the stage was poor Mr. Irving walking about, talking—I know not what. On I rushed, said my lines, gave him my lobster-coloured wet hand to kiss—a pretty contrast to my ashen cheeks, and when the curtain fell, I dissolved in tears.

"Mr. Irving sent for me to his room. In fear and trembling I went.

"'This was terrible,' he said. 'How did it happen?'

"'I forgot, I forgot, why I know not, but I forgot,' I said, and my tears flowed again. He patted me on the back.

"'Never mind,' he said kindly, 'but please don't let it occur again.'"

Once when I was talking to this clever little lady the conversation turned on games.

"Games!" she exclaimed. "I know nothing of them: as a child I never had time to play, and when I was sixteen years old I had to keep myself and my family. Of late years I have been far too busy even to take up golf."

Mrs. Maude has two charming daughters, quaint, old-fashioned little creatures, and some years their junior is a small brother.

Miss Winifred Emery and Mr. Cyril Maude in "The School for Scandal."

Photo by Window & Grove, Baker Street, W.

The two girls were once invited to a fancy dress ball in Harley Street: it happened to be a Saturday, and therefore *matinée* day. Their mother arranged their dresses. The elder was to wear the costume of Lady Teazle, an exact replica of the one reproduced in this volume, and which Mrs. Maude wore when playing that part, while the younger was to be dressed as a Dutch bride, also a copy of one of Miss Emery's dresses in the *Black Tulip*. They all lunched together, and as the mother was going off to the theatre, she told the nurse to see that the children were dressed properly, and take them to the house at a certain hour.

"Oh, but, mummy, we can't go unless you dress us," exclaimed the elder child; "we should never be right." And therefore it was settled that the two little people should be arrayed with the exception of the final touches, and then driven round by way of the Haymarket Theatre, so that their mother might attend to their wigs, earrings, hat or cap, as the case might be.

What a pretty idea. The mother, who was attracting rounds of applause from a crowded house every time she went on the stage, running back to her dressing-room between the scenes, to drop down on her knees and attend to her little girls, so that they should be all right for their party.

Admiring the costume of the younger one, I said:

"Why, you have got on your mother's dress."

"No, it's not mother's," she replied. "It's *my* dress, and *my* shoes, and *my* stockings—all my very own; but it's mother's gold cap, and mother's earrings, and mother's necklace, and mother's apron—with a tuck in," and she nodded her wise little head.

This was a simple child, not like the small American girl whose mother was relating wonderful stories of her precocity to an admiring friend, when a shrill voice from the corner called out:

"But you haven't told the last clever thing I said, mamma," evidently wishing none of her brilliant wit to be lost.

They looked sweet, those two children of Mrs. Maude's, and the way the elder one attended upon her smaller sister was pretty to see.

In a charming little house near the Brompton Oratory Mrs. Maude lived for years, surrounded by her family, perfectly content in their society. She is in every sense a thoroughly domesticated woman, and warmly declares she "loves housekeeping."

One cannot imagine a happier home than the Maudes', and no more charming gentleman walks upon the stage than this well-known descendant of many distinguished army men. Mr. Maude was at Charterhouse, one of our best public schools, and is a most enthusiastic old Carthusian. So is General Baden-Powell, whose interest in the old place went so far as to make him spend his last night in England among his old schoolfellows at the City Charterhouse when he returned invalided on short leave from the Transvaal. The gallant soldier gave an excellent speech, referring to Founders' Day, which they were then commemorating, and delighted his boy hearers and "Ancient Brethren" equally.

On Charterhouse anniversaries Mr. Maude drops his jester's cap and solemnly, long stick in hand, takes part in the ceremony at the old Carthusian Church made popular by Thackeray's *Newcomes*.

Cyril Maude was originally intended for another profession, but, in spite of family opposition, elected to go upon the stage, and as his parents did not approve of such a proceeding, he commenced his theatrical career in America, where he went through many vicissitudes. He began in a Shakespearian *règpertoire* company, playing through the Western mining towns of the States, where he had to rough it considerably.

"I even slept on a bit of carpet on a bar-room floor one night," he said; "but our beautiful company burst up in 'Frisco, and I had to come home emigrant fashion, nine days and nine nights in the train, with a little straw mattress for my bed, and a small tin can to hold my food. They were somewhat trying experiences, yet most interesting, and gave great opportunities for studying mankind. I have played in every conceivable sort of play, and once 'walked on' for months made up as Gladstone in a burlesque, to a mighty dreary comic song."

So Mr. Maude, like the rest who have climbed to the top, began at the bottom of the ladder, and has worked his way industriously up to his present position, which he has held at the Haymarket since 1896, and where—he laughingly says— he hopes to die in harness.

Cyril Maude gives rather an amusing description of his first theatrical performance. When he was a boy of eighteen his family took a house at Dieppe for six months, and he was sent every day to study French with *Monsieur le Pasteur*.

"One day, when I had been working with him for three or four weeks, he asked me what I was going to make my profession.

"'Comédien,' I replied.

"'Comment? Comédien? Etes-vous fou?' he exclaimed, horrified and astounded at such a suggestion, and added more gravely, 'I am quite sure you have not the slightest idea how to act; so, my boy, you had better put such a ridiculous idea out of your head and stick to your books. Besides, you must choose a profession fit for a gentleman.'

"Of course I felt piqued, and as I walked home that evening I just wondered if there were not some way by which I could show the old man that I *could* act if I chose.

"The Pasteur had a resident pupil of the name of Bishop, a nice young fellow, and to him I related my indignation.

"'Of course you can act,' he said; so between us we concocted the brilliant idea that I should dress up as Bishop's aunt and go and call upon the Pasteur, with the ostensible view of sending another nephew to his excellent establishment. Overjoyed at the scheme I ransacked my mother's wardrobe, and finally dressed myself up to resemble a somewhat lean, cadaverous English old maid.

"I walked down the street to the house, and to my joy the servant did not recognise me. The old man received me with great cordiality and politeness. I told him in very bad French, with a pronounced Cockney accent, that I was thinking of sending another of my nephews to him if he had room. At this suggestion the Pasteur was delighted, took me upstairs, showed me all the rooms, and made quite a fuss over me. Then he called 'my nephew,' who nearly gave the show away by choking with laughter when I affectionately greeted him with a chaste salute. This was the only part of the business I did not really enjoy! As we were coming downstairs, the Pasteur well in front, I smiled—perhaps I winked—at Bishop, anyhow I slipped, whereupon the polite old gentleman turned round, was most *désolé* at the accident, gave me his arm, and assisted me most tenderly all the rest of the way to the dining-room, his wife following and murmuring:—

"'Prenez garde, madame, prenez garde.'

"Having arrived at the *salle-à-manger* the dear old Pasteur said he would leave me for a moment with his wife, in case there was anything I might like to discuss with her, and to my horror I was left closeted with madame, nervously fearing she might touch on subjects fit only for ladies' ears, but not for the tender years of my manly youth. Needless to say I escaped from her clutches as quickly as possible.

"For two days I kept up the joke. Then it became too much for me, and as we were busily working at French verbs, in the curé's study, I changed my voice and returned to the old lady's Cockney French intonations, which was not in the least difficult, as my own French was none of the brightest. The Pasteur turned round, looked hard at me for a moment, and then went back to the verbs. I awaited another opportunity, and began again. This time he almost glared at me, and then, clapping his hands to his head and bursting into laughter, he exclaimed:

"'Mais c'était vous, c'était vous la tante de Bishop?'

"It turned out he had written that morning to Bishop's real aunt, accepting her second nephew as a pupil, and arranging all the details of his arrival. How surprised the good lady must have been."

June 3rd, 1899, was the eleventh anniversary of Cyril Maude and Winifred Emery's wedding day, and they gave a delightful little luncheon party at their pretty house in Egerton Crescent, where they then lived. The host certainly looked ridiculously young to have been married eleven years, or to be the father of the big girl of nine and the smaller one of six who came down to dessert.

Their home was a very cosy one—not big or grand in those days, but thoroughly carried out on a small scale, with trees in the gardens in front, trees in the back-yard behind, and the aspect was refreshing on that frightfully hot Oaks day.

Winifred Emery had a new toy—a tiny little dog, so small that it could curl itself up quite happily in the bottom of a man's top hat, but yet wicked enough to do a vast amount of damage, for it had that morning pulled a blouse by the sleeves from the bed to the floor, and had calmly dissevered the lace from the cambric.

The Maudes are a most unconventional theatrical pair. They love their home and their children, and seem to wish to get rid of every remembrance of the theatre once they pass their own front door. And yet it is impossible to get rid of the theatre in the summer, for besides having eight performances a week of *The Manœuvres of Jane* at that time—which was doing even better business at the end of nine months than it was at the beginning—those unfortunate people were giving charity performances every week for seven consecutive weeks, which of course necessitated rehearsals apart from the performances themselves. Really the charity distributed by the theatrical world is enormous.

We had a delightful luncheon: much of my time was spent gazing at Miss Ellaline Terriss, who is even prettier off the stage than she is on.

When Mrs. Maude said she had been married for eleven years, with the proudest air in the world Mrs. Hicks remarked:

"And we have been married nearly six."

But certainly to look at Ellaline Terriss and Seymour Hicks made it seem impossible to believe that such could be the case. Hard work seems to agree with some people, and the incessant labour of the stage had left no trace on these young couples.

After luncheon the Maudes' eldest little girl recited a French poem she had learnt at school, and it was quite ridiculous to see the small child already showing inherited talent. She was calm and collected, and when she had done and I congratulated her, she said in the simplest way in the world:

"I am going to be an actress when I am grown up, and so is Baby," nodding her head at the other small thing of six, for the boy had not then arrived to usurp "Baby's" place.

"Oh yes, so am I," said little six-year-old. But when I asked her to recite something, she said:

"I haven't learnt yet, but I shall soon."

The Maudes were then eagerly looking forward to some weeks' holiday which they always enjoy every autumn.

"I like a place where I need not wear gloves, and a hat is not a necessity," she said. "I have so much dressing-up in my life that it is a holiday to be without it."

Somehow the conversation turned on a wedding to which they had just been, and Winifred Emery exclaimed:

"I love going to weddings, but I always regret I am not the bride."

"Come, come," said her husband, "that would be worse than the Mormons. However many husbands would you have?"

"Oh, I always want to keep my own old husband, but I want to be the bride." At which he laughed immoderately, and said:

"I declare, Winifred, you are never happy unless you are playing the leading lady."

"Of course not," she retorted; "women always appreciate appreciation."

They were much amused when I told them the story of my small boy, who, aged about seven, was to go to a wedding as a page in gorgeous white satin with lace ruffles and old paste buttons.

"I don't want to go," he remarked; "I hate weddings"—for he had officiated twice before. Something he said leading me to suppose he was a little shy, I soothingly answered:

"Oh, well, every one will be so busy looking at the bride that they will never look at you."

To which the small gentleman indignantly replied:

"If they aren't even going to look at me, then I don't see why I need go at all!"

So after all there is a certain amount of vanity even in a small boy of seven.

"I cannot bear a new play," Mrs. Maude once said. "I am nervous, worried, and anxious at rehearsal, and it is not until I have got on my stage clothes that it ceases to be a trouble to me. Not till I have played it for weeks that I feel thoroughly at home in a new part.

"It is positively the first real holiday I have ever had in my life," she exclaimed to me at the time of her illness; "for although we always take six weeks' rest in the summer, plays have to be studied and work is looming ahead, whereas now I have six months of complete idleness in front of me. It is splendid to have time to tidy my drawers in peace, ransack my bookshelves, see to a hundred and one household duties without any hurry, have plenty of time to spend with the children, and actually to see something of my friends, whom it is impossible to meet often in my usually busy life."

So spoke Miss Winifred Emery, and a year later Mrs. Kendal wrote, "I've had ten days' holiday this year, and am now rehearsing literally day and night."

After that who can say the life of the successful actress is not a grind? A maidservant or shopgirl expects her fortnight's holiday in a twelvemonth, while one of the most successful actresses of modern times has to be content with ten days during the same period. Yet Mrs. Kendal is not a girl or a beginner, she is in full power and at the top of her profession.

All theatrical life is not a grind, however, and it has its brighter moments. For instance, one beautiful warm sunny afternoon, the anniversary of their own wedding day—the Cyril Maudes gave an "At Home" at the Haymarket. Guests arrived by the stage door at the back of the famous theatre, and to their surprise found themselves at once upon the stage, for the back scene and Suffolk Street are almost identical. Mrs. Maude, with a dear little girl on either side, received her friends, and an interesting group of friends they were. Every one who was any one seemed to have been bidden thither. The stage was, of course, not large enough for this goodly throng, so a great staircase had been built down from the footlights to where the stalls usually stand. The stalls, however, had gone—disappeared as though they had never existed—and where the back row generally cover the floor a sumptuous buffet was erected. It was verily a fairy scene, for the dress-circle (which at the Haymarket is low down) was a sort of winter garden of palms and flowers behind which the band was ensconced.

What would the players of old, Charles Mathews, Colley Cibber, Edmund Kean, Liston, and Colman, have said to such a sight? What would old Mr. Emery have thought could he have known that one day his grand-daughter would reign as a very queen on the scene of his former triumphs? What would he have said had he known that periwigs and old stage coaches would have disappeared in favour of closely-cut heads, electric broughams, shilling hansoms with C springs and rubber tyres, or motor cars? What would he have thought of the electric light in place of candle dips and smelling lamps? How surprised he would have been to find neatly coated men showing the audience to their seats at a performance, instead of fat rowdy women, to see the orange girls and their baskets superseded by dainty trays of tea and ices, and above all to note the decorous behaviour of a modern audience in contrast to the noisy days when Grandpapa Emery trod the Haymarket boards.

Almost the most youthful person present, if one dare judge by appearances, was the actor-manager, Cyril Maude. There is something particularly charming about Mr. Maude—there is a merry twinkle in his eyes, with a sound of tears in his voice, and it is this combination, doubtless, which charms his audience. He is a low comedian, a character-actor, and yet he can play on the emotional chord when necessity arises. He and his co-partner, Mr. Harrison, are warm friends—a delightful situation for people so closely allied in business.

Immediately off the stage is the green-room, now almost unused. Formerly the old green-room on the other side of the stage was a fashionable resort, and the green-rooms at the Haymarket and Drury Lane were crowded nightly at the beginning of the last century with all the fashionable men of the day. Kings went there to be amused, plays began at any time, the waits between the acts were of any length, and general disorder reigned in the candle and oil-lighted theatres—a disorder to which a few visitors did not materially add. All is changed nowadays. The play begins to the minute, and ends with equal regularity. Actors do not fail to appear without due notice, so that the under-study has time to get ready, and order reigns both before and behind the footlights. Therefore at the Haymarket no one is admitted to the green-room, in fact, no one is allowed in the theatre "behind the scenes" at all, except to the dressing-room of the particular star who has invited him thither.

Mrs. Maude made a charming hostess at that party.

I think the hour at which we were told on the cards "to leave" was 6.0, or it may have been 6.30; at any rate, we all streamed out reluctantly at the appointed time, and the stage carpenters streamed in. Away went the palms, off came the bunting, down came the staircase, and an hour later the evening audience were pouring in to the theatre, little knowing what high revelry had so lately ended.

Some people seem to be born old, others live long and die young; judging by their extraordinary juvenility, Mr. Seymour Hicks and his charming wife, *née* Ellaline Terriss, belong to the latter category. They are a boyish man and a girlish woman, in the best sense of lighthearted youthfulness, yet they have a record of successes behind them, of which many well advanced in years might be proud. No daintier, prettier, more piquante little lady trips upon our stage than Ellaline Terriss. She is the personification of everything mignonne, and whether dressed in rags as *Bluebell in Fairyland,* or as a smart lady in a modern play, she is delightful.

It is a curious thing that so many of our prominent actors and actresses have inherited their histrionic talents from their parents and even grandparents, and Mrs. Hicks is no exception, for she is the daughter of the late well-known actor, William Terriss. She was not originally intended for the stage, and her adoption of it as a profession was almost by chance. A letter of her own describes how this came about.

"I was barely sixteen when Mr. Calmour, who wrote *The Amber Heart* and named the heroine after me, suggested we should surprise my father one day by playing *Cupid's Messenger* in our drawing-room, and that I should take the leading part. We had a brass rod fixed up across the room, and thus made a stage, and on the preceding night informed a few friends of the morrow's performance. The news greatly astonished my father, who laughed. I daresay he was secretly pleased, though he pretended not to be. A couple of months passed, and I heard that Miss Freke was engaged at the Haymarket to play the part I had sustained. Oh, how I wished it was I! Little did I think my wish was so near fulfilment. I was sitting alone over the fire one day when a telegram was handed to me, which ran:

> "'*Haymarket Theatre. Come up at once. Play Cupid's Messenger, to-night.*'

"I rushed to catch a train, and found myself at the stage door of the theatre at 7.15 p.m. All was hurry and excitement. I did not know how to make-up. I did not know with whom I was going to appear, and Miss Freke's dress was too large for me. The whole affair seemed like a dream. However, I am happy to say Mr. Tree stood by and saw me act, and I secured the honour of a 'call.' I played for a week, when Mr. Tree gave me a five-pound note, and a sweet letter of thanks. My father then said that if it would add to my happiness I might go on the stage, and he would get me an engagement."

How proud the girl must have been of that five-pound note, for any person who has ever earned even a smaller sum knows how much sweeter money seems when acquired by one's own exertions. Five-pound notes have come thick and fast since then, but I doubt if any gave the actress so much pleasure as Mr. Beerbohm Tree's first recognition of her talent.

Thus it really was quite by accident Miss Terriss entered on a theatrical career. Her father, knowing the hard work and many disappointments attendant on stage life, had not wished his daughter to follow his own calling. But talent will out. It waits its opportunity, and then, like love, asserts itself. The opportunity came in a kindly way; the talent was there, and Miss Terriss was clever and keen enough to take her chance when it came and make the most of it. From that moment she has never been idle, even her holidays have been few and far between.

Every one in London must have seen *Bluebell in Fairyland*, which ran nearly a year. Indeed, at one time it was being played ten times a week. Think of it. Ten times a week. To go through the same lines, the same songs, the same dances, to look as if one were enjoying oneself, to enter into the spirit and fun of the representation, was indeed a herculean task, and one which the Vaudeville company successfully carried through. But poor Mrs. Hicks broke down towards the close, and was several times out of the bill.

Mr. and Mrs. Seymour Hicks.

Photo by London Stereoscopic Co., Ltd., Cheapside, E.C.

It is doubtful whether Seymour Hicks will be better known as an actor or an author in the future, for he has worked hard at both professions successfully. He was born at St. Heliers, Jersey, in 1871, and is the eldest son of Major Hicks, of the 42nd Highlanders. His father intended him for the army, but his own taste did not lie in that direction, and when only sixteen and a half he elected to go upon the stage, and five years later was playing a principal light comedy part at the Gaiety Theatre. Like his wife, he has been several times in America, where both have met with success, and when not acting, at which he is almost constantly employed, this energetic man occupies his time by writing plays, of a light and musical nature, which are usually successful. *One of the Best, Under the Clock, The Runaway Girl, Bluebell in Fairyland*, and *The Cherry Girl* have all had long runs.

When the Hicks find time for a holiday their idea of happiness is an out-of-door existence, with rod or gun for companions. Most of our actors and actresses, whose lives are necessarily so public, love the quiet of the country coupled with plenty of exercise when able to take a change. The theatre is barely closed before they rush off to moor or fen, to yacht or golf—to anything, in fact, that carries them completely away from the glare of the footlights.

Another instance of theatrical heredity is Ben Webster, whose talent for acting doubtless comes from his grandfather. Originally young Ben read for the Bar with that eminent and amusing man, Mr. Montagu Williams. It was just at that time that poor Montagu Williams's throat began to trouble him: later on, when no longer able to plead in court, he was given an appointment as magistrate. I only remember meeting him once—it was at Ramsgate. When walking along the Esplanade one day—I think about the year 1890—I found my father talking to a neat, dapper little gentleman in a fur coat, thickly muffled about the throat. He introduced his friend as Montagu Williams, a name very well known at that time. Alas! the eminent lawyer was hardly able to speak—disease had assailed his throat well-nigh to death, and the last time I saw that wonderful painter and charming man Sir John Everett Millais, at a private view at the Royal Academy, he was almost as speechless, poor soul.

Well, Montagu Williams was made a magistrate, and young Ben Webster, realising his patron's influence was to a certain extent gone, and his own chances at the Bar consequently diminished, gladly accepted an offer of Messrs. Hare and Kendal to play a companion part to his sister in the *Scrap of Paper*, then on tour. He had often acted as an amateur; and earned some little success during his few weeks' professional engagement, so that when he returned to town and found Montagu Williams removed from active practice at the Bar, he went at once to Mr. Hare and asked for the part of Woodstock in *Clancarty*. Thus he launched himself upon the stage, although his grandfather had been dead for three years, and so had not directly had anything to do with his getting there.

Old Grandfather Ben seems to have been a very irascible old gentleman, and a decidedly obstinate one. On one occasion his obstinacy saved his life, however, so his medical man stoutly declared.

The doctor had given Ben Webster up: he was dying. Chatterton and Churchill were outside the room where he lay, and the medico when leaving told them "old Ben couldn't last an hour."

"Ah, dear, dear!" said Chatterton; "poor old Ben going at last," and he sadly nodded his head as he entered the room.

"Blast ye! I'm not dead yet," roared a voice from the bed, where old Ben was sitting bolt upright. "I'm not going to die to please any of you."

He fell back gasping; but from that moment he began to get better.

Another eminent theatrical family, the Sotherns, were born on the stage, so to speak, and took to the profession as naturally as ducks to water, while their contemporaries the Irvings and Boucicaults have done likewise.

It must have been towards the end of the seventies that my parents took a house one autumn in Scarborough. We had been to Buxton for my father's health, and after a driving tour through Derbyshire, finally arrived at our destination. To my joy, Mr. Sothern and his daughter, who was then my schoolfellow in London, soon appeared upon the scene. He had come in consequence of an engagement to play at the Scarborough Theatre in *Dundreary* and *Garrick*, and had secured a house near us. Naturally I spent much of my time with my girl friend, and we used often to accompany her father in a boat when he went on his dearly-loved fishing expeditions. Never was there a merrier, more good-natured, pleasanter gentleman than this actor. He was always making fun which we children enjoyed immensely. Practical jokes to him seemed the essence of life, and I vaguely remember incidents which, though amusing to him, rather perturbed my juvenile mind. At the time I had been very little to theatres, but as he had a box reserved every night, I was allowed now and then to go and gaze in wild admiration at *Garrick* and *Dundreary*.

One afternoon I went to the Sotherns for a meat tea before proceeding to the theatre, but the great comedian was not there. "Pops," for so he was called by his family, had gone out at four o'clock that morning with a fisherman, and still remained absent. The weather had turned rough, and considerable anxiety was felt as to what could have become of him. His eldest son, Lytton, since dead, appeared especially distressed. He had been down to the shore to inquire of the boatmen, but nothing could be heard of his father. We finished our meal—Mr. Sothern's having been sent down to be kept warm—and although he had not appeared, it was time to go to the theatre. Much perturbed in his mind, Lytton escorted his sister and myself thither, and leaving us in the box, went off once more to inquire if his father had arrived at the stage door; again without success.

This seemed alarming; the wind was still boisterous and the stage manager in a fright because he knew the only attraction to his audience was the appearance of Edward Sothern as Lord Dundreary. It was the height of the season, and the house was packed. Lytton started off again to the beach, this time in a cab; the stage manager popped his head into our box to inquire if the missing hero had by chance arrived, the orchestra struck up, but still no Mr. Sothern. It was a curious experience. The "gods" became uneasy, the pit began to stamp, the orchestra played louder, and at last, dreading a sudden tumult, the stage manager stepped forward and began to explain that "Mr. Sothern, a devoted fisherman, had gone out at four o'clock that morning; but had failed to return. As they knew, the weather was somewhat wild, therefore, they could only suppose he had been detained by the storm——"

At this juncture an unexpected and dishevelled figure appeared on the scene.

The usually spick-and-span, carefully groomed Mr. Sothern, with his white locks dripping wet and hanging like those of a terrier dog over his eyes, hurried up, exclaiming:

"I am here, I am here. Will be ready in a minute," and the weird apparition disappeared through the opposite wing. Immense relief and some amusement kept the audience in good humour, while with almost lightning rapidity the actor changed and the play began.

In one of the scenes the hero goes to bed and draws the curtain to hide him from the audience. Mr. Sothern went to bed as usual, but when remarks should have been heard proceeding from behind the curtain, no sound was forthcoming. The other player went on with his part; still silence from the bed. The stage manager became alarmed, knowing that Sothern was terribly fatigued and had eaten but little food, he tore a small hole in the canvas which composed the wall of the room, and, peeping through, saw to his horror that the actor was fast asleep. This was an awkward situation. He called him—no response. The poor man on the stage still gagged on gazing anxiously behind him for a response, till at last, getting desperate, the stage manager seized a broom and succeeded in poking Sothern's ribs with the handle. The actor awoke with a huge yawn, quite surprised to find himself in bed wearing Dundreary whiskers, which proved a sharp reminder he ought to have been performing antics on the stage.

Actor and fisherman had experienced a terrible time in their boat. The current was so strong that when they turned to come back they were borne along the coast, and as hour after hour passed poor Sothern realised that not only might he not be able to keep his appointment at the theatre, but was in peril of ever getting back any more. He made all sorts of mental vows never to go out fishing again when he was due to play at night; never to risk being placed in such an awkward predicament, never to do many things; but in spite of this experience, when once safe on land, his ardour was not damped, for he was off fishing again the very next day.

When I went to America in 1900 Mrs. Kendal kindly gave me some introductions, and one among others to Mr. Frohman. His is a name to conjure with in theatrical circles on that side of the Atlantic, and is becoming so on this side, for he controls a vast theatrical trust which either makes or mars stage careers.

I called one morning by appointment at Daly's Theatre, and as there happened to be no rehearsal in progress all was still except at the box office. I gave my card, and was immediately asked to "step along to Mr. Frohman's room."

Up dark stairs and along dimly lighted passages I followed my conductor, till he flung open the door of a beautiful room, where at a large writing-table sat Mr. Frohman. He rose and received me most kindly, and was full of questions concerning the Kendals and other mutual friends, when suddenly, to my surprise, I saw a large photograph hanging on the wall, of a Hamlet whose face I seemed to know.

"Who is that?" I asked.

"Mr. Edward Sothern, the greatest Hamlet in America, the son of the famous

Dundreary."

"I had the pleasure of playing with that Hamlet many times when I was a little girl," I remarked; "for although 'Eddy' was somewhat older, he used often to come to the nursery in Harley Street to have games with us children when his mother lived a few doors from the house in which I was born."

Mr. Frohman was interested, and so was I, to hear of the great success of young Edward Sothern, for of course Sam Sothern is well known on the English stage.

The sumptuous office of Mr. Frohman is at the back of Daly's Theatre. It is a difficult matter to gain admittance to that sacred chamber, but preliminaries having been arranged, the attendant who conducts one thither rings a bell to inform the great man that his visitor is about to enter. Mr. Frohman was interesting and affable. He evidently possesses a fine taste, for pieces of ancient armour, old brocade, and the general air of a *bric-à-brac* shop pervaded his sitting-room.

"English actors are as successful over here," he said, "as Americans are in London, and the same may be said of plays, the novelty, I suppose, in each case."

The close alliance between England and America is becoming more emphasised every day. Why, in the matter of acting alone we give them our best and they send us their best in return. So much is this the case that most of the people mentioned in these pages are as well known in New York as in London; for instance, Sir Henry Irving, Miss Ellen Terry, Mr. and Mrs. Kendal, Mr. Weedon Grossmith, Mr. E. S. Willard, Miss Fay Davis, Madame Sarah Bernhardt, Miss Winifred Emery, Mr. Cyril Maude, Miss Ellaline Terriss, Mr. Seymour Hicks, Mr. and Mrs. Beerbohm Tree, Mr. W. S. Gilbert, Mr. Anthony Hope, Mr. A. W. Pinero, and a host of others. Sir Henry Irving has gone to America, for the eighth time during the last twenty years, with his entire company. That company for the production of *Dante* consists of eighty-two persons, and no fewer than six hundred and seventy-three packages, comprising scenery, dresses, and properties.

"No author should ever try to dramatise his own books: he nearly always fails," Mr. Frohman added later during our pleasant little chat, after which he took me round his theatre, probably the most celebrated in the United States, for it was built by the famous Daly, and still maintains its position at the head of affairs. On the whole, American theatres are smaller than our own, the entire floor is composed of stalls which only cost 8s. 4d. each, and there is no pit. In the green-room, halls, and passages Mr. Frohman pointed out with evident delight various pictures of Booth as Hamlet, since whose time no one had been so successful till Edward Sothern junior took up that *rôle* in 1900. There was also a large portrait of Charlotte Cushman, and several pictures of Irving, Ellen Terry, Jefferson, and others, as well as some photographs of my old friend Mr. Sothern.

I have quoted the Terrys, Kendals, Ellaline Terriss, Ben Webster, Winifred Emery, and the Sotherns as products of the stage, but there are many more, including Dion and Nina Boucicault, whose parents were a well-known theatrical couple, George and Weedon Grossmith, the sons of an entertainer, and George's son is also on the stage. Both the Irvings are sons of Sir Henry of that ilk, and so on *ad infinitum*.

From the above list it will be seen that most of our successful actors and actresses were cradled in the profession. They were "mummers" in the blood, if one may be forgiven the use of such a quaint old word to represent the modern exponents of the drama.

CHAPTER IV

PLAYS AND PLAYWRIGHTS

Interview with Ibsen—His Appearance—His Home—Plays Without
Plots—His Writing-table—His Fetiches—Old at Seventy—A Real
Tragedy and Comedy—Ibsen's First Book—Winter in Norway—
An Epilogue—Arthur Wing Pinero—Educated for the Law—As
Caricaturist—An Entertaining Luncheon—How Pinero writes his
Plays—A Hard Worker—First Night of *Letty*.

PROBABLY the man who has had the most far-reaching influence on modern
drama is Henrik Ibsen. Half the dramatic world of Europe admire his work as
warmly as the other half deplore it.

Ibsen has a strange personality. The Norwegian is not tall, on the contrary,
rather short and thick-set—one might almost say stout—in build, broad-shoul-
dered, and with a stooping gait. His head is splendid, the long white hair is a
glistening mass of tangled locks. He has an unusually high forehead, and in true
Norse fashion wears his plentiful hair brushed straight back, so that, being long, it
forms a complete frame for the face. He has whiskers, which, meeting in the middle, beneath his chin, leave the chin and mouth bare. Under the upper lip one sees
by the indentation the decision of the mouth, and the determination of those thin
lips, which through age are slightly drawn to one side. He has a pleasant smile
when talking; but in repose the mouth is so firmly set that the upper lip almost
disappears.

The great dramatist has lived for many years in Christiania, and it was in that
town, on a cold snowy morning in 1895 I first met him. The streets were completely buried in snow; even the tram-lines, despite all the care bestowed upon
them, were embedded six or seven inches below the surface of the frozen mass.
It can be very cold during winter in Christiania, and frost-bite is not unknown,
for the thermometer runs down many degrees below zero. That is the time to see
Norway. Then everything is at its best. The sky clear, the sun shining—all Nature
bright, crisp, and beautiful. Icicles many feet long hung like a sparkling fringe
in the sunlight as I walked—or rather stumbled—over the snow to the Victorian
Terrasse to see the celebrated man. Tall posts leaning from the street gutters to the
houses reminded pedestrians that deep snow from the roofs might fall upon them.

The name of Dr. Henrik Ibsen was written in golden letters at the entrance to
the house, with the further information that he lived on the first floor. There was
nothing grand about his home, just an ordinary Norwegian flat, containing eight

or ten good rooms; and yet Ibsen is a rich man. His books have been translated into every tongue, his plays performed on every stage. His work has undoubtedly revolutionised the drama. He started the idea of a play without plot, a character-sketch in fact, a psychological study, and introduced the "no-ending" system. Much he left to the imagination, and the imagination of various nationalities has run in such dissimilar lines that he himself became surprised at the thoughts he was supposed to have suggested.

Brilliant as much of his work undoubtedly is, there is quite as much which is repellent and certainly has not added to the betterment of mankind. His characters are seldom happy, for they too often strive after the impossible.

The hall of his home looked bare, the maid was capless and apronless, according to Norwegian fashion, while rows of goloshes stood upon the floor. The girl ushered me along a passage, at the end of which was the great man's study. He rose, warmly shook me by the hand, and finding I spoke German, at once became affable and communicative. He is of Teutonic descent, and in many ways has inherited German characteristics. When he left Norway in 1864—when, in fact, Norway ceased to be a happy home for him—he wandered to Berlin, Dresden, Paris, and Rome, remaining many years in the Fatherland.

"The happiest summer I ever spent in my life was at Berchtesgaden in 1880," he exclaimed. "But to me Norway is the most lovely country in the world."

Ibsen's writing-table, which is placed in the window so that the dramatist may look out upon the street, was strewn with letters, all the envelopes of which had been neatly cut, for he is faddy and tidy almost to the point of old-maidism. He has no secretary, it worries him to dictate, and consequently all communications requiring answers have to be written by the Doctor himself. His calligraphy is the neatest, smallest, roundest imaginable. It is representative of the man. The signature is almost like a schoolboy's—or rather, like what a schoolboy's is supposed to be—it is so carefully lettered; the modern schoolboy's writing is, alas! ruined by copying "lines" for punishment, time which could be more profitably employed learning thought-inspiring verses.

On the table beside the inkstand was a small tray. Its contents were extraordinary—some little wooden carved Swiss bears, a diminutive black devil, small cats, dogs, and rabbits made of copper, one of which was playing a violin.

"What are those funny little things?" I ventured to ask.

"I never write a single line of any of my dramas unless that tray and its occupants are before me on the table. I could not write without them. It may seem strange—perhaps it is—but I cannot write without them," he repeated. "Why I use them is my own secret." And he laughed quietly.

Are these little toys, these fetishes, and their strange fascination, the origin of those much-discussed dolls in *The Master Builder*? Who can tell? They are Ibsen's secret.

Dr. Henrik Ibsen.

In manner Henrik Ibsen is quiet and reserved; he speaks slowly and deliberately, so slowly as to remind one of the late Mr. Bayard, the former American Minister to the Court of St. James, when he was making a speech. Mr. Bayard appeared to pause between each word, and yet the report in the papers the following day read admirably. This slowness may with Ibsen be owing to age, for he was born in

1828 (although in manner and gait he appears at least ten years older), or it may be from shyness, for he is certainly shy. How men vary. Ibsen at seventy seemed an old man; General Diaz, the famous President of Mexico, young at the same age. The one drags his feet and totters along; the other walks briskly with head erect. Ibsen was never a society man in any sense of the word, a mug of beer and a paper at the club being his idea of amusement. Indeed, in Christiania, until 1902, he could be seen any afternoon at the chief hotel employed in this way, for after his dinner at two o'clock he strolled down town past the University to spend a few hours in the fashion which pleased him.

Norwegian life is much more simple than ours. The inhabitants dine early and have supper about eight o'clock. Entertainments are hospitable and friendly, but not as a rule costly, and although Ibsen is a rich man, the only hobby on which he appears to have spent much money is pictures. He loves them, and wherever he has wandered his little gallery has always gone with him.

Ibsen began to earn his own living at the age of sixteen, and for five or six years worked in an apothecary's shop, amusing himself during the time by reading curious books and writing weird verses. Only twenty-three copies of his first book were sold, the rest were disposed of as waste paper to buy him food. Those long years of struggle doubtless embittered his life, but relief came when he was made manager of the Bergen Theatre with a salary of £67 a year. For seven years he kept the post, and learnt the stage craft which he later utilised in his dramas.

A strange comedy and tragedy was woven into the lives of Ibsen and Björnson. As young men they were great friends; then politics drove them apart; they quarrelled, and never met for years and years. Strange fate brought the children of these two great writers together, and Björnson's daughter married Ibsen's only child. The fathers met after years of separation at the wedding of their children.

Verily a real comedy and tragedy, woven into the lives of Scandinavia's two foremost writers of tragedy and comedy.

I spent part of two winters in Norway, wandering about on snow-shoes (ski) or in sledges, and during various visits to Christiania tried hard to see some plays by Ibsen or Björnson acted; but, strange as it may seem, plays by a certain Mr. Shakespeare were generally in the bill, or else amusing doggerel such as *The Private Secretary*.

At last, however, there came a day when *Peer Gynt* was put on the stage. This play has never been produced in England, and yet it is one of Ibsen's best, at all events one of his most poetic. The hero is supposed to represent the Norwegian character, vacillating, amusing, weak, bound by superstition, and lacking worldly balance. The author told me he himself thought it was his best work, though *The Master Builder* gave him individually most satisfaction.

In 1898 Ibsen declared, "My life seems to me to have slipped by like one long, long, quiet week"; adding that "all who claimed him as a teacher had been wrong—all he had done or tried to do was faithfully, closely, objectively to paint human nature as he saw it, leaving deductions and dogmatism to others." He declared he had never posed as a reformer or as a philosopher; all he had attempted was to try and work out that vein of poetry which had been born in him. "Poetry has served me as a bath, from which I have emerged cleaner, healthier, freer." Thus spoke of himself the man who practically revolutionised modern drama.

In the early days of the twentieth century Ibsen finished his life's work—he relinquished penmanship. The celebrity he had attained failed to interest him, just as attack and criticism had failed to arouse him in earlier years. His social and symbolical dramas done, his work in dramatic reform ended, he folded his hands to await the epilogue of life. It is a pathetic picture. He who had done so much, aroused such enthusiasm and hatred, himself played out—he whose works had been read in every Quarter of the globe, living in quiet obscurity, waiting for that end which comes to all.

It is a proud position to stand at the head of English dramatists; a position many critics allot to Arthur Wing Pinero. The Continent has also paid him the compliment of echoing that verdict by translating and producing many of his plays: and if in spite of translation they survive the ordeal of different interpretations and strange surroundings, may it not be taken as proof that they soar above the ordinary drama?

About the year 1882 Mr. Pinero relinquished acting as a profession—like Ibsen, it was in the theatre he learnt his stage craft—and devoted himself to writing plays instead. Since that period he has steadily and surely climbed the rungs of that fickle ladder "Public Opinion" and planted his banner on the top.

Look at him. See the strength of the man's mind in his face. Those great shaggy eyebrows and deep-set, dark, penetrating eyes, that round bald head, within which the brain is apparently too busy to allow anything outside to grow. Though still young he is bald, so bald that his head looks as if it had been shaven for the priesthood. The long thin lips and firm mouth denote strength of purpose, which, coupled with genius make the man. Under that assumed air of self-possession there is a merry mind. His feelings are well under control—part of the actor's art— but he is human to the core. Pinero is no ordinary person, his face with its somewhat heavy jaw is full of thought and strength. He has a vast fund of imagination, is a keen student of human nature, and above all possesses the infinite capacity for taking pains, no details being too small for him. He and Mr. W. S. Gilbert will, at rehearsals, go over a scene again and again. They never get angry, even under the most trying circumstances; but politely and quietly show every movement, every gesture, give every intonation of the voice, and in an amiable way suggest:

"Don't you think that so and so might be an improvement?"

They always get what they want, and no plays were ever more successful or better staged.

Mr. Pinero believes in one-part dramas, and women evidently fascinate him. Think of *Mrs. Tanqueray* and *Mrs. Ebbsmith*, for instance, both are women's plays; in both are his best work. He is always individual; individual in his style, and individual in the working out of his characters. During the whole of one August Mr. Pinero remained in his home near Hanover Square finishing a comedy of which he superintended rehearsals in the September following. He must be alone when he works, and apparently barred windows and doors, and a charwoman and her cat, when all London is out of town, give him inspiration.

London is particularly proud of Arthur Pinero, who was born amid her bustle in 1855. The only son of a solicitor in the City, he was originally intended for the law, but when nineteen he went upon the stage, where he remained for about seven years. One can only presume, however, that he did not like it, or he would not so quickly have turned his attention to other matters. Those who remember his stage life declare he showed great promise as a young actor. But be this as it may, it is a good thing he turned his back upon that branch of the profession and adopted the *rôle* of a dramatist, for therein he has excelled. Among his successful plays are *The Magistrate, Dandy Dick, Sweet Lavender, The Cabinet Minister, The Second Mrs. Tanqueray, The Notorious Mrs. Ebbsmith, Trelawny of the Wells, The Gay Lord Quex*, and *Iris*.

Among other attributes not usually known, Mr. Pinero is an excellent draughtsman, and can make a remarkable caricature of himself in a few moments. His is a strong and striking head which lends itself to caricature, and he is one of those people who, while poking fun at others, does not mind poking fun at himself.

When asked to what he attributed his success, Mr. Pinero replied:

"Such success as I have obtained I attribute to small powers of observation and great patience and perseverance."

His work is always up-to-date, for Mr. Pinero is modern to his finger-tips.

How delightful it is to see people who have worked together for years remaining staunch friends. One Sunday I was invited to a luncheon the Pineros gave at Claridge's. The room was marked "Private" for the occasion, and there the hospitable couple received twenty guests, while beyond was a large dining-room, to which we afterwards adjourned. That amusing actor and charming man, John Hare, with whom Pinero has been associated for many years, was present; Miss Irene Vanbrugh, his Sophy Fullgarney in the *Gay Lord Quex*, and Letty, in the play of that name, that dainty and fascinating American actress, Miss Fay Davis, and Mr. Dion Boucicault. There they were, all these people who had worked so long together, and were still such good friends as to form a merry, happy little family party.

Gillette, the American hero of the hour, was also present, and charming indeed he proved to be; but he was an outsider, so to speak, for most of the party had acted in Pinero's plays, and that was what seemed so wonderful; because just as a secretary sees the worst side of his employer's character, the irritability, the moments of anxious thought and worry, so the actor generally finds out the angles and corners of a dramatist. Only those who live in the profession can realise what such a meeting as that party at Claridge's really meant, what a fund of good temper it proclaimed, what strength of character it represented, what forbearance on all sides it proved.

That party was representative of friendship, which, like health, is seldom valued until lost.

Mr. Arthur W. Pinero.

Photo by Langfier, 23a, Old Bond Street, London, W.

There are as many ways of writing a play as there are of trimming a hat. Some people, probably most people, begin at the end, that is to say, they evolve some grand climax in their minds and work backwards, or they get hold of the chief situations as a nucleus, from which they work out the whole. Some writers let the play write itself, that is to say, they start with some sort of idea which develops as they go on, but the most satisfactory mode appears to be for the writer to decide everything even to the minutest detail, and then sketch out each situation. In a word, he ought to know exactly what he means to do before putting pen to paper.

The plots of Mr. Pinero's plays are all conceived and born in movement. He walks up and down the room. He strolls round Regent's Park, or bicycles further afield, but the dramas are always evolved while his limbs are in action, mere exercise seeming to inspire him with ideas.

It is long before he actually settles down to write his play. He thinks and ponders, plans and arranges, makes and remakes his plots, and never puts pen to paper until he has thoroughly realised, not only his characters, but the very scenes amid which these characters are to move and have their being.

He knows every room in which they are to enact their parts, he sees in his mind's eye every one of his personalities, he dresses them according to his own individual taste, and so careful is he of the minutest details that he draws a little plan of the stage for each act, on which he notifies the position of every chair, and with this before him he moves his characters in his mind's eye as the scene progresses. His play is finished before it is begun, that is to say, before a line of it is really written.

His mastery of stage craft is so great that he can definitely arrange every position for the actor, every gesture, every movement, and thus is able to give those minute details of stage direction which are so well known in his printed plays.

In his early days he wrote *Two Hundred a Year* in an afternoon; *Dandy Dick* occupied him three weeks; but as time went on and he became more critical of his own work, he spent fifteen months in completing *The Notorious Mrs. Ebbsmith*, nine months over *The Second Mrs. Tanqueray*, and six months over *The Gay Lord Quex*, helped in the latter drama, as he said, "by the invigorating influence of his bicycle."

He is one of the most painstaking men alive, and over *Letty* he spent two years.

"I think I have done a good day's work if I can finish a single speech right," he remarked, and that sums up the whole situation.

Each morning he sees his secretary from eleven to twelve, dictates his letters, and arranges his business; takes a walk or a ride till luncheon, after which he enjoys a pipe and a book, and in the afternoon lies down for a couple of hours' quiet.

When he is writing a play he never dines out, but after his afternoon rest enjoys a good tea (is it a high tea?), shuts the baize doors of that delightful study overlooking Hanover Square, and works until quite late, when he partakes of a light supper.

No one dare disturb him during those precious hours, when he smokes incessantly, walks about continually, and rarely puts a line on paper until he feels absolutely certain he has phrased that line as he wishes it to remain.

Pinero's writing-table is as tidy as Ibsen's; but while Ibsen's study is small and simply furnished, Pinero's is large, contains handsome furniture, interesting books, sumptuous *Éditions de luxe*, charming sketches, portraits, caricatures, handsome carpets, and breathes an air of the owner's luxurious taste.

Like his writing-table, his orthography is a model of neatness. When he has completed an act he carefully copies it himself in a handwriting worthy of any clerk, and sends it off at once to the printers. But few revisions are made in the proof, so sure is the dramatist when he has perfected his scheme.

Mr. Pinero keeps a sort of "day-book," in which he jots down characters, speeches, and plots likely to prove of use in his work. It is much the same sort of day-book as that kept by Mr. Frankfort Moore, the novelist, who has the nucleus of a hundred novels ever in his waistcoat pocket.

Formerly men jotted down notes on their shirt-cuffs, from which the laundress learned the wicked ways of society. The figures now covering wristbands are merely the winnings or losings at Bridge.

The dramatist loves ease and luxury, and his plays represent such surroundings.

"Wealth and leisure," he remarked, "are more productive of dramatic complications than poverty and hard work. My characters force me in spite of myself to lift them up in the world. The lower classes do not analyse or meditate, do not give utterance either to their thoughts or their emotions, and yet it is easier to get a low life part well played than one of high society."

Mr. Pinero is a delightful companion and he has the keenest sense of humour. He tells a good story in a truly dramatic way, and his greatest characteristic is his simple modesty. He never boasts, never talks big; but is always a genial, kindly, English gentleman. He rarely enters a theatre; in fact, he could count on his fingers the times he has done so during the last twenty years. Life is his stage, men and women its characters, his surroundings the scenes. He does not wish a State theatre, and thinks Irving has done more for the stage than any man in any time. He has the greatest love for his old master, and considers Irving's Hamlet the "most intelligent performance of the age." He waxes warm on the subject of Irving's "magnetic touch," which influences all that great actor's work. Pinero's love for, and belief in, the powers of the stage for good or ill are deep-seated, and each year finds him more given to careful psychological study, the only drawback to which is the fear that in over-elaboration freshness somewhat vanishes. Ibsen always took two years over a play, and Pinero seems to be acquiring the same habit.

A Pinero first night is looked upon as a great theatrical event, and rightly so. It was on a wet October evening (1903) that the long-anticipated *Letty* saw the light.

Opposite is the programme.

Duke of York's Theatre,
ST. MARTIN'S LANE, W.C.

Proprietors   Mr. & Mrs. FRANK WYATT.

Sole Lessee and Manager   CHARLES FROHMAN.

EVERY EVENING at a Quarter to Eight

CHARLES FROHMAN

Presents

A Drama, in Four Acts and an Epilogue, entitled

By ARTHUR W. PINERO.

Nevill Letchmere		Mr. H. B. IRVING
Ivor Crosbie		Mr. IVO DAWSON
Coppinger Drake		Mr. DORRINGTON GRIMSTON
Bernard Mandeville		Mr. FRED KERR
Richard Perry		Mr. DION BOUCICAULT
Neale	(*A Commercial Traveller*)	Mr. CHARLES TROODE
Ordish	(*Agent for an Insurance Company*)	Mr. JERROLD ROBERTSHAW
Rugg	(*Mr. Letchmere's Servant*)	Mr. CLAYTON GREENE
Frédéric	(*A Maître d'Hôtel*)	M. EDOUARD GARCEAU
Waiters		Mr. W. H. HAIGH & Mr. WALTER HACK
Mrs. Ivor Crosbie		Miss SARAH BROOKE
Letty Shell	*Clerks at Dugdale's*	Miss IRENE VANBRUGH
Marion Allardyce		Miss BEATRICE FORBES ROBERTSON
Hilda Gunning	*An Assistant at Madame Watkins's*	Miss NANCY PRICE
A Lady's-maid		Miss MAY ONSLOW

The Scene is laid in London:—the First and Fourth Acts at Mr. Letchmere's Flat in Grafton Street, New Bond Street; the Second at a house in Langham Street; the Third in a private room at the Café Régence; and the Epilogue at a photographer's in Baker Street. The events of the four acts of the drama, commencing on a Saturday in June, take place within the space of a few hours. Between the Fourth Act and the Epilogue two years and six months are supposed to elapse.

THE PLAY PRODUCED UNDER THE PERSONAL
DIRECTION OF THE AUTHOR.

The Scenery Painted by Mr. W. HANN.

FIRST MATINÉE SATURDAY, OCTOBER 17th, at 2.

General Manager   (for CHARLES FROHMAN)   W. LESTOCQ.

For once the famous dramatist descended from dukes and duchesses to a typewriter girl and a Bond Street swell. For once he left those high-class folk he finds so full of interest, moods, whims, ideas, self-analysis, and the rest of it, and cajoled a lower stratum of life to his pen.

Almost the first actor to appear was H. B. Irving—what a reception he received, and, brilliant cynic-actor though he be, his nervousness overpowered him to the point of ashen paleness and unrestrained twitching of the fingers. His methods, his tact, his cynicism were wonderful, and as Nevill Letchmere his resemblance to his father was remarkable.

What strikes one most in a Pinero play is the harmony of the whole. Every character is a living being. One remembers them all. The limelight is turned on each in turn, and not as at so many theatres on the actor-manager only. The play is a complete picture—not a frame with the actor-manager as the dominant person. He is so often the only figure on the canvas, his colleagues mere side-show puppets, that it is a real joy to see a play in England where every one is given a chance. Mr. Pinero does that. He not only creates living breathing studies of humanity, but he sees that they are played in a lifelike way. What is the result? A perfect whole. A fine piece of mosaic work well fitted together. We may not altogether care for the design or the colour, but we all admire its aims, its completeness, and feel the touch of genius that permeates the whole.

No more discriminating audience than that at the first night of *Letty* could possibly have been brought together. Every critic of worth was there. William Archer sat in the stalls immediately behind me, W. L. Courtney and Malcolm Watson beyond, J. Knight, A. B. Walkley, and A. E. T. Watson near by. Actors and actresses, artists, writers, men and women of note in every walk of life were there, and the enthusiasm was intense. Mr. Pinero was not in the house, no call of "author" brought him before the footlights, but his handsome wife—a prey to nervousness—was hidden behind the curtains in the stage box.

CHAPTER V

THE ARMY AND THE STAGE

Captain Robert Marshall—From the Ranks to the Stage—£10 for a
Play—How Copyright is Retained—I. Zangwill as Actor—Copy-
right Performance—Three First Plays (Pinero, Grundy, Sims)—
Cyril Maude at the Opera—*Mice and Men*—Sir Francis Burnand,
Punch, Sir John Tenniel, and a Cartoon—Brandon Thomas and
Charley's Aunt—How that Play was Written—The Gaekwar of
Baroda—Changes in London—Frederick Fenn at Clement's Inn—
James Welch on Audiences.

ONE of our youngest dramatists, for it was only in 1897 that Captain Robert
Marshall's first important play appeared, has suddenly leapt into the front
rank. His earlier days were in no way connected with the stage.

It is not often a man can earn an income in two different professions; such
success is unusual. True, Earl Roberts is a soldier and a writer; Forbes Robertson,
Weedon Grossmith, and Bernard Partridge are actors as well as artists; Lumsden
Propert, the author of the best book on miniatures, was a doctor by profession;
Edmund Gosse and Edward Clodd have other occupations besides literature. Although known as a writer, W. S. Gilbert could earn an income at the Bar or in Art;
A. W. Pinero is no mean draughtsman; Miss Gertrude Kingston writes and illus-
trates as well as acts; and Harry Furniss has shown us he is as clever with his pen
as with his brush in his *Confessions of a Caricaturist*. Still, it is unusual for any one
to succeed in two ways.

Nevertheless Captain Robert Marshall, once in the army, is now a successful
dramatist. He was born in Edinburgh in 1863, his father being a J.P. of that city.
Educated at St. Andrews, the ancient town famous for learning and golf, he later
migrated to Edinburgh University. While studying there his brother entered Sand-
hurst at the top of the list, and left in an equally exalted position. This inspired the
younger brother with a desire for the army, and he enlisted in the Highland Light
Infantry, then stationed in Ireland. The ranks gave him an excellent training, besides affording opportunities for studying various sides of life. Three years later he
entered the Duke of Wellington's West Riding Regiment as an officer, receiving his
Captaincy in 1895, after having filled the post of District Adjutant at Cape Town
and A.D.C. to the Governor of Natal, Sir W. Hely-Hutchinson.

No one looking at Captain Marshall now would imagine that ill-health had
ever afflicted him; such, however, was the case, and but for the fact that a delicate

chest necessitated retiring from the army, he would probably never have become a dramatist by profession. It was about 1898 that he left the Service; but he has made good use of the time since then, for such plays as *His Excellency the Governor*, *A Royal Family*, *The Noble Lord*, and *The Second in Command* have followed in quick succession. Then came an adaptation of M.M. Scribe and Legouvé's *Bataille de Dames*, which he called *There's Many a Slip*, but which T. Robertson translated with immense success as *The Ladies' Battle* some years before.

Mrs. Kendal, *àpropos* of this, writes me the following:

"My dear brother Tom had been dead for years before I ever played in *The Ladies' Battle*. He translated and sold it to Lacy, an old theatrical manager and agent, for about £10. Mr. Kendal and Mr. Hare revived it at the Court Theatre when I was under their management."

What would a modern dramatist say to a £10 note? What, indeed, would Captain Marshall say for such a small reward, instead of reaping a golden harvest as he did with his translation of the very same piece. Times have changed indeed during the last few years, for play-writing is now a most remunerative profession when it proves successful.

I remember once at a charming luncheon given by the George Alexanders at their house in Pont Street, hearing Mr. Lionel Monckton bitterly complaining of the difficulty of getting royalties for musical plays from abroad. Since then worse things have happened, and pirated copies of favourite songs have been sold by hundreds of thousands in the streets of London for which the authors, composers, and publishers have never received a cent. Mr. J. M. Barrie, who was sitting beside me, joined in, and declared, if I am not mistaken, that he had never got a penny from *The Little Minister* in America, or *The Window in Thrums*; indeed, it was not till *Sentimental Tommy* appeared in 1894 that he ever received anything at all from America, so *The Little Minister*, like *Pinafore*, was acted thousands of times without any royalties being paid to the respective authors by the United States.

Of course there was no copyright at all in England till 1833, and until that date a play could be produced by any one at any time without payment. The idea was preposterous, and so much abused that the Royal Assent was given in Parliament to a copyright bill proposed by the Hon. George Lamb, and carried through by Mr. Lytton Bulwer, who afterwards became famous as Lord Lytton. Still, even this, unfortunately, does not prevent piracy. Pirate thieves of other people's brains have had a good innings lately.

The only way to safeguard against the confiscation of a play without the author receiving any dues is to give a "copyright performance." With this end in view the well-known writer, Mr. I. Zangwill, gave an amusing representation of his play called *Merry Mary Ann*, founded on his novel of the same name. The performance took place at the Corn Exchange, Wallingford, and Mr. Zangwill was himself stage manager. This took place a week before it was given with such success in Chicago, and secured the English copyright to its author as well as the American.

The *modus operandi* under these circumstances is:

(1) To pay a two-guinea fee for a licence.

(2) To hire a hall which is licensed for stage performances.

(3) To notify the public by means of posters that the play will take place.

To make some one pay for admission. If only one person pay one guinea, that person constitutes an audience, which, if small, is at least unanimous.

Having arranged all these preliminaries the author and his friends proceed to read, or whenever possible act, the parts of the drama, and a very funny performance it sometimes is.

Mr. Zangwill's caste was certainly amusing. Mr. Jerome K. Jerome, author of *Three Men in a Boat*, was particularly good; but then he is an old actor. He lives at Wallingford-on-Thames, where he represents literature and journalism, G. F. Leslie, R.A., representing art; both joined forces for one afternoon at that strange performance which was in many ways a record. Sir Conan Doyle, of Sherlock Holmes fame, was to have played; but was called away at the last moment.

Mr. Zangwill is an old hand at this sort of thing; when a copyright performance of Hall Caine's *Mahdi* was given at the Haymarket Theatre he began at first by playing his allotted part; but as one performer after another threw up their *rôles* he was finally left to act them all. The female parts he played in his shirt-sleeves, with a high pitched voice. Mr. Clement Scott gave a long and favourable notice in the *Daily Telegraph* next day. Mr. Zangwill has lately taken unto himself a wife, none too soon, as he was the only member left in his Bachelor Club!

It is rather amusing to contrast the first plays of various men; for instance, Mr. Pinero, writing in the *Era Annual*, graphically described his beginning thus:

"First play of all: *Two Hundred a Year*. This was written for my old friends Mr. R. C. Carton and Miss Compton (Mrs. Carton) as a labour of love when I was an actor, and was produced at the Globe in 1877. The love, however, was and is more considerable than the composition, which did not employ me more than a single afternoon. My next venture was in the same year, and entitled *Two Can Play at the Game*, a farce produced at the Lyceum Theatre by Mrs. Bateman in order really to provide myself with a part. I acted in this many times in London, and afterwards under Mr. Irving, as he then was, throughout the provinces. By the way, Mrs. Bateman paid me five pounds for this piece."

Mr. Sydney Grundy tells the following story:

"In 1872 I amused myself by writing a comedietta. I had it printed, and across the cover of one copy I scrawled in a large bold hand, "You may play this for nothing," addressed it to J. B. Buckstone, Esq., Haymarket Theatre, London, posted it, and forgot all about it. A week afterwards I received a letter in these terms: 'Dear Sir,—Mr. Buckstone desires me to inform you that your comedietta is in rehearsal, and will be produced at his forthcoming Benefit. Mr. and Mrs. Kendal will play the principal parts.—Yours faithfully, F. Weathersby.' New authors were such rare phenomena in those days, that Mr. Buckstone did not know how to announce me, so adopted the weird expedient of describing me as 'Mr. Sydney Grundy, of Manchester.' The comedietta was a great success and received only one bad review.

One critic was so tickled by the circumstance that the author lived in Manchester that he mentioned it no fewer than three times in his 'notice.'"

G. R. Sims describes his initial attempt thus:

"My first play was produced at the Theatre Royal, 113, Adelaide Road, and was a burlesque of *Leah*; the parts were played by my brothers and sisters and some young friends. The price of admission to the day nursery, in which the stage was erected, was one shilling, which included tea, but visitors were requested to bring their own cake and jam. The burlesque was in four scenes. Many of the speeches were lifted bodily from the published burlesque of Henry J. Byron.

"That was my first play as an amateur. My first professional play *was*, *One Hundred Years Old*, and *is* now twenty-seven years old. It was produced July 10th, 1875, at a *matinée* at the Olympic Theatre, by Mr. E. J. Odell, and was a translation or adaptation of *Le Centenaire*, by D'Ennery and another. It was less successful than my amateur play. It did not bring me a shilling. The burlesque brought me two—one paid by my father and one by my mother."

Such were the first experiences of three eminent dramatic authors.

It must be delightful when author and actor are in unison. Such a thing as a difference of opinion cannot be altogether unknown between them; but no more united little band could possibly be found than that behind the scenes at the Haymarket Theatre, where the rehearsals are conducted in the spirit of a family party. The tyrannical author and the self-assertive representatives of his creations all work in harmony.

"As one gets up in the Service," amusingly said Captain Marshall, "one receives a higher rate of pay, and has proportionately less to do. Thus it was I found time for scribbling; it was actually while A.D.C. and living in a Government House that I wrote *His Excellency the Governor*. Three days after it came out I left the army."

"Was that your first play?" I inquired.

"No. My first was a little one-act piece which Mr. Kendal accepted. It dealt with the flight of Bonnie Prince Charlie from Scotland in 1746. My first acted play appeared at the Lyceum, and was another piece in one act, called *Shades of Night*, which finally migrated to the Haymarket."

It is curious how success and failure follow one on the other. No play of Captain Marshall's excited more criticism than *The Broad Road* at Terry's; but nevertheless it was a failure. It was succeeded immediately by *A Royal Family* at the Court, which proved popular. He has worked hard during the last few years, and deserves any meed of praise that may be given him by the public. Many men on being told to relinquish the profession they loved because of ill-health would calmly sit down and court death. Not so Robert Marshall. He at once turned his attention elsewhere, chose an occupation he could take about with him when driven by necessity to warmer climes, lived in the fresh air, did as he was medically advised, with the result that to-day he is a comparatively strong man, busy in a life that is full of interest.

As a subaltern in the army the embryo dramatist once painted the scenery for a performance of *The Mikado* in Bermuda, and was known to write, act, stage-manage, and paint the scenes of another play himself. Enthusiasm truly; but it was all experience, and the intimate knowledge then gained of the difficulties of stage craft have since stood him in good stead.

Captain Marshall is a broad, good-looking man, retiring by disposition, one might almost say shy—for that term applies, although he emphatically denies the charge—and certainly humble and modest as regards his own work. The author of *The Second in Command* is athletically inclined; he is fond of golf, fencing, and tennis—the love of the first he doubtless acquired in his childhood's days, when old Tom Morris was so well known on the St. Andrews links.

The playwright is also devoted to music, and nothing gives him greater pleasure than to spend an evening at the Opera. One night I happened to sit in a box between him and Mr. Cyril Maude, and probably there were no more appreciative listeners in the house than these two men, both intensely interested in the representation of *Tannhäuser*. Poor Mr. Maude having a sore throat, had been forbidden to act that evening for fear of losing the little voice which remained to him. As music is his delight, and an evening at the Opera an almost unknown pleasure, he enjoyed himself with the enthusiasm of a child, feeling he was having a "real holiday."

Captain Marshall is so fond of music that he amuses himself constantly at his piano or pianola in his charming flat in town.

"I like the machine best," he remarked laughingly, "because it makes no mistakes, and with a little practice can be played with almost as much feeling as a pianoforte."

When in London Captain Marshall lives in a flat at the corner of Berkeley Square; but during the winter he migrates to the Riviera or some other sunny land. The home reflects the taste of its owner; and the dainty colouring, charming pictures, and solid furniture of the flat denote the man of artistic taste who dislikes show without substance even in furniture.

The first time I met Robert Marshall was at W. S. Gilbert's delightful country home at Harrow Weald. The Captain has a most exalted opinion of Mr. Gilbert's writings and witticisms. He considers him a model playwright, and certainly worships—as much as one man can worship at the shrine of another—this originator of modern comedy.

One summer, when Captain Marshall found the alluring hospitality of London incompatible with work, he took a charming house at Harrow Weald, and settled himself down to finish a play. He could not, however, stand the loneliness of a big establishment by himself—a loneliness which he does not feel in his flat. Consequently that peace and quiet which he went to the country to find, he himself disturbed by inviting friends down on all possible occasions, and being just as gay as if he had remained in town. He finished his play, however, between the departure and arrival of his various guests.

Two of the most successful plays of modern times have been written by women; the first, by Mrs. Hodgson Burnett, was founded on her own novel, *Little Lord Fauntleroy*, of which more anon. The second had no successful book to back it, and yet it ran over three hundred nights.

This as far as serious drama is concerned—for burlesque touched up may run to any length—is a record.

Mice and Men, by Mrs. Ryley, must have had something in it, something special, or why should a play from an almost unknown writer have taken such a hold on the London public? It was well acted, of course, for that excellent artist Forbes Robertson was in it; but other plays have been well acted and yet have failed.

Why, then, its longevity?

Its very simplicity must be the answer. It carried conviction. It was just a quaint little idyllic episode of love and romance, deftly woven together with strong human interest. It aimed at nothing great, it merely sought to entertain and amuse. Love rules the world, romance enthrals it, both were prettily depicted by a woman, and the play proved a brilliant success. To have written so little and yet made such a hit is rare.

On the other hand, one of our most successful playwrights has been very prolific in his work. Sir Francis Burnand has edited *Punch* for more than thirty years, and yet has produced over one hundred and twenty plays. 'Tis true one of the most successful of these was written in a night. Mr. Burnand, as he was then, went to the St. James's Theatre one evening to see *Diplomacy*, and after the performance walked home. On the way the idea for a burlesque struck him, so he had something to eat, found paper and pens, and began. By breakfast-time next morning *Diplomacy* was completed, and a few days later all London was laughing over it. There is a record of industry and speed.

The stage, however, has not claimed so much of his attention of late years as his large family and Mr. Punch. Sir Francis is particularly neat and dapper, with a fresh complexion and grey hair. He wears a pointed white beard, but looks remarkably youthful. He is a busy man, and spends hours of each day in his well-stocked library at the Boltons (London, Eng.: as our American friends would say), or at Ramsgate, his favourite holiday resort, where riding and sea-boating afford him much amusement, and time for reflection. He is a charming dinner-table companion, always full of good humour and amusing stories.

It was when dining one night at the Burnands' home in the Boltons that I met Sir John Tenniel after a lapse of some years, for he virtually gave up dining out early in the '90's in order to devote his time to his *Punch* cartoon. One warm day in July, 1902, however, John Tenniel was persuaded to break his rule, and proved as kind and lively as ever. Although eighty-two years of age he drew a picture for me after dinner. There are not many men of eighty-two who could do that; but then, did he not draw the *Punch* cartoon without intermission for fifty years?

"What am I to draw?" he asked. "I have nothing to copy and no model to help me."

"Britannia," I replied. "That ever-young lady is such an old friend of yours, you must know every line in her face by heart." And he did. The dear old man's hand was very shaky, until he got the pencil on to the paper, and then the lines themselves were perfectly clear and distinct; years of work on wood blocks had taught him precision which did not fail him even when over fourscore.

Every one loves Sir John. He never seems to have given offence with his cartoons as so many have done before and since. Cartoonists and caricaturists ply a difficult trade, for so few people like to be made fun of themselves, although they dearly love a joke at some one else's expense.

A few doors from the Burnands' charming house in Bolton Gardens lives the author of *Charley's Aunt*.

When in the city of Mexico, one broiling hot December day in 1900, I was invited to dine and go to the theatre. I had only just arrived in that lovely capital, and was dying to see and do everything.

"Will there be any Indians amongst the audience?" I inquired.

"Si, Señora. The Indians and half-castes love the theatre, and always fill the cheaper places."

This sounded delightful; a Spanish play acted in Castilian with beautiful costumes of matadors and shawled ladies—what could be better? Gladly I accepted the invitation to dine and go to the theatre afterwards, where, as subsequently proved, they have a strange arrangement by which a spectator either pays for the whole performance, or only to witness one particular act.

We arrived. The audience looked interesting: few, however, even in the best places wore dress-clothes, any more than they do in the United States. The performance began.

It did not seem very Spanish, and somehow appeared familiar. I looked at the programme. "LA TIA DE CARLOS."

What a sell! I had been brought to see *Charley's Aunt*.

One night after my return to London I was dining with William Heinemann, the publisher, to meet the great "Jimmy" Whistler. I was telling Mr. Brandon Thomas, the author of *Charley's Aunt*, this funny little experience, when he remarked:

"I can tell you another. My wife and I had been staying in the Swiss mountains, when one day we reached Zürich. 'Let us try to get a decent dinner,' I said, 'for I am sick of *table d'hôtes*.' Accordingly we dined on the best Zürich could produce, and then asked the waiter what play he would recommend.

"'The theatres are closed just now,' he replied.

"'But surely something is open?'

"'Ah, well, yes, there's a sort of music hall, but the *Herrschaften* would not care to go there.'

"'Why not?' I exclaimed, longing for some diversion.

"'Because they are only playing a very vulgar piece, it would not please the *gnädige Frau*, it is a stupid English farce.'

"'Never mind how stupid. Tell me its name.'

"'It is called,' replied the waiter, '*Die Tante*.'"

Poor Brandon Thomas nearly collapsed on the spot, it was his very own play. They went. Needless to say, however, the author hardly recognised his child in its new garb, although he never enjoyed an evening more thoroughly in his life.

The first draft of this well-known piece was written in three weeks, and afterwards, as the play was considerably cut in the provinces, Mr. Thomas restored the original matter and entirely re-wrote it before it was produced in London, when the author played the part of Sir Francis Chesney himself.

I have another recollection in connection with *Charley's Aunt*. It must have been about 1895 that my husband and I were dining with that delightful little gentleman and great Indian Prince, the Gaekwar of Baroda, and the Maharanee (his wife), and we all went on to the theatre to see *Charley's Aunt*. At that time His Highness the Gaekwar was very proud of a grand new theatre he had built in Baroda, and was busy having plays translated for production. Several Shakespearian pieces had already been done. He thought *Charley's Aunt* might be suitable, but as the play proceeded, turning to me he remarked:

"This would never do, it would give my people a bad idea of English education; no, no—I cannot allow such a mistake as that."

So good is His Highness's own opinion of our education that his sons are at Harrow and Oxford as I write.

Charley's Aunt has been played in every European language—verily a triumph for its author. How happy and proud a man ought to be who has brought so much enjoyment into life; and yet Brandon Thomas feels almost obliged to blush every time the title is mentioned. When Mr. Penley asked him to write a play, in spite of being in sad need of cash, he was almost in despair. His eye fell upon the photograph of an elderly relative, and showing it to Penley he asked:

"How would you like to play an old woman like that?"

"Delighted, old chap; I've always wanted to play a woman's character." And when the play was written Penley acted the part made up like the old lady in the photograph which still stands on Brandon Thomas's mantelshelf.

London is changing terribly, although *Charley's Aunt* seems as if it would go on for ever. Old London is vanishing in a most distressing manner. Within a few months Newgate has been pulled down, the Bluecoat School has disappeared, and now Clifford's Inn has been sold for £100,000 and is to be demolished. Many of the sets of chambers therein contained beautiful carving, and in one of these sets dwelt Frederick Fenn, the dramatist, son of Manville Fenn, the novelist. He determined to have a bachelor party before quitting his rooms, and an interesting party it proved.

I left home shortly after nine o'clock with a friend, and when we reached Piccadilly Circus we found ourselves in the midst of the crowd waiting to watch

President Loubet drive past on his way to the Gala performance at Covent Garden (July, 1903). The streets were charmingly decorated, and must have given immense satisfaction not only to the President of France but to the entire Republic he represented. From the Circus through Leicester Square the crowd was standing ten or fifteen deep on either side of the road, and we had various vicissitudes in getting to our destination at all. The police would not let us pass, and we drove round and round back streets, unable to get into either the Strand or St. Martin's Lane. However, at last a mighty cheer told us the royal party had passed, and we were allowed to drive on our way to Clifford's Inn. Up a dark alley beyond the Law Courts we trudged, and rang the big sonorous bell for the porter to admit us to the courtyard surrounded by chambers.

Ascending a spiral stone staircase, carpeted in red for the occasion, we passed through massive oak doors with their low doorways and entered Mr. Fenn's rooms.

"How lovely! Surely those carvings are by the famous Gibbons?"

"They are," he said, "or at any rate they are reputed to be, and in a fortnight will be sold by auction to the highest bidder."

This wonderful decoration had been there for numbers of years, the over-doors, chimneypieces and window-frames were all most beautifully carved, and the whole room was panelled from floor to ceiling. The furniture was in keeping. Beautiful inlaid satinwood tables, settees covered with old-fashioned brocade, old Sheffield cake-baskets, were in harmony with the setting.

It was quite an interesting little party, and I thoroughly enjoyed my chat with James Welsh, the clever comedian, who played in the *New Clown* for eighteen months consecutively. Such an interesting little man, with dark round eyes and pale eyelashes, and a particularly broad crown to his head.

"I don't mind a long run at all," he said, "because every night there is a fresh audience. Sometimes they are so dull we cannot get hold of them at all till the second act, and sometimes it is even the end of the second act before they are roused to enthusiasm; another time they will see the fun from the first rise of the curtain. Personally I prefer the audience to be rather dull at the beginning, for I like to work them up, and to work up with them myself. The most enthusiastic audiences to my mind are to be found in Scotland—I am of course speaking of low comedy. In Ireland they may be as appreciative, but they are certainly quieter. Londoners are always difficult to rouse to any expression of enthusiasm. I suppose they see too many plays, and so become *blasé*."

CHAPTER VI

DESIGNING THE DRESSES

Sarah Bernhardt's Dresses and Wigs—A Great Musician's Hair—
Expenses of Mounting—Percy Anderson—*Ulysses*—*The Eternal
City*—A Dress Parade—Armour—Over-elaboration—An Under-
study—Miss Fay Davis—A London Fog—The Difficulties of an
Engagement.

MADAME SARAH BERNHARDT is an extraordinary woman. A young artist of my acquaintance did much work for her at one time. He designed dresses, and painted the Egyptian, Assyrian, and other trimmings. She was always most grateful and generous. Money seemed valueless to her; she dived her hand into a bag of gold, and holding it out bid him take what would repay him for his trouble. He was a true artist and his gifts appealed to her.

"More, more," she often exclaimed. "You have not reimbursed yourself sufficiently—you have only taken working-pay and allowed nothing for your talent. It is the talent I wish to pay for."

And she did.

On one occasion a gorgeous cloak he had designed for her came home; a most expensive production. She tried it on.

"Hateful, hateful!" she cried. "The bottom is too heavy, bring me the scissors," and in a moment she had ripped off all the lower trimmings. The artist looked aghast, and while he stood—

"Black," she went on—"it wants black"; and thereupon she pinned a great black scarf her dresser brought her over the mantle. The effect was magical. That became one of her most successful garments for many a day.

"Ah!" said the artist afterwards, "she has a great and generous heart—she adores talent, worships the artistic, and her taste is unfailing."

Wonderful effects can be gained on the stage by the aid of the make-up box— and the wig-maker.

Madame Sarah Bernhardt declares Clarkson, of London, to be the "king of wig-makers," and he has made every wig she has worn in her various parts for many years.

"She is a wonderful woman," Mr. Clarkson said, "she knows exactly what she wants, and if she has not time to write and enclose a sketch—which, by the way, she does admirably — she sends a long telegram from Paris, and expects the wig to be despatched almost as quickly as if it went over by a 'reply-paid process.'"

"But surely you get more time than that usually?"

Drawing of Costume for Juliet.

By Percy Anderson.

"Oh yes, of course; but twice I have made wigs in a few hours. Once for Miss Ellen Terry. I think it was the twenty-fifth anniversary of *The Bells* — at any rate she was to appear in a small first piece for one night. At three o'clock that afternoon the order came. I set six people to work on six different pieces, and at seven o'clock took them down to the theatre and pinned them on Miss Terry's head. The other wig I had to make so quickly was for Madame Eleonora Duse. She arrived in London October, 1903, and somehow the wigs went astray. She wired to Paris to inquire who made the one in *La Ville Morte* with which Madame Bernhardt strangled her victim. When the reply came she sent for me, and the same night Madame Duse wore the new wig in *La Gioconda*."

By-the-bye, Madame Duse has a wonderful wig-box. It is a sort of miniature cupboard made of wood, from which the front lets down. Inside are six divisions. Each division contains one of those weird block-heads on which perruques stand when being redressed, and on every red head rests a wig. These are for her different parts, the blocks are screwed tight into the box, and the wigs are covered lightly with chiffon for travelling. When the side of the box falls down those six heads form a gruesome sight!

Most of the hair used in wig-making comes from abroad, principally from the mountain valleys of Switzerland, where the peasant-girls wear caps and sell their hair. A wig costs anything from £2 to £10, and it is wonderful how little the good ones weigh. They are made on the finest net, and each hair is sewn on separately.

When Clarkson was a boy of twelve and a half years old he first accompanied his father, who was a hairdresser, to the opera, and thus the small youth began his profession. He still works in the house in which he was born, so he was reared literally in the wig trade, and now employs a couple of hundred persons. What he does not know can hardly be worth knowing—and he is quite a character. Not only does he work for the stage; but detectives often employ him to paint their faces and disguise them generally, and he has even decorated a camel with whiskers and grease paint.

The most expensive wig he ever made was for Madame Sarah Bernhardt in *La Samaritaine*. It had to be very long, and naturally wavy hair, so that she could throw it over her face when she fell at the Saviour's feet. In *L'Aiglon* Madame Bernhardt wore her own hair for a long time, and had it cut short for the purpose: but she found it so difficult to dress off the stage that she ultimately ordered a wig.

If Madame Bernhardt is particular about her wigs and her dresses she has done much to improve theatrical costumes—she has stamped them with an individuality and artistic grace.

A well-known musician travelled from a far corner in Europe to ask a wig-maker to make him a wig. He arrived one day in Wellington Street in a great state of distress and told his story. He had prided himself on his beautiful, long, wavy hair, through which he could pass his fingers in dramatic style, and which he could shake with leonine ferocity over a passage which called for such sentiments. But alas! there came a day when the hair began to come out, and the locks threatened to disappear. He travelled hundreds of miles to London to know if the wig-maker could copy the top of his head exactly before it was too late. Of course he could, and consequently those raven curls were matched, and one by one were sewn into the fine netting to form the toupet. Having got the semi-wig exactly to cover his head, the great musician sallied forth and had his head shaved. Then, with a little paste to catch it down in front and at the sides, the toupet was securely placed upon the bald cranium. For six months that man had his head shaved daily. The effect was magical. When he left off shaving a new crop of hair began to grow with lightning rapidity, and he is now the happy possessor of as beautiful a head of hair as ever.

Little by little the public has been taught to expect the reproduction of correct historical pictures upon the stage, and such being the case, artists have risen to the occasion, men who have given years of their lives to the study of apparel of particular periods.

Designing stage dress is no easy matter; long and ardent research is necessary for old costume pieces, and men who have made this their speciality read and sketch at museums, and sometimes travel to far corners of the world, to get exactly what they want. As a rule the British Museum provides reliable material for historical costume.

Think of the hundreds, aye hundreds, of costumes necessary for a heavy play at the Lyceum or His Majesty's—think of what peasantry, soldiers, to say nothing of fairies, require, added to which four or five dresses for each of the chief performers, not only cost months of labour to design and execute, but need large sums of money to perfect. As much as £10,000 has often been spent in the staging of a single play.

This is no meagre sum, and should the play fail the actor-manager who has risked that large amount (or his syndicate) must bear the loss.

Some wonderful stage pictures have been produced within the last few years—and not a few of them were the work of Mr. Percy Anderson, Sir Alma-Tadema, and Mr. Percy Macquoid. It is an interesting fact that, while the designs for *Ulysses* cost Mr. Anderson six months' continual labour, he managed to draw the elaborate costumes for Lewis Waller's production of *The Three Musketeers* in three days, working eighteen hours out of the twenty-four, because the dresses were wanted immediately.

Percy Anderson did not start as an artist in his youth, he was not born in the profession, but as a mature man allowed his particular bent to lead him to success. He lives in a charming little house bordering on the Regent's Park, where he works with his brush all day, and his pencil far into the night. His studio is a pretty snuggery built on at the back of the house, which is partly studio, partly room, and partly greenhouse. Here he does his work and accomplishes those delightfully sketchy portraits for which he is famous, his innumerable designs for theatrical apparel.

When I asked Mr. Anderson which costumes were most difficult to draw, he replied:

"Either those in plays of an almost prehistoric period, when the materials from which to work are extremely scanty, or those that introduce quite modern and up-to-date ceremonial.

"As an instance of the former *Ulysses* proved an exceedingly difficult piece for which to design the costumes, because the only authentic information obtainable was from castes and sketches of remains found during the recent excavations at Knossus, in Crete, that have since been exhibited at the Winter Exhibition at Burlington House, but which were at the time reposing in a private room at the British Museum, where I was able to make some rough sketches and notes by the courtesy of Mr. Sidney Colvin."

"How did you manage about colour?"

"My guide as to the colours in use at that remote period of time was merely a small fragment of early Mycenean mural decoration from Knossus, in which three colours, namely, yellow, blue, and a terra-cotta-red, together with black and white, were the only tones used, and to these three primary colours I accordingly confined myself, but I made one introduction, a bright apple-green dress which served to throw the others into finer relief. From these extremely scanty materials I had to design over two hundred costumes, none of which were exactly alike."

The brilliancy of the result all playgoers will remember. The frontispiece shows one of the designs.

As an instance of a play introducing intricate modern ceremonial for which every garment worn had some special significance, *The Eternal City* may be mentioned. In that Mr. Anderson had the greatest difficulty in discovering exactly what uniform or vestment would be worn by the Pope's *entourage* on important private occasions, such as the scene in the Gardens of the Vatican, where His Holiness was carried in and saluted by the members of his guard before being left to receive his private audiences.

Mr. Anderson, however, received invaluable assistance in these matters from Mr. De La Roche Francis, who, besides having relatives in high official positions in Rome, had himself been attached to the Papal Court. All orders and decorations worn by the various characters in *The Eternal City* were modelled from the originals. Mr. Anderson usually makes a separate sketch for every costume to be worn by each character, in order to judge of the whole effect, which picture he supplements by drawings of the back and side views, reproductions of hats, head-dresses, hair, and jewellery.

This is thoroughness—but after all thoroughness is the only thing that really succeeds. From these sketches the articles are cut out and made after Mr. Anderson has passed the materials as satisfactory submitted to him. Sometimes nothing proves suitable, and then something has to be woven to meet his own particular requirements.

Mr. Anderson received orders direct from Beerbohm Tree for *King John, Midsummer Night's Dream, Herod, Ulysses, Merry Wives of Windsor, Resurrection,* and *The Eternal City,* but in some cases the orders come from the authors. For instance, Mr. Pinero wrote asking him to design those delightful Victorian costumes for *Trelawny of the Wells.* Captain Basil Hood arranged with him about the dresses for *Merrie England,* and J. M. Barrie for those in *Quality Street.*

Some of the old-style dresses do not allow of much movement, and therefore it is sometimes necessary to make the garments in such a way that, while the effect remains, the actor has full play for his limbs. For instance, much adaptation of this sort was necessary for *Richard II.* at His Majesty's. Mr. Anderson was about three months designing the two hundred and fifty dresses for this marvellous spectacle. He sought inspiration at the British Museum and Westminster, the Bluemantle at the Heralds' College giving him valuable information with regard to the heraldry. All this shows the pains needed and taken to produce an accurate and harmonious stage picture.

The designer is given a free hand, he chooses his own materials to the smallest details—often a guinea a yard is paid for silks and velvets—and he superintends everything, even the grouping of the crowds, so as to give most effect to his colouring. "Dress parades," of which there are several, are those in which all the chorus and crowds have to appear, therefore their dresses are usually made first, so as to admit of ample study of colour before the "principals" receive theirs. The onlooker hardly recognises the trouble this entails, nor how well thought out the scheme of colour must be, so that when the crowd breaks up into groups the dresses shall not clash. The artist must always work up to one broad effect in order to make a decorative scene.

It may be interesting to note that there is one particular colour—French blue—practically the shade of hyacinths, which is particularly useful for stage effect as it does not lose any of its tint by artificial light. It can only be dyed in one river at Lyons, in France, where there is some chemical in the water which exactly suits and retains the particular shade desired. We are improving in England, however, and near Haslemere wonderful fabrics and colours are now produced. There are excellent costumiers in England, some of the best, in fact, many of whom lay themselves out for work of a particular period; but all the armour is still made in France. That delightful singer and charming man, Eugene Oudin, wore a beautiful suit of chain armour as the Templar in *Ivanhoe*, which cost considerably over £100, and proved quite light and easy to wear. (During the last five years armour has become cheaper.) It was a beautiful dress, including a fine plumed helmet, and as he and my husband were the same size and build he several times lent it to him for fancy balls. It looked like the old chain armour in the Tower of London or the Castle of Madrid, and yet did not weigh as many ounces as they do pounds, so carefully had it been made to allow ease and movement to the singer.

After all, it is really a moot question whether tremendous elaboration of scenery is a benefit to dramatic production. At the present time much attention is drawn from the main interest, and instead of appreciating the acting or the play, it is the stage carpentering and gorgeous "mounting" that wins the most applause.

This is all very well to a certain extent, but it is hardly educating the public to grasp the real value of play or acting if both be swamped by scenery and silks. Lately we had an opportunity of seeing really good performances *without* their being enhanced by scenic effect, such as *Twelfth Night*, by the Elizabethan Stage Society, and *Everyman*. These representations were an intellectual treat, such as one seldom enjoys, and were certainly calculated to raise the standard of purely theatrical work. Strictness of detail may do much to make the *tout ensemble* perfect, but does not the piece lose more than it gains?

Again, the careful rehearsing which is now in fashion tends to make the performers more or less puppets in the hands of the stage manager or author, rather than real individual actors. Individuality except in "stars" is not wanted nor appreciated. Further, *long runs* are the ruin of actors. Instead of being kept up to the mark, alert, their brains active by constantly learning and performing new *rôles*, they simply become automata, and can almost go through their parts in their sleep. Surely this is not *acting*.

Every important *rôle* has an understudy. Generally some one playing a minor part in the programme is allowed the privilege of understudying a star. By this arrangement he is at the theatre every night, and if the star cannot shine, the minor individual goes on to twinkle instead, his own part being played by some lesser luminary. Many a man or woman has found an opening and ultimate success in this way, through the misfortune of another.

At some theatres the understudy is paid for performing, or is given a present of some sort in recognition of his services, while at others, even good ones, he gets nothing at all, the honour being considered sufficient reward.

No one misses a performance if he can possibly help it; there are many reasons for not doing so; and sometimes actors go through this strain when physically unfit for work, rather than be out of the bill for a single night. Theatrical folk go through many vicissitudes in their endeavour to keep faith with the public.

For instance, one terribly foggy night in 1902 during the run of *Iris* all London was steeped in blackness. It was truly an awful fog, just one of those we share with Chicago and Christiania. Miss Fay Davis, that winsome American actress, was playing the chief part in Pinero's play and went down to the theatre every night from her home in Sloane Square in a brougham she always hired, with an old coachman she knew well.

She ate her dinner in despair at the fog, her mother fidgeted anxiously and wondered what was to happen, when the bell rang, long before the appointed time, and the carriage was announced.

"Oh, we'll get there somehow, miss," the old coachman remarked; so, well wrapped up in furs, the daring lady started for her work. They did get there after an anxious journey, assisted by policemen and torches, Miss Davis alighted, saying:

"I daresay it will be all right by eleven, but anyway you must fetch me on foot if you can't drive."

"Aye, aye, ma'am," replied her worthy friend, and off he drove. Miss Davis went to her dressing-room, feeling a perfect heroine for venturing forth, and when she was half ready there came a knock at the door.

"No performance to-night, miss."

"What?"

"Only half the actors have turned up, and there isn't a single man or woman in the theatre—pit empty, gallery empty, everything empty—so they've decided not to play *Iris* to-night. No one can see across the footlights."

It was true; so remarkable was that particular fog, several of the playhouses had to shut-up-shop for the night. How Miss Davis got home remains a mystery.

A very beautiful actress of my acquaintance rarely has an engagement. She acts well, she looks magnificent, and has played many star parts in the provinces, yet she is constantly among the unemployed. "Why," I once asked, "do you find it so difficult to get work?"

"Because I'm three inches too tall. No man likes to be dwarfed by a woman on the stage. In a ball-room the smaller the man the taller the partner he chooses, and this sometimes applies to matrimony, but on the stage never."

"Can you play with low heels?" she is often asked when seeking an engagement.

"Certainly," is the reply.

"Would you mind standing beside me?"

"Delighted."

"Too tall, I'm afraid," says the man.

"But I can dress my hair low and wear small hats."

"Too tall all the same, I'm afraid."

And for this reason she loses one engagement after another. Most of the actor-managers have their own wives or recognised "leading ladies," so that in London, openings for new stars are few and far between, and when the actress, however great her talent or her charm, makes the leading actor look small, she is waved aside and some one inferior takes her place.

On one occasion it was a woman who refused to act with my friend. She had been engaged for a big part—but when this woman—once the darling of society, and a glittering star upon the stage—saw her fellow-worker, she said:

"I can't act with you, you would make me look insignificant; besides, you are too good-looking."

CHAPTER VII

SUPPER ON THE STAGE

ONE of the most delightful theatrical entertainments I ever remember was held by Mr. George Alexander on the stage of the St. James's Theatre. It was in honour of the Coronation of Edward VII., and given to the Indian Princes and Colonial visitors.

The play preceding the reception was that charming piece *Paolo and Francesca*. I sat in the stalls, and on my right hand was a richly attired Indian, who wore a turban lavishly ornamented with jewels. I had seen him a short while previously at a Court at Buckingham Palace, one of those magnificent royal evening receptions Queen Alexandra has instituted instead of those dreary afternoon Drawing-rooms. This gentleman had been there when the Royalties received the Indian Princes in June, 1902, the occasion when the royal *cortége* promenaded through those spacious rooms with such magnificent effect. It was the Court held a few days prior to the date first fixed for the Coronation—a ceremony postponed, as all the world knows, till some weeks later in consequence of the King's sudden illness.

My princely neighbour was very grand. He wore that same huge ruby at the side of his head, set in diamonds and ornamented with an osprey, which had excited so much admiration at Buckingham Palace. Although small he was a fine-looking man and had charming manners. He read his programme carefully and seemed much interested in the performance, then he looked through his opera-glasses and appeared puzzled; suddenly I realised he wanted to know something.

"You follow the play?" I asked; "or can I explain anything to you?"

"Thank you so much," he replied in charming English. "I can follow it pretty well, but I cannot quite make out whether the lovely young lady is really going to marry that hump-backed man. Surely she ought to marry the handsome young fellow. She is so lily-lovely."

"No, Francesca marries Giovanni."

"Ah, it is too sad, poor thing," answered the Indian gentleman, apparently much grieved. He turned to his neighbour, who did not speak English, and retailed the information. Their distress was really amusing. Evidently the lovely white lady (Miss Millard) deserved a better fate according to their ideas, for he repeatedly expressed his distress as the play proceeded. Before he left the theatre that night he crossed the stage, and making a profound bow, thanked me for helping him to understand the play. His gratitude and Oriental politeness were charming.

The St. James's presented a gay scene. The Indian dresses, the diamonds, and extra floral decorations rendered it a regular gala performance. At the usual hour the curtain descended. The general public left; but invited guests remained. We rose from our seats and conversed with friends, while a perfect army of stage carpenters and strange women, after moving out the front row of stalls, brought flights of steps and made delightfully carpeted staircases lead up to either side of the stage. Huge palms and lovely flowers banked the banisters and hid the orchestra. Within a few moments the whole place resembled a conservatory fitted up as for a rout. It was all done as if by magic. Methinks Mr. Alexander must have had several "stage rehearsals" to accomplish results so admirable with such rapidity.

The curtain rose, the stage had been cleared, and there at the head of the staircase stood the handsome actor-manager in plain dress clothes, washed and cleaned from his heavy make-up, and with his smiling wife ready to receive their guests.

At the back of the stage the scenery had been arranged to form a second room, wherein supper was served at a buffet.

It was all admirably done. Most of the Colonial Premiers were there, many of the Indian Princes, and a plentiful sprinkling of the leading lights of London. Of course a stage is not very big and the numbers had to be limited; but about a couple of hundred persons thoroughly enjoyed that supper behind the footlights at the St. James's Theatre. Many of the people had never been on a stage before, and it was rather amusing to see them peeping behind the flies, and asking weird questions from the scene-shifters. Some were surprised to find the floor was not level, but a gentle incline, for all audiences do not know the necessity of raising the back figures, so that those in front of the house may see all the performers.

A party on the stage is always interesting, and generally of rare occurrence, although Sir Henry Irving and Mr. Beerbohm Tree both gave suppers in honour of the Coronation, so England's distinguished visitors had several opportunities of enjoying these unique receptions. At the supper at His Majesty's Theatre a few nights later the chief attractions besides the Beerbohm Trees were Mrs. Kendal and Miss Ellen Terry, the latter still wearing her dress as Mistress Page. Every one wanted to shake hands with her, and not a few were saddened to see her using

those grey smoked glasses she always dons when not actually before the footlights.

Mr. George Alexander.

Photo by Langfier, 23A, Old Bond Street, London, W.

George Alexander has had a most successful career, but he was not cradled on the stage. His father was an Ayrshire man and the boy was brought up for business. Not liking that he turned to medicine, and still being dissatisfied he abandoned the doctor's art at an early stage and took a post in a silk merchant's office. This brought him to London. From that moment he was a constant theatre-goer, and in September, 1879, made his first bow behind the footlights. He owes much of his success to the training he received in Sir Henry Irving's Company at the Lyceum. There is no doubt much of the business learned in early youth has stood him in good stead in his theatrical ventures, and much of the artistic taste and desire for perfection in stage-mounting so noticeable at the St. James's was imbibed in the early days at the Lyceum. It takes a great deal to make a successful actor-manager; he must have literary and artistic taste, business capacity, and withal knowledge of his craft.

In 1891 he took the St. James's Theatre and began a long series of successes. He has gone through the mill, worked his way from the bottom to the top, and being possessed of an exceptionally clear business head, has made fewer mistakes than many others in his profession.

Mr. Alexander tells a good story about himself:

"For many months I continually received very long letters from a lady giving me her opinion not only on current stage matters, but on the topics of the hour, with graphic descriptions of herself—her doings—her likes and dislikes. She gave no address, but her letters usually bore the postmark of a country town not a hundred miles from London. She confided in me that she was a spinster, and that she did not consider her relations sympathetic. She was obviously well-to-do—I gathered this from her account of her home and her daily life as she described them. Suddenly her letters ceased, and I wondered what had happened. Almost two months after I received her last letter, I had a communication from a firm of lawyers asking for an appointment. I met them—two very serious-looking gentlemen they were too! After a good deal of preliminary talk they came to their point.

"'You know Miss — —' said the elder of the men.

"'No,' I replied.

"'But you do,' he said. 'She has written to you continually.'

"This was very puzzling, but following up the slight clue, I asked:

"'Is her Christian name Mary?'

"'Yes,' he replied.

"'And she lives at— —?'

"Then I knew whom they meant. Their mission, it seemed, was to tell me that the lady had been very ill, and fearing she was going to die, had expressed a wish to alter her will in my favour. As the lawyers had acted for her family for many years, and were friends of her relations, they had taken her instructions quietly, but after much discussion in private had decided to call on me and inform me of the facts, and they asked me to write a letter to them stating that such a course would be distasteful to me and unfair to her relations. I did so in strong terms, and so I lost a little fortune."

When Mr. Alexander learns a new part he and his wife retire to their cottage at Chorley Wood to study. I bicycled thither one day from Chalfont St. Peter's, when to my disappointment the servant informed me they were "out."

"Oh dear, how sad!" I said, "for it is so hot, and I'm tired and wanted some tea."

Evidently this wrung her heart, for she said she would "go and see." She went, and immediately Mr. Alexander appeared to bid me welcome.

"I'm working," he said, "and the maid has orders not to admit any one without special permission."

What a pretty scene. Lying in a hammock in the orchard on that hot summer's day was the actor-manager of the St. James's Theatre. Seated on a garden chair was his wife, simply dressed in white serge and straw hat. On her lap lay the new typewritten play in its brown paper covers, and at her feet was Boris, the famous hound. The Alexanders had been a fortnight at the cottage working hard at the play, and at the moment of my arrival Mrs. Alexander was hearing her husband his part. Not only does she do this, but she makes excellent suggestions. She studies the plays, too, and her taste is of the greatest value as regards dresses, stage decorations, or the arrangement of crowds. Although she has never played professionally, Mrs. Alexander knows all the ins and outs of theatrical life, and is of the greatest help to her husband in the productions.

Had a stranger entered a compartment of a train between Chorley Wood and London a few days later, he might have thought George Alexander and I were about to commit murder, suicide, or both.

"What have you got there?" asked the actor when we met on the platform.

"A gun," was my reply.

"A gun?"

"Yes, a gun. I'm taking it to London to be mended."

"Ha ha! I can beat that," he laughed. "See what I have here," and opening a little box he disclosed half a dozen razors.

"Razors!" I exclaimed.

"Yes, razors; so be wary with your sanguinary weapon, for mine mean worse mischief."

He was taking the razors to London to be sharpened.

It was fortunate no accident happened to that train, or a gun and six razors might have formed food for "public inquiry."

It is a curious thing how many actors and actresses like to shake the dust of the stage from their feet on leaving the theatre. They seem to become satiated with publicity, to long for the country and an outdoor, freer life, and in many instances they not only long for it, but actually succeed in obtaining it, and the last trains on Saturday night are often full of theatrical folk seeking repose far from theatres till Monday afternoon.

Recreation and entire change of occupation are absolutely necessary to the brain-worker, and the man is wise who realises this. If he does, and seeks complete rest from mental strain, he will probably have a long and successful career; otherwise the breakdown is sure to come, and may come with such force as to leave the victim afflicted for life, so it is far wiser for the brain-worker of whatever profession or business to realise this at an early stage. In this respect actors are as a rule wiser than their fellow-workers, and seek and enjoy recreation on Sunday and Monday, which is more than can be said of many lawyers, doctors, painters, or literary men.

The strain of theatrical life is great. No one should attempt to go upon the stage who is not strong. If there be any constitutional weakness, theatrical life will find it out. Extremes of heat and cold have to be borne. Low dresses or thick furs have to be worn in succeeding acts. The atmosphere of gas and sulphur is often bad, but must be endured.

A heavy part exhausts an actor in a few minutes as much as carrying a hod of bricks all day does a labourer. He may have to change his underclothing two or three times in an evening, in spite of all his dresser's rubbing down. The mental and physical strain affects the pores of the skin and exhausts the body, that is why one hardly ever finds an actor fat. He takes too much physical exercise, takes too much out of himself, ever to let superfluous flesh accumulate upon his bones.

Yes, the actor's life is often a mental strain, of which the following is a striking instance. A very devoted couple were once caused much anxiety by the wife's serious and protracted illness. Months wore on, and every night the husband played his part, wondering what news would greet him when he returned home. At last it was decided that an operation was necessary. It was a grave operation, one of life and death, but it had to be faced.

One morning the wife bade her bairns and her home good-bye, and drove off with her spouse to a famous surgical home. That night the poor actor had to play his comic part, with sad and anxious heart he had to smile and caper and be amusing. Think of the mockery of it all. Next morning he was up early, toying with his breakfast, in order to be at the home before nine o'clock, when that serious operation was to be performed. He did not see his wife—that would have upset them both—but like a caged lion he walked up and down, up and down in an adjoining room. At last came the glad tidings that it was over, and all had so far gone satisfactorily.

Back to the theatre he went that night, having heard the latest bulletin, and played his part with smiling face, knowing his wife was hovering between life and death. Next morning she was not so well. It was a *matinée* day, and in an agony of anxiety and excitement that poor man played two performances, receiving wires about her condition between the acts. Think of it! We often laugh at men and women, who may be for all we know, acting with aching hearts. Comedy and tragedy are closely interwoven in life, perhaps especially so in theatrical life.

By way of recreation from work George Alexander rushes off to his cottage at Chorley Wood to play golf. Sir Charles Wyndham and Sir Squire and Lady Bancroft for many years enjoyed rambles in Switzerland. Sir Henry Irving is a tremendous smoker and never happy without a cigar. Ellen Terry is so devoted to her son and daughter, she finds recreation in their society. Cyril Maude loves shooting and all country pursuits. Winifred Emery never mentions the theatre after she leaves the stage door, and finds relaxation in domesticity. Mrs. Kendal knits. Lewis Waller motors. Dan Leno retires to the suburbs to look after his ducks. Arthur Bourchier is fond of golfing whenever he gets a chance. Miss Marie Tempest lives in a musical set, and is as devoted to her friends as they are to her.

The world is governed by fads. Fads are an antidote to boredom—a tonic to the overworked, and actors enjoy fads like the rest of us; for instance:

Eugene Oudin, that most delightful operatic singer, who was cut off just as he stepped on the top rung of Fame's ladder, was a splendid photographer. In 1890 photography was not so much the fashion as it is nowadays, but even then his pictures were works of art. He portrayed his contemporaries—the De Reskes, Van Dyck, Calvé, Hans Richter, Mascagni, Joachim, Tosti, Alma-Tadema, John Drew, Melba, and dozens more at their work, or in some way that would make a picture as well as a photograph. Then these worthies signed the copies, which were subsequently hung round the walls of Oudin's private study.

Miss Julia Neilson has a passion for collecting fans. Herbert Waring is a brilliant whist-player. Mrs. Patrick Campbell adores small dogs, and nearly always has one tucked under her arm. Many actresses have particular mascots. Miss Ellen Terry, Miss Lily Hanbury, and a host more have their lucky ornaments which they wear on first nights. Miss Irene Vanbrugh is devoted to turquoises, and has a necklace composed of curious specimens of these stones, presents from her many friends.

Miss Violet Vanbrugh declares she is "one of those people who somehow never contrive actively or passively to be the heroine of any little stage joke." This is rather an amusing assertion for a lady who is continually playing stage heroines. Her husband, Mr. Arthur Bourchier, however, tells a good story against himself.

"My present servant, or 'dresser,' as they are called at the theatre, was one of the original Gallery First Nighters and a member of the celebrated Gaiety Gallery Boys. Of course when he joined me I imagined he had forsaken the auditorium for the stage. One night, however, a play was produced by me, the dress rehearsal of which he had seen, and I noticed that he seemed particularly gloomy and morose at its conclusion. On the first night, when I came back to my dressing-room from the stage, I found the door locked. Here was a pretty predicament. It was clear that he had got the key and had mysteriously disappeared. I had the door broken open, for dress I must as time was pressing, and sent another man to search for my missing servant. The sequel is as follows. He was caught red-handed in the gallery among his old associates loudly 'booing' his master. Arraigned before me, he maintained the firmest attitude possible, and asserted boldly:

"'No, sir, I am your faithful servant behind the scenes, but as an independent *man* and honest gallery *boy* I am bound to express my unbiased opinion either for or against any play which I may happen to see at a first night!'"

Mr. Hare, like most men, has his hobby, and it is racing: he loves a horse, and he loves a race meeting. In fact, on one occasion report says he nearly missed appearing at the theatre in consequence.

John Hare is one of the greatest character-actors of our day. He is a dapper little gentleman, and lives in Upper Berkeley Street, near Portman Square. His house is most tasteful, and while his handsome wife has had much to say to the decoration, the actor-manager has decided views of his own in these matters. He has a delightful study at the back of the house, round the sides of which low book-cases run, while the walls reflect copper and brass pots, and old blue china. It is here he is at his best, as he sits smoking a cigarette, perched on the high seat in front of the fire.

What an expressive face his is. The fine-chiselled features, the long thin lips are like a Catholic priest of æsthetic tendency; but as the expression changes with lightning speed, and the dark deep-set eyes sparkle or sadden, one realises the actor-spirit.

Evidence of fads may often be seen in an actor's dressing-room, where the walls are decorated according to the particular taste of its occupant.

Cyril Maude has a particularly interesting dressing-room at the Haymarket Theatre. It is veritably a studio, for he has persuaded his artistic friends to do sketches for him on the distempered walls, and a unique little collection they make. Phil May, Harry Furniss, Dudley Hardy, Holman Clarke, Bernard Partridge, Raven Hill, Tom Brown, are among the contributors, and Leslie Ward's portrait of Lord Salisbury is one of the finest ever sketched of the late Prime Minister. It is a quaint and original idea of Mr. Maude's, but unfortunately those walls are so precious he will never dare to disturb the grime of ages and have them cleaned.

The St. James's Theatre, as it stands, is very modern, and therefore Mr. Alexander is the proud possessor of a charming sitting-room with a little dressing-room attached. It is quite near the stage, and has first-floor windows which look out on King Street, next door to Willis's Rooms, once so famous for their dinners, and still more famous at an earlier date as Almack's, where the *beaux* and *belles* of former days disported themselves.

Both Mr. Alexander and his wife are fond of artistic surroundings, and his little room at the theatre is therefore charming. Here on *matinée* days the actor-manager dines, an arrangement which saves him much time and trouble, and his huge dog Boris—the famous boarhound which appeared in *Rupert of Hentzau*—is his companion, unless Mrs. Alexander pops in with some little delicacy to cheer him over his solitary meal.

That is one of the drawbacks of the stage, the poor actor generally has to eat alone. He cannot expect ordinary mortals to dine at his hours, and he cannot accommodate himself to theirs. The artist who appears much in public is forced to live much by himself, and his meals are consequently as lonely as those of a great Indian potentate.

If we are to follow Mr. Pinero's advice we shall all have to eschew dinner and adopt a "high-tea" principle before the play; but as all the audience are not agreed upon the subject there seems to be some difficulty about it.

Why not have the evening performance as late as usual on *matinée* days, to allow the players time to take food and rest, and early on other days to suit those folk who prefer the drama from seven to ten instead of nine to twelve? By this means early comers and late diners would both be satisfied. Instead of which, as matters stand in London, the late diners arrive gorged and grumbling half through the first act to disturb every one, and the 'bus and train folk struggle out halfway through the last act, sad and annoyed at having to leave.

Most theatrical folk dine at five o'clock. Allowing an hour for this meal, they are able to get a little rest before starting for the theatre, which generally has to be reached by seven.

Preparing for the stage is a serious matter. All that can be put on beforehand is of course donned. Ladies have been known to wear three pairs of stockings, so that a pair might be taken off quickly between each act. Then a long time is required to "make up." For instance in such a part as Giovanni Malatesta (*Paolo and Francesca*), Mr. Alexander spent an hour each day painting his face and arranging his wig. He did not look pretty from the front, but the saffron of his complexion and the blue of his eyes became absolutely hideous when beheld close at hand. That make-up, however, was really a work of art.

An actor's day, even in London, is often a heavy one. Breakfast between nine and ten is the rule, then a ride or some form of exercise, and the theatre at eleven or twelve for a "call," namely, a rehearsal. This "call" may go on till two o'clock or later, at which hour light luncheon is allowed; but if the rehearsal be late, and the meal consequently delayed, it is impossible to eat again between five and six, consequently the two meals get merged into one. Rehearsals for a new play frequently last a whole month, and during that month the players perform eight times a week in the old piece, and rehearse, or have to attend the theatre nearly all day as well. Three months is considered a good run for a play—so, as will be seen, the company scarcely recover from the exertions of one play before they have to commence rehearsing for another, to say nothing of the everlasting rehearsals for charity performances. The actor's life is necessarily one of routine, and routine tends to become monotonous.

A well-known actor was a very absent-minded man except about his profession, where habit had drilled him to punctuality. One Sunday he was sitting in the Garrick Club when a friend remarked he was dining at A——.

"God bless me, so am I."

He rushed home, dressed, and went off to the dinner, during the course of which his neighbour asked him if he were going to the B.'s.

"I'd really forgotten it—but if you are going I'll go too."

So he went.

About midnight he got home. His wife was sitting in full evening dress with her gloves and cloak on.

"You are very late," she said.

"Late? I thought it was early. It is only a quarter past twelve."

"I've been waiting for nearly two hours."

"Waiting — what for?"

"Why, you arranged to fetch me a little after ten o'clock to go to the B's."

"God bless me — I forgot I had a dinner-party, forgot there was a *soirée*, and forgot I had a wife."

"And where's your white tie?" asked his wife stiffly.

"Oh dear, I must have forgotten that too! Dear, dear, what a man I am away from the stage and my dresser!"

There is a wonderful *bonne camaraderie* among all people engaged in the theatrical profession.

Theatrical people are as generous to one another in misfortune as the poor. In times of success they are apt to be jealous; but let a comrade fall on evil days, let him be forced to "rest" when he wants to work, and his old colleagues will try and procure him employment, and when work and health fail utterly, they get up a benefit for him. These benefits take much organising; they often entail endless rehearsals and some expense, and yet the profession is ever ready to come forward and help those in need.

People on the stage have warm hearts and generous purses, but to give gracefully requires as much tact as to receive graciously.

It is a curious thing how few actors have died rich men. Many have made fortunes, but they have generally contrived to lose them again. Money easily made is readily lost. He who buys what he does not want ends in wanting what he cannot buy. Style and show begun in flourishing times are hard to relinquish. Capital soon runs away when drawn upon because salary has ceased, even temporarily. Many an actor, once a rich man, has died poor. Kate Vaughan, once a wealthy woman, died in penury, and so on *ad infinitum*.

Actors, like other people, have to learn there is no disgrace in being poor — it is merely inconvenient.

Theatrical salaries are sometimes enormous, although George Edwardes has informed the public that £100 a week is the highest he ever gives, because he finds to go beyond that sum does not pay him.

It seems a great deal for a pretty woman, not highly born, nor highly educated, nor highly gifted — merely a pretty woman who has been well drilled by author, stage manager, and conductor, to be able to command £100 a week in a comic opera, but after all it is not for long. It is never for fifty-two weeks in the year, and only for a few years at most. Beauty fades, flesh increases, the attraction goes, and she is relegated to the shelf, a poorer, wiser woman than before. But meanwhile her scintillating success, the glamour around her, have acted as a bait to induce others to rush upon the stage.

The largest salary ever earned by a man was probably that paid to Charles Kean, who once had a short engagement at Drury Lane for £50 a night, and on one occasion he made £2,000 by a benefit. Madame Vestris, however, beat him, for she had a long engagement at the Haymarket at £40 a night, or £240 a week, a sum unheard of to-day.

It may be here mentioned that salaries are doled out according to an old and curious custom.

"Treasury day" is a great event; theatrical folk never speak of "pay": it is always "salaries" and "treasury day." Each "house" has its own methods of procedure, but at a great national theatre like Drury Lane the "chiefs" are paid by cheque, while every Friday night the treasurer and his assistants with trays full of "salary" go round the theatre and distribute packets in batches to the endless persons who combine to make a successful performance. The money is sealed up in an envelope which bears the name of the receiver, so no one knows what his neighbour gets. It takes five or six hours for the treasurer and his two assistants to pay off a thousand people at a pantomime, and check each salary paid.

There is no field where that little colt imagination scampers more wildly than in the matter of salaries. For instance, a girl started as "leading lady" in a well-known play on a provincial tour. Her name, in letters nearly as big as herself, met her on the hoardings of every town the company visited. She was given the star dressing-room, and a dresser to herself. This all meant extra tips and extra expenses everywhere, for she was the "leading lady"! Wonderful notices appeared in all the provincial papers and this girl was the draw. The manager knew that, and advertised her and pushed her forward in every way. All the company thought she began at a salary of £10 a week, and rumour said this sum had been doubled after her success. Such was the story. Now for the truth. She was engaged for the tour at £3 a week, and £3 a week she received without an additional penny, although the tour of weeks extended into months. She was poor, others were dependent on her, and she dared not throw up that weekly sixty shillings for fear she might lose everything in her endeavour to get more.

This is only one instance: there are many such upon the stage.

"I suppose A — — has given more time to rehearsals this year," said the wife of a well-known actor, "than any man in London, and yet he has only drawn ten weeks' salary. Everything has turned out badly; so we have had to live for fifty-two weeks on ten weeks' pay and thirty-four weeks' work."

Large sums and well-earned salaries have, of course, been made—in fact, Sir Henry Irving was earning about £30,000 a year at the beginning of the century, an income very few actor-managers could boast.

Among thrifty theatrical folk the Bancrofts probably take front rank. Marie

Wilton and her husband amused England for thirty years, and had the good sense always to spend less than they made. The result was that, while still young enough to enjoy their savings they bought a house in Berkeley Square, retired, and have enjoyed a well-earned rest. More than that, Sir Squire Bancroft stands unique as regards charities. Although not wishing to be tied any more to the stage, he does not mind giving an occasional "Reading" of Dickens's *Christmas Carol*, and he has elected to give his earnings to hospitals and other charities, which are over £15,000 the richer for his generosity. Could anything be more delightful than for a retired actor to give his talent for the public good?

I was brought up on Mrs. Bancroft and Shakespeare, so to speak. The Bancrofts at that time had the Haymarket Theatre, and their Robertson pieces were considered suitable to my early teens by way of amusement, while I was taken to Shakespeare's plays by way of instruction. I remember I thought the Robertson comedies far preferable, and should love to see them again.

It is always averred by old playgoers that Marie Wilton (Lady Bancroft) was the originator of modern comedy. She and her husband at one time had a little play-house in an unfashionable part of London, to which they attracted society people of that day. The theatre was not then what it is now, the "upper ten" seldom visited the play at that time, and yet the Prince of Wales' Theatre known as "The Dust-hole" drew all fashionable London to the Tottenham Court Road to laugh with Marie Wilton over Robertson's comedies.

Her company consisted of men and women who are actor-managers to-day: people went forth well drilled in their profession, accustomed to expending minute care over details, each in their turn to inculcate the same thoroughness in the next generation. These people numbered John Hare, Mr. and Mrs. Kendal (Madge Robertson was the younger sister of the dramatist), H. J. Montague, and Arthur Cecil. Again one finds the best succeeds, and there is always room at the top, hence the Bancroft triumph.

One of their innovations was to rope off the front rows of the pit, which then occupied the entire floor of the house, and call them "stalls," for which they dared ask 6/- apiece. They got it—more were wanted. Others were added, and gradually the price rose to 10/6, which is now the charge: but half-guinea stalls, though now universal, are a modern institution.

At a dinner given by the Anderson Critchetts in 1891 I sat between Squire Bancroft and G. Boughton, R.A. Mr. Bancroft remarked in the course of conversation that he was just fifty, though he looked much younger. His tall figure was perfectly erect, and his white hair showed up the freshness of his complexion. I asked him if he did not miss acting, the applause, and the excitement of the theatre.

"No," he replied. "It will be thirty years this September since I first went on the stage, and it is now nearly six since I gave it up. No, I don't think I should mind much if I never entered a theatre again, either as spectator or actor—and my wife feels the same. My only regret about our theatrical career is that we never visited America, but no dollars would induce Mrs. Bancroft to cross the sea, so we never went."

He surprised me by saying that during the latter years of their theatrical life they never took supper, but dined at 6.0 or 6.30 as occasion required, and afterwards usually walked to the theatre. During the performance they had coffee and biscuits, or sometimes, on cold nights, a little soup, and the moment the curtain was down they jumped into their carriage, and were in their own house in Cavendish Square, where they then lived, by 11.30, and in bed a few minutes later. They were always down to breakfast at 9 o'clock year in year out; an early hour for theatrical folk.

I spoke of the autograph photographs which I had seen in the Haymarket green-room.

"How curious," he said, "that you should mention them to-night. We have always intended to take them away, and only yesterday, after an interval of six years, I gave the order for their removal. This evening as we started for dinner they arrived in Berkeley Square. A strange coincidence."

Lady Bancroft has the merriest laugh imaginable. I used to love to see her act when I was quite a girl, and somehow Miss Marie Tempest reminds me strongly of her to-day. She has the same lively manner.

Lady Bancroft's eyes are her great feature—they are deeply set, with long dark lashes, and their merry twinkle is infectious. When she laughs her eyes seem to disappear in one glorious smile, and every one near her joins in her mirth. Mrs. Bancroft was comparatively a young woman when she retired from the stage, and one of her greatest joys at the time was to feel she was no longer obliged to don the same gown at the same moment every day.

At some theatres a dress rehearsal is a great affair. The term properly speaking means the whole performance given privately right through, without even a repeated scene. The final dress rehearsal, as a rule, is played before a small critical audience, and the piece is expected to run as smoothly as on the first night itself—to be, in fact, a sort of prologue to the first night. This is a dress rehearsal proper, such as is given by Sir Henry Irving, Messrs. Beerbohm Tree, Cyril Maude, George Alexander, or the old Savoy Company.

Before this, however, there are endless "lighting rehearsals," "scenic rehearsals," or "costume parades," all of which are done separately, and with the greatest care. As we saw before, Mrs. Kendal disapproves of a dress rehearsal, but she is almost alone in her opinion. It is really, therefore, a matter of taste whether the whole performance be gone through in separate portions or whether one final effort be made before the actual first night. As a rule Sir Henry Irving has three dress rehearsals, but the principals only appear in costume at one of them. They took nine weeks to rehearse the operetta *The Medal and the Maid*, yet Irving put *The Merchant of Venice* with all its details on the Lyceum stage in twenty-three days.

Sir Henry strongly objects to the public being present at any rehearsal. "The impression given of an incomplete effort cannot be a fair one," he says. "It is not fair to the artistes. A play to be complete must pass through one imagination, one intellect must organise and control. In order to attain this end it is necessary to experiment: no one likes to be corrected before strangers, therefore rehearsals—or in other words 'experiments' — should be made in private. Even trained intellect in an outsider should not be admitted, as great work may be temporarily spoiled by some slight mechanical defect."

In Paris rehearsals used to be great institutions. They were opportunities for meeting friends. In the *foyers* and green-rooms of the theatres, at *répètitions générales*, every one talked and chatted over the play, the actors, and the probable success or failure. This, however, gradually became a nuisance, and early in this twentieth century both actors and authors struck. They decided that even privileged persons should be excluded from final rehearsals, which are always in costume in Paris. As a sort of salve to the offended public, it was agreed that twenty-four strangers should be admitted to the last great dress rehearsal before the actual production of a new piece, hence everybody who is anybody clamours to be there.

CHAPTER VIII

MADAME SARAH BERNHARDT

Sarah Bernhardt and her Tomb—The Actress's Holiday—Love of her Son—Sarah Bernhardt Shrimping—Why she left the Comédie Française—Life in Paris—A French Claque—Three Ominous Raps—Strike of the Orchestra—Parisian Theatre Customs—Programmes—Late Comers—The *Matinée* Hat—Advertisement Drop Scene—First Night of *Hamlet*—Madame Bernhardt's own Reading of *Hamlet*—Yorick's Skull—Dr. Horace Howard Furness—A Great Shakespearian Library.

It is not every one who cares to erect his own mausoleum during his life.

There are some quaint and weird people who prefer to do so, however: whether it is to save their friends and relations trouble after their demise, whether from some morbid desire to face death, or whether for notoriety, who can tell? Was it not one of our dukes who built a charming crematorium for the benefit of the public, and beside it one for himself, the latter to be given over to general use after he himself had been reduced to spotless ashes within its walls? He was a public benefactor, for his wise action encouraged cremation, a system which for the sake of health and prosperity is sure to come in time.

Madame Sarah Bernhardt has not erected a crematorium, but on one of the highest spots of the famous *Père Lachaise* Cemetery in Paris she has placed her tomb. It is a solid stone structure, like a large sarcophagus, but it is supported on four arches, so that light may be seen beneath, and the solidity of the slabs is thereby somewhat lessened. One word only is engraven on the stone:

BERNHARDT.

This is the mausoleum of one of the greatest actresses the world has ever known. What is lacking in the length of inscription is made up by the size of the lettering.

Upon the tomb lay one enormous wreath on the *Jour des Morts*, 1902, and innumerable people paid homage to it, or stared out of curiosity at the handsome erection.

Though folk say Madame Bernhardt courts notoriety, there are moments when she seeks solitude as a recreation, and she has a great love of the sea.

Every year for two months she disappears from theatrical life. She forgets that such a thing as the stage exists, she never reads a play, and as far as theatrical matters are concerned she lives in another sphere. That is part of her holiday. It is not a holiday of rest, for she never rests; it is a holiday because of the change of scene, change of thought, change of occupation. Her day at her seaside home is really a very energetic one.

Madame Sarah Bernhardt as Hamlet.

Photo by Lafayette, New Bond Street.

At five the great artiste rises, dons a short skirt, country boots, and prepares to enjoy herself. Often the early hours are spent in shooting small birds. She rarely misses her quarry, for her artistic eye helps her in measuring distance, and her aim is generally deadly. Another favourite entertainment is to shrimp. She takes off her shoes and stockings and for a couple of hours will stand in the water shrimping, for her "resting" is as energetic as everything else she does. She plies her net in truly professional style, gets wildly enthusiastic over a good catch, and loves to eat her freshly boiled fish at *déjeuner*. Perhaps she has a game with her ten lovely Russian dogs before that mid-day meal.

Her surroundings are beautiful. She adores flowers—flowers are everywhere; she admires works of art—works of art are about her, for she has achieved her own position, her own wealth, and why should she not have all she loves best close at hand?

After *déjeuner* the guests, of whom there are never more than two or three, such as M. Rostand (author of *Cyrano de Bergerac*) and his wife, rest and read. Not so Madame Bernhardt. She sits in the open air, her head covered with a shady hat, and plays Salta with her son. This game is a kind of draughts, and often during their two months' holiday-making she and her only child Maurice will amuse themselves in this way for two or three hours in the afternoon; generally she wins, much to her joy. She simply loves heat, like the Salamanders, and, even in July, when other people feel too hot, she would gladly wear furs and have a fire. She can never be too warm apparently. Her own rooms are kept like a hothouse, for cold paralyses her bodily and mentally.

How she adores her son—she speaks of him as a woman speaks of her lover; Maurice comes before all her art, before all else in the world, for Maurice to her is life. He has married a clever woman, a descendant of a Royal house, and has a boy and two girls adored by their grandmother almost as much as their father. She plays with them, gets up games for them, dances with them, throws herself as completely into their young lives as she does into everything else.

About 3.30 *au tennis* is the cry. Salta is put aside and every one has to play tennis. Away to tennis she trips. Sarah never gets hot, but always looks cool in the white she invariably wears. She wants an active life, and if her brain is not working her body must be, so she plays hard at the game, and when tea is ready in the arbour close at hand, about 6.30, she almost weeps if she has to leave an unfinished "sett."

She must be interested, or she would be bored; she must be amused, or she would be weary; thus she works hard at her recreations, the enforced rest while reading a novel being her only time of repose during her summer holiday. She walks when she has nothing else to do, and rambles for miles around her seaside home, only occasionally going on long carriage expeditions, with her tents and her servants, to pitch camp for the night somewhere along the coast.

Then comes dinner—dinner served with all the glories of a Parisian *chef*, for Madame, although a small eater, believes well-cooked food necessary to existence. There is no hurry over dinner, and "guess" games are all the fashion, games which she cleverly arranges to suit the children. No evening dresses are allowed, nor *décolleté* frocks; except for flowers and well-cooked food, Madame likes to feel she is in the country and far removed from Paris, therefore a dainty blouse is all that is permitted. Music is often enjoyed in the evening. Sometimes on a fine night Madame will exclaim:

"Let us go and fish," and off they all go. Down the endless steps cut in the rock the party stumble, and on the seashore they drag their nets. Up those same steps every night toil men with buckets of salt water, for the great actress has a boiling salt water bath every morning, to which she attributes much of her good health. Fishermen throw nets for the evening's catch, but "Sarah" is most energetic in hauling them in, and gets wildly excited at a good haul. Her unfailing energy is thrown even into the fishing, and she will stay out till the small hours enjoying the sport. One summer Madame Bernhardt caught a devil fish—this delighted her. She took it home and quickly modelled a vase from her treasure. Seaweed and shells formed its stand, the tail its stem. She seldom sculpts nowadays, but the power is still there.

It was in 1880 that she retired from the *Comédie Française*, not being content with her salary of £1,200 a year, and she then announced her intention of making sculpture and painting her profession. After a rest, however, she fortunately changed her mind, or the stage would have lost one of the greatest actresses the world has known. Perhaps the apotheosis of her life was in December, 1896, when she was acclaimed Queen of the French stage, and the leading poets of her country recited odes in her honour. On that occasion the heroine of the *fête* declared:

"For twenty-nine years I have given the public the vibrations of my soul, the pulsations of my heart, and the tears of my eyes. I have played 112 parts, I have created thirty-eight new characters, sixteen of which are the work of poets. I have struggled as no other human being has struggled.... I have ardently longed to climb the topmost pinnacle of my art. I have not yet reached it. By far the smaller part of my life remains for me to live; but what matters it? Every day brings me nearer to the realisation of my dream. The hours that have flown away with my youth have left me my courage and cheerfulness, for my goal is unchanged, and I am marching towards it."

She was right; there is always something beyond our grasp, and those who think they have seized it must court failure from that moment. Those nearest perfection best know how far they really are from it.

Madame Bernhardt's mind is penetrating, yet her body never rests. She can do with very little sleep—can live without butcher's meat, rarely drinks alcohol, and prefers milk to anything. Perhaps this is the reason of her perpetual youth. She loves her holiday, she loves the simple life of the country, the repose from the world, the knowledge that autograph hunters and reporters cannot waylay her, and in the country she ceases to be an actress and can enjoy being a woman.

In Paris her life is very different. She resides in a beautiful hotel surrounded by works of art, and keeps a *table ouverte* for her friends. She rises at eleven, when she has her *masseuse* and her boiling bath, sees her servants, and gives personal orders for everything in the establishment. She is one of those women who find time for all details, and is capable of seeing to most matters well. At 12.30 is *déjeuner*, rarely finished till 2 o'clock, as friends constantly drop in. Then off to the theatre, where she rehearses till six. There she sits in a little box, from which point of vantage she can see everything and yet be out of draughts. She always wears white, even in the theatre, and looks as smart as though at a party instead of on business bent. Dresses are brought her for inspection, she alters, changes, admires, or deplores as fancy takes her; she arranges the lighting, decides a little more blue or a little less green will give the tone required; but then she has that inner knowledge of harmony and the true painter spirit. She is never out of tune. At six high-tea is served in her dressing-room, for she rarely leaves the theatre. The meal consists mostly of fish—lobster, crab, cray-fish, shrimps, scallops cooked or raw—with a little tea and lots of milk. A chat with a friend, a peep at a new play, and then it is time to dress for the great work of the day. She changes quickly. After the performance is over she sees her manager, and rarely leaves the theatre in Paris before 1.30, when she returns home to a good hot supper. But her day is not ended even then. She will have a play read to her or read it herself, study a new part, write letters, and do dozens of different things before she goes to bed. She can do with little rest, and seems to have the energy of many persons in one. In spite of this she has never mastered English, although she can read it.

Madame Bernhardt will ever be associated in my mind with a night spent at a theatre behind a French *claque*. That *claque* was terrible, but the actress was so wonderful I almost forgot its existence, and sat rapt in admiration of her first night of *Hamlet*.

Till quite lately there was a terrible institution in France known as the *claque*, nothing more or less than a paid body of men whose duty it was to applaud actors and actresses at certain points duly marked in their play-books.

At the *Comédie Française* of Paris a certain individual known as the *Chef de Claque* had been retained from 1881 for over twenty years at a monthly salary of three hundred francs, that is to say, he received £12 a month, or £3 a week, for "clapping" when required. He was a person of great importance. Though disliked by the public, he was petted and feasted by actors and actresses, for a clap at the wrong moment, or want of applause at the right, meant disaster; besides, there was a sort of superstitious fear that being on bad terms with the *Chef de Claque* foreboded ill luck.

After performing his duties for twenty-one years with considerable success, the *Chef de Claque* was dismissed, and it was decided that professional applause should be discontinued. Naturally the *Chef* was indignant, and in the autumn of 1902 sued the *Comédie Française* for 30,000 francs damages or a pension. Paris, however, found relief in the absence of the original *claque*, and gradually one theatre after another began to dispense with a nuisance it had endured for long. History says that during the early days of the *claque* there was an equally obnoxious institution, a sort of organised opposition known as *siffleurs*. It was then as fashionable to whistle a piece out of the world as to clap it into success. There was a regular instrument made for the purpose, known as a *sifflet*, which was wooden and emitted a harsh creaking noise. No man thought of going to the theatre without his *sifflet*—but the *claque* gradually clapped him away. Thus died out the official dispensers of success or failure.

It so chanced that having bicycled through France from Dieppe along the banks of the Seine, my sister and I were leaving Paris on the first occasion of Sarah Bernhardt's impersonation of Hamlet—that is to say, in May, 1899. We were so anxious to see her first performance, however, that we decided to stay an extra day. So far all was well, but not a single ticket could be obtained. Here was disappointment indeed. Of course our names were not on the first night list in Paris and, as in England, it is well-nigh impossible for any ordinary member of the public to gain admittance on such an occasion.

The gentleman in the box office became sympathetic at beholding our distress, and finally suggested he might let us have seats upstairs.

"It is very high up, but you will see and hear everything," he added.

We decided to ascend to the gods, where, instead of finding ourselves beside Jupiter and Mars, Venus or Apollo, we were seated immediately behind the *claque.*

Never, never shall I forget my own personal experience of the performance of a *claque.* Six men sat together in the centre of the front row. The middle one had a marked book—fancy Shakespeare's *Hamlet* marked for applause!—and according to that book's instructions the *Chef* and his friends clapped once, twice, thrice.

On ordinary occasions the *claque* slept or read, and only woke up to make a noise when called upon by the *Chef,* who seemed to have free passes for his supporters every night, and took any one he liked to help him in his curious work. The noise those men made at *Hamlet* was deafening. The excitement of the leader lest the play should not go off well on a first night was terrible—and if their hands were not sore, and their arms did not ache, it was a wonder indeed. They were so appallingly near us, and so overpowering and disturbing, nothing but interest in the divine Sarah could have kept us in our seats during all those hot, stuffy, noisy hours. It was a Saturday night, the piece began at 8 p.m., and ended at 2 a.m.

Think of it, ye London first-nighters! Especially in a French theatre, where the seats are torture racks, the heat equal to Dante's Inferno, and no sweet music soothes the savage breast, only long dreary *entr'actes* and the welcome—if melancholy—three raps French playgoers know so well.

Two years later, when I was again in Paris, there were different excitements in the air, one a strike of coal-miners, the other—and in Paris apparently the more important—a strike of the orchestras at the theatres. A few years previously there could not have been a strike, for the sufficient reason there were no orchestras; but gradually our plan of having music during the long waits crept in. The musicians at first engaged as an experiment were badly paid. When they became an institution they naturally asked for more money, which was promptly refused.

Then came the revolt. From the first violin to the big drum all demanded higher pay. It seems that theatre, music hall, and concert orchestras belong to a syndicate of *Artistes Musiciens* numbering some sixteen hundred members. During the strike I chanced to be present at a theatre where there was generally an orchestra—that night one small cottage piano played by a lady usurped its place. She managed fairly well—but a piano played by a mediocre musician, does not add to the gaiety of a theatre although it may decrease its melancholy. When November came, the strike ceased. The managers capitulated.

The orchestra in an English theatre is a little world to itself. The performers never mix with the actors, they have their own band-room, and there they live when not before the curtain. At the chief theatres, as is well known, the performers are extremely good, and that is because they are allowed to "deputise"; when there is a grand concert at the St. James's Hall or elsewhere, provided they find some one to take their place in their own orchestra, they may go and play. Consequently, when there is a big concert several may be away from their own theatre. Many of these performers remain in the same orchestra for years. For instance, Mr. Alexander told me he met a man one day roving at the back of the stage, so he stopped and asked whom he wanted. The man smiled and replied:

"I am in your orchestra, sir, and have been for eleven years."

"Ah, yes, so you are; I thought I knew your face; but I am accustomed to look at it from above, you see!"

In many London theatres the orchestra is hidden under the stage, a decided advantage with most plays.

Parisian theatres are strange places. They are very fashionable, and yet they are most uncomfortable. The seats are invariably too small and too high. The result is there is nowhere to lay a cloak or coat, and short people find their little legs dangling high above the ground. All this causes inconvenience which ends in annoyance, and the hangers-on at the theatres are a veritable nuisance. Ugly old women in blue aprons, without caps, pounce upon one on entering and pester for wraps. It is difficult to know which is the worse evil, to cling to one's belongings in the small space allotted each member of the audience, or to let one of those women take them away. In the latter case before the last act she returns with a great deal of fuss, hands over the articles, and demands her sous. If the piece be only in three acts, one pays for being free of a garment for two of them and is annoyed by its presence during the third. Again, when one enters a box these irritating *ouvreuses* demand tips *pour le service de la loge, s'il vous plaît,* and will often insist on forcing footstools under one's feet so as to claim the *pourboires* afterwards. The *pourboires* of the *vestiaire* are also a thorn in the flesh, and the system which exacts payment from these women turns them from obliging servants into harpies. How Parisians put up with these disagreeable creatures is surprising, but they do.

The stage is conservative in many ways; for instance, that tiresome plan of charging for programmes still exists in England in some theatres, and even good theatres too. Programmes cost nothing: the expense of printing is paid by the advertisements. Free distribution, therefore, does not mean that the management are out of pocket. Why, then, do they not present them gratis? As things are it is most aggravating. Suppose two ladies arrive; as they are shown to their seats, holding their skirts, opera-bags and fans in their hands, they are asked for sixpence. While they endeavour to extract their money they are dropping their belongings and inconveniencing their neighbours: in the case of a man requiring change the same annoyance is felt by all around, especially if the play has begun.

Programmes and their necessary "murmurings" are annoying, and so is the meagreness of the space between the rows of stalls. There are people who openly declare they never go to a theatre because they have not got room for their knees. This is certainly much worse in Parisian theatres, where the seats are high and narrow as well; but still, when people pay for a seat they like room to pass to and fro without inconveniencing a dozen persons *en route*.

Matinée hats and late arrivals are sins on the part of the audience so cruel that no self-respecting person would inflict either upon a neighbour. But some women are so inconsiderate that we shall soon be reduced to an American notice like the following, "Ladies who cannot, or are unwilling to, remove their hats while occupying seats in this theatre, are requested to leave at once; their money will be returned at the box office." A gentlewoman never wears a picture hat at the play; if she arrives in one she takes it off. In the same way a gentleman makes a point of being in time. People who offend in these respects belong to a class which apparently knows no better, a class which complacently talks, or makes love, through a theatrical entertainment!

Another strange Parisian custom is the advertisement drop-scene. At the end of the act, a curtain descends literally covered with pictures and puffs of pills, automobiles, corsets, or tobacco. After a tragedy the effect is comical, but this is an age of advertisement.

But to return to Madame Bernhardt's Hamlet. When the great Sarah appeared upon the scene I did not recognise her. Why? Because she looked so young and so small. This woman, who was nearly sixty, appeared quite juvenile. This famous *tragédienne*, who had always left an impression of a tall, thin, willowy being in her wonderful scenes in *La Tosca*, or *Dame aux Caméllias*, deprived of her train appeared quite tiny. She had the neatest legs, encased in black silk stockings, the prettiest feet with barely any heel to give her height, while her flaxen wig which hung upon her shoulders, made her look a youth, in the sixteenth century clothes she elected to wear. At first I felt woefully disappointed; she did not act at all, and when she saw her father's ghost, instead of becoming excited, as we are accustomed to Hamlet's doing in this country, she insinuated a lack of interest, an "Oh, is that really my father's ghost!" sort of style, which seemed almost annoying; but as she proceeded, I was filled with admiration—her players' scene was a great *coup*.

On the left of the stage a smaller one was arranged for the players' scene, and before it half a dozen torches were stuck in as footlights. On the right there was a high raised daïs with steps leading up on either side—a sort of platform erection. The King and Queen sat upon two seats at the top, the courtiers grouped themselves upon the stairs. Immediately below the Royal pair sat Ophelia, and at her feet, upon a white polar-bear-skin rug, reclined Sarah Bernhardt, with her elbow upon Ophelia's knee and her hand upon some yellow cushions. As the play went on she looked up to catch a glimpse of the King, but he was too high above her, the wall of the platform hid him from view. Very quietly she rose from her seat, crawled round to the back, where she gradually and slowly pulled herself up towards the daïs, getting upon a stool in her eagerness to see her victim's face. The

King, in his excitement, rose from his seat at the fatal moment, and putting his hand upon the balustrade, peered downwards upon the play-actors.

At that instant Sarah Bernhardt rose, and the two faces came close together across the barrier in eager contemplation of each other. It was a magnificent piece of acting, one which sent a thrill through the whole house; and as the "divine Sarah" saw the guilt depicted upon her uncle's face she gave a shriek of triumph, a perfectly fiendish shriek of joy, once heard never to be forgotten, and springing down from her post, rushed to the torch footlights, and seizing one in her hand stood in the middle of the stage, her back to the audience, waving it on high and yelling with wild exultant delight as the King and all his courtiers slunk away, to the fall of the curtain. It was a brilliant ending to a great act, and Sarah triumphed not only in the novelty of her rendering, but in the manner of its execution.

Another hit that struck me as perfectly wonderful in its contrasting simplicity, was, when she sat upon a sofa, her feet straight out before her, a book lying idle upon her lap, and murmured, *mots, mots*, or again, when she came in through the arch at the back of the stage, and leaning against its pillar repeated quietly and dreamily the lines "To be, or not to be."

Apropos of *Hamlet*, Madame Bernhardt wrote to the *Daily Telegraph*:

"Hamlet rêve quand il est seul; mais quand il y a du monde il parle; il parle pour cacher sa pensée....

"On me reproche, dans la scène de l'Oratoire, de m'approcher trop près du Roi; mais, si Hamlet veut tuer le Roi, il faut bien qu'il s'approche de lui. Et quand il l'entend prier des paroles de repentir, il pense que s'il le tue il l'enverra au ciel, et il ne tue pas le Roi; non pas parcequ'il est irrésolu et faible, mais parcequ'il est tenace et logique; il veut le tuer dans le péché, non dans le repentir, car il veut qu'il aille en enfer, et pas au ciel. On veut absolument voir, dans Hamlet, une âme de femme, hésitante, imponderée; moi, j'y vois l'âme d'un homme, résolue mais refléchie. Aussitôt que Hamlet voit l'âme de son père et appréhend le meurtre, il prend la résolution de le venger; mais, comme il est le contraire d'Othello, qui agit avant de penser, lui, Hamlet, pense avant d'agir, ce qui est le signe d'une grande force, d'une grande puissance d'âme.

"Hamlet aime Ophélie! il renonce à l'amour! il renonce à l'étude! il renonce à tout! pour arriver à son but! Et il y arrive! Il tue le Roi quand il est pris dans le péché le plus noir, le plus criminel; mais il ne le tue que lorsqu'il est absolument sûr. Lorsqu'on l'envoie en Angleterre, à la première occasion qu'il rencontre il bondit tout seul sur un bateau ennemi et il se nomme pour qu'on le fasse prisonnier, sûr qu'on le ramenera. Il envoie froidement Rosencrantz et Guildenstern à la mort. Tout cela est d'un être jeune, fort et résolu!

"Quand il rêve: c'est à son projet! c'est à sa vengeance! Si Dieu n'avait pas défendu le suicide, il se tuerait par dégoût du monde!

mais, puisqu'il ne peut pas se tuer, il tuera!

"Enfin, Monsieur, permettez-moi de vous dire que Shake-speare, par son génie colossal, appartient à l'Univers! et qu'un cerveau Français, Allemand, ou Russe a le droit de l'admirer et de le comprendre.

"SARAH BERNHARDT.

"LONDRES, *le 16 Juin, 1899.*"

Madame Bernhardt made Hamlet a man, and a strong man—there was nothing of the halting, hesitating woman about her performance, one which she herself loves to play.

It was a fine touch also when she went into her uncle's room, where, finding him on his knees, she crept up close behind, and taking out her dagger, prepared to kill him. She said nothing, but her play was marvellous, her expression of hatred and loathing, her pause to contemplate, and final decision to let the man alone, were done in such a way as only Sarah Bernhardt could render them.

Another drama took place on this memorable first night of Hamlet. Two famous men when discussing whether Hamlet ought to be fat or thin, struck one another in the face and finally arranged a duel—a duel fought two or three days later, which nearly cost one of them his life.

Opposite is the programme of the first night of Sarah Bernhardt's Hamlet.

LA TRAGIQUE HISTOIRE D'

HAMLET

PRINCE DE DANEMARK

Drame en 15 Tableaux de **William SHAKESPEARE**

Traduction en prose de MM. EUGÈNE MORAND et MARCEL SCHWOB

Mme SARAH BERNHARDT

HAMLET

MM.

BREMONT	Le Roi
MAGNIER	Laertes
CHAMEROY	Polonius
DENEUBOURG	Horatio
RIPERT	Le Spectre
SCHUTZ	Premier fossoyeur
LACROIX	Deuxième fossoyeur
TESTE	Le Roi Comédien

Scheler	Osric
Jean Darav	Rosencrantz
Jahan	Voltimand
Colas	Bernardo
Krauss	Marcellus
Laurent	Guildenstern
Barbier	Fortinbras
Stebler	Deux^me comédien
Cauroy	Francesco
Lahor	Un Prêtre
Bary	Cornélius
Caillere	Trois^me comédien
Bertaut	Un Gentilhomme
MM^mes	
Marthe Mellot	Ophélie
Marcya	La Reine Gertrude
Boulanger	La reine comédienne

Prêtres, Comédiens, Marins, Officiers, Soldats, etc.

There is a famous Hamlet skull in America, known as Yorick's skull, which is in the possession of Dr. Horace Howard Furness, of Philadelphia.

Dr. Furness is one of the greatest Shakespearian scholars of the day. Dr. Georg Brandes, of Copenhagen, Mr. Sydney Lee, of London, and he probably know more of the work of this great genius than any other living persons.

When I was in America I had the pleasure of spending a few days at Dr. Furness's delightful home at Wallingford, on the shores of the Delaware River. The place might be in England, from its appearance—a low, rambling old house with wide balconies, creeper-grown with roses, and honey-suckle hugging the porch. The dear old home was built more than a century ago, by some of Dr. Furness's ancestors, and one sees the love of those ancestors for the old English style manifest at every turn. The whole interior bespeaks intellectual refinement.

He stood on the doorstep to welcome me, a grey-headed man of some sixty-eight years, with a ruddy complexion, and closely cut white moustache. His manner was delightful; no more polished gentleman ever walked this earth than Horace Howard Furness, the great American writer. His father was an intimate friend of Ralph Waldo Emerson, whose famous portrait at the Philadelphia Art Gallery was painted by the doctor's brother; so young Horace was brought up amid intellectual surroundings.

At the back of the house is the world-renowned iron-proof Shakespearian library, the collection of forty ardent years. It is a veritable museum with its upper galleries, its many tables, and its endless cases of treasures. The books which line the walls were all catalogued by the doctor himself. He has many of the earlier editions of Shakespeare besides other rare volumes. Some original MSS. of Charles Lamb, beautifully written and signed Elia, are there; a delightful sketch of Mary Anderson by Forbes Robertson; Lady Martin's (Helen Faucit) own acting editions of the parts she played marked by herself; and in a special glass case lie a pair of grey gauntlet gloves, richly embroidered in silver, which were worn by Shakespeare himself when an actor. If I remember rightly they came from David Garrick, and the card of authenticity is in the case. Then there are Garrick's and Booth's walking-sticks, and on a small ebony stand, the famous Yorick skull handled in the grave-digging scene by all the great actors who have visited Philadelphia, and signed by them—Booth, Irving, Tree, Sothern, etc.

I never spent a more delightful evening than one in October, 1900, when the family went off to Philadelphia to see the dramatisation of one of Dr. Weir Mitchell's novels by his son, and I was left alone with Dr. Furness for some hours.

What a charming companion. What a fund of information and humour, what a courtly manner, what a contrast to the ruggedness of Ibsen, or the wild energy of Björnsen. Here was repose and strength. Not an originator, perhaps, but a learned disciple. How he loved Shakespeare, with what reverence he spoke of him. He scoffed at the mere mention of Bacon's name, and was glad, very glad, so little was known of the private life of Shakespeare.

"He was too great to be mortal; I do not want to associate any of Nature's frailties with such a mind. His work is the thing, for the man as a man I care nothing." This was unlike Brandes, whose brilliant books on Shakespeare deal chiefly with the man.

There was something particularly delightful about Horace Furness and his home. Even the dinner-table appointments were his choice. The soup-plates were of the rarest Oriental porcelain, and the meat-plates were of silver with mottoes chosen by himself round the borders.

"I loved my china, but it got broken year by year, until in desperation I looked about for something that could not break—solid and plain, like myself, eh?" he chuckled. The mottoes were well chosen and the idea as original as everything else about Dr. Furness.

It was Mrs. Kemble's readings that first awakened his love for Shakespeare; but he was nearly forty years old when he gave up law and devoted himself to writing; much the same age as Dr. Samuel Smiles when he exchanged business for authorship.

Dr. Furness loves his Shakespeare and thoroughly enjoys his well-chosen library; but still an Englishwoman cannot help hoping that when he has done with them, he will bequeath his treasures to the Shakespeare Museum at Stratford-on-Avon.

CHAPTER IX

AN HISTORICAL FIRST NIGHT

An Interesting Dinner—Peace in the Transvaal—Beerbohm Tree as a Seer—How he cajoled Ellen Terry and Mrs. Kendal to Act—First-nighters on Camp-stools—Different Styles of Mrs. Kendal and Miss Terry—The Fun of the Thing—Bows of the Dead—Falstaff's Discomfort—Amusing Incidents—Nervousness behind the Curtain—An Author's Feelings.

THE scene was changed.

It was the 1st of June. I remember the date because it was my birthday, and this particular June day is doubly engraven on my mind as the most important Sunday in 1902. It was a warm summer's evening as I drove down Harley Street to dine with Sir Anderson and Lady Critchett, whose dinners are as famous as his own skill as an oculist.

Most of the company had assembled. Mr. and Mrs. Kendal were already there, Frank Wedderburn, K.C., Mr. Luke Fildes, R.A., who had just completed his portrait of the King, Mr. Orchardson, R.A., Mr. Lewis Coward, K.C., and their wives, Mr. and Mrs. Edward Sassoon, Mr. and Mrs. W. L. Courtney, when the Beerbohm Trees were announced. He bore a telegram in his hand.

"Have you heard the news?" he asked.

"No," every one replied, guessing by his face it was something of importance.

"Peace has been officially signed," was the reply.

Great was the joy of all present. There had been a possibility felt all day that the good news from South Africa might be confirmed on that Sunday, although it was supposed it could not be known for certain until Monday. Sunday is more or less a *dies non* in London, but as the tape is always working at the theatre, Mr. Tree had instructed a clerk to sit and watch the precious instrument all day, so as to let him have the earliest information of so important an event. As he was dressing for dinner in Sloane Street, in rushed the clerk, breathless with excitement, bearing the news of the message of Peace that had sped across a quarter of the world.

This in itself made that dinner-party memorable, but it was memorable in more ways than one, as among the twenty people round that table sat four of the chief performers in *The Merry Wives of Windsor*, which was to electrify London as a Coronation performance ten days later.

Sir Anderson himself is connected with the drama, for his brother is Mr. R. C. Carton, the well-known dramatic author. Sir Anderson is also an indefatigable first-nighter, and being an excellent *raconteur*, knows many amusing stories of actors of the day. In his early years an exceptionally fine voice almost tempted him on to the lyric stage, but he has had no cause to regret that his ultimate choice was ophthalmic surgery.

It was a stroke of genius, the genius of the seer, on the part of Beerbohm Tree, to invite the two leading actresses of England to perform at his theatre during Coronation season.

It came about in this way. On looking round the Houses, Mr. Tree noticed that, although Shakespeare was to the fore in the provinces, filling two or three theatres, there happened to be no Shakespearian production—except an occasional *matinée* at the Lyceum—going on in London during the Coronation month. Of course London without Shakespeare is like *Hamlet* without the Dane to visitors from the Colonies and elsewhere. Something must be done. He decided what. A good all-round representation, played without any particular star part would suit the purpose, and a record cast would suit the stranger. Accordingly Mr. Tree jumped into a hansom and drove to Mrs. Kendal's home in Portland Place, where he was announced, and exclaimed:

"I have come to ask you to act for me at His Majesty's for the Coronation month. Your own tour will be finished by that time."

For one hour they talked, Mrs. Kendal declaring she had not played under any management save her husband's for so many years that the suggestion seemed well-nigh impossible.

"Besides," she added, "you should ask Ellen Terry, who is my senior, and stands ahead of me in the profession. She has not yet appeared since she returned from America. There is your chance."

Whereupon there ensued further discussion, till finally Mrs. Kendal laughingly remarked:

"Well, if you can get Ellen Terry to act, I will play with you both with pleasure."

Off went Mr. Tree to the hansom, and directed the driver to take him at once to Miss Terry's house, for he was determined not to let the grass grow under his feet. He brought his personal influence to bear on the famous actress for another hour, at the end of which time she had consented to play *if* Sir Henry Irving would allow her. This permission was quickly obtained, and two hours after leaving Portland Place Mr. Tree was back to claim Mrs. Kendal's promise. It was sharp work; one morning overcame what at the outset seemed insurmountable obstacles, and thus was arranged one of the best and luckiest performances ever given. For weeks and weeks that wonderful cast played to overflowing houses. The month wore on, but the public taste did not wear out, July found all these stars still in the firmament, and even in August they remained shining in town.

Moral: the very best always receives recognition. The "best" lay in the acting, for as a play the *Merry Wives* is by no means one of Shakespeare's best. It is said he wrote it in ten days by order of Queen Elizabeth. How delighted Bouncing Bess would have been if she could have seen the Coronation performance!

Mr. Beerbohm Tree as Falstaff.

Photo by London Stereoscopic Co., Ltd., Cheapside, E.C.

I passed down the Haymarket early in the morning preceding that famous first night. There, sitting on camp-stools, were people who had been waiting from 5 a.m. to get into the pit and gallery that evening. They had a long wait, over twelve hours some of them, but certainly they thought it worth while if they enjoyed themselves as much as I did. It was truly a record performance.

The house was packed; in one box was the Lord Chief Justice of England, in the stalls below him Sir Edward Clarke, at one time Solicitor-General, and who has perhaps the largest practice at the Bar of any one in London. Then there was Mr. Kendal not far off, watching his wife. Mr. and Mrs. Beerbohm Tree's daughter—showing a strong resemblance to both parents—was in a box; Princess Colonna was likewise there; together with some of the most celebrated doctors, such as Sir Felix Semon, learned in diseases of the throat, Sir Anderson Critchett, our host of a few nights before, while right in the front sat old Mrs. Beerbohm, watching her son with keen interest and enjoyment, and, a little behind, that actor's clever brother, known on an important weekly as "Max," a severe and caustic dramatic critic.

The enthusiasm of the audience was extraordinary. When some one had called for the feminine "stars" at one of the rehearsals, Mrs. Kendal, with ready wit, seized Ellen Terry by the hand, exclaiming:

"Ancient Lights would be more appropriate, methinks!"

Below is the programme.

TUESDAY, JUNE 10th, 1902, at 8.15
SHAKESPEARE'S COMEDY

The Merry Wives of Windsor

Sir John Falstaff		Mr. TREE
Master Fenton		Mr. GERALD LAWRENCE
Justice Shallow		Mr. J. FISHER WHITE
Master Slender	(*Cousin to Shallow*)	Mr. CHARLES QUARTERMAIN
Master Ford	} *Gentlemen dwelling*	{ Mr. OSCAR ASCHE
Master Page	} *at Windsor*	{ Mr. F. PERCIVAL STEVENS
Sir Hugh Evans	(*a Welsh Parson*)	Mr. COURTICE POUNDS
Dr. Caius	(*a French Physician*)	Mr. HENRY KEMBLE
Host of the "Garter" Inn		Mr. LIONEL BROUGH
Bardolph	}	{ Mr. ALLEN THOMAS
Nym	} *Followers of Falstaff*	{ Mr. S. A. COOKSON
Pistol	}	{ Mr. JULIAN L'ESTRANGE
Robin	(*Page to Falstaff*)	Master VIVYAN THOMAS
Simple	(*Servant to Slender*)	Mr. O. B. CLARENCE
Rugby	(*Servant to Dr. Caius*)	Mr. FRANK STANMORE

Mistress Page		Miss ELLEN TERRY (By the Courtesy of Sir HENRY IRVING)
Mistress Anne Page	(*Daughter to Mrs. Page*)	Mrs. TREE
Mistress Quickly	(*Servant to Dr. Caius*)	Miss ZEFFIE TILBURY
Mistress Ford		Mrs. KENDAL (By the Courtesy of Mr. W. H. KENDAL)

The Merry Wives of Windsor is a comedy, but it was played on the first night as a comedy of comedies, every one, including Lionel Brough as the Innkeeper, being delightfully jovial. Every one seemed in the highest spirits, and all those sedate actors and actresses thoroughly enjoyed a romp. When the two ladies of the evening appeared on the scene hand in hand, convulsed with laughter, they were clapped so enthusiastically that it really seemed as if they would never be allowed to begin.

What a contrast they were, in appearance and style. They had played together as children, but never after, till that night. During the forty years that had rolled over Ellen Terry's head since those young days she has developed into a Shakespearian actress of the first rank. Her life has been spent in declaiming blank verse, wearing mediæval robes, and enacting tragedy and comedy of ancient days by turn, and added to her vast experience, she has a great and wonderful personality.

Mrs. Kendal, on the other hand, who stands at the head of the comedians of the day, and is also mistress of her art, has played chiefly modern parts and depicted more constantly the sentiment of the time; but has seldom attacked blank verse; therefore, the two leading actresses of England are distinctly dissimilar in training and style. No stronger contrast could have been imagined; and yet, although neither part actually suited either, the finished actress was evident in every gesture, every tone, every look of both, and it would be hard to say which achieved the greatest triumph, each was so perfect in her own particular way.

Miss Ellen Terry did not know her words—she rarely does on a first night, and is even prone to forget her old parts. Appearing in a new character that she was obliged to learn for the occasion, she had not been able to memorise it satisfactorily; but that did not matter in the least. She looked charming, she was charming, the prompter was ever ready, and if she did repeat a line a second time while waiting to be helped with the next, no one seemed to think that of any consequence. When she went up the stairs to hide while Mrs. Kendal (Mrs. Ford) made Tree (Falstaff) propose to her, Mrs. Kendal packed her off in great style, and then wickedly and with amusing emphasis remarked:

"Mistress Page, remember your cue," which of course brought down the house.

Their great scene came in the third act, when they put Falstaff into the basket. Mr. Tree was excellent as the preposterously fat knight—a character verily all stuff and nonsense. He is a tall man, and in his mechanical body reaches enormous girth. Falstaff and the Merry Wives had a regular romp over the upset of the basket, and the audience entering into the fun of the thing laughed as heartily as they did. Oh dear, oh dear! how every one enjoyed it.

A few nights later during this same scene Mr. Tree was observed to grow gradually thinner. He seemed to be going into a "rapid decline," for his belt began to slip about, and his portly form grew less and less. Ellen Terry noticed the change: it was too much for her feelings. With the light-hearted gaiety of a child she was convulsed with mirth. She pointed out the phenomenon to Mrs. Kendal, who at once saw the humour of it, as did the audience, but the chief actor could not fathom the cause of the immoderate hilarity until his belt began to descend. Then he realised that "Little Mary"—which in his case was an air pillow—had lost her screw, and was rapidly fading away.

But to return to that memorable first night; as the curtain fell on the last act the audience clapped and clapped, and not content with having the curtain up four or five times, called and called until the entire company danced hand in hand across the stage in front of the curtain. Even that was not enough, although poor Mrs. Kendal lost her enormous horned head-dress during the dance. The curtain had to be rung up again and again, till Mr. Tree stepped forward and said he had no speech to make beyond thanking the two charming ladies for their assistance and support, whereupon these two executed *pas seuls* on either side of the portly Falstaff.

It was a wonderful performance, and although the two women mentioned stood out pre-eminently, one must not forget Mrs. Tree, who appeared as "Sweet Anne Page." She received quite an ovation when her husband brought her forward to bow her acknowledgments. Bows on such an occasion or in such a comedy are quite permissible; but was ever anything more disconcerting than to see an actor who has just died before us in writhing agony, spring forward to bow at the end of some tragedy—to rise from the dead to smile—to see a man who has just moved us to tears and evoked our sympathy, stand gaily before us, to laugh at our sentiment and cheerily mock at our enthusiasm? Could anything be more inartistic? A "call" often spoils a tragedy, not only in the theatre but at the opera. Over zeal on the part of the audience, and over vanity on the side of the actor, drags away the veil of mystery which is our make-believe of reality, and shows glaringly the make-believe of the whole thing.

Mr. Beerbohm Tree never hesitates to tell a story against himself, and he once related an amusing experience in connection with his original production of *The Merry Wives of Windsor*.

In the final scene at Herne's oak, where Falstaff is pursued by fairy elves and sprites, the burly knight endeavours to escape from his tormentors by climbing the trunk of a huge tree. In order to render this possible the manager had ordered some pegs to be inserted in the bark, but on the night of the final dress rehearsal these necessary aids were absent. A carpenter was summoned, and Mr. Tree, pointing to his namesake, said in tones of the deepest reproach:

"No pegs! No pegs!"

When the eventful first night came Falstaff found to his annoyance and amazement that he was still unable to compass the climb by which he hoped to create much amusement. On the fall of the curtain the delinquent was again called into the managerial presence and addressed in strong terms. He, however, quickly cut short the reproof by exclaiming:

"'Ere, I say, guvnor, 'old 'ard: what was your words last night at the re-'earsal? 'No pegs,' you said—'no pegs'—well, there ain't none," and he gave a knowing smack of the lips as if to insinuate another kind of peg would be acceptable.

Experience has shown Mr. Tree that he can give the necessary appearance of bloated inflation to the cheeks of the fat knight by the aid of a paint-brush alone; but then Mr. Tree mixes his paints with brains. When he first essayed the character of Falstaff he relied for his effect on cotton wool and wig-paste. Even now his nose is deftly manipulated with paste to increase its size and shape, and I once saw him give it a tweak after a performance with droll effect. A little lump of nose-paste remained in his hand, while his own white organ shone forth in the midst of a rubicund countenance.

On an early occasion at the Crystal Palace Mr. Tree was delighted at a burst of uproarious merriment on the part of the audience, and flattered himself that the scene was going exceptionally well. Happening to glance downwards, however, he saw that the padding had slipped from his right leg, leaving him with one lean shank while the other leg still assumed gigantic proportions. He looked down in horror. The audience were not laughing *with* him, but *at* him. He endeavoured to beat a hasty retreat, but found he could not stir, for one of his cheeks had fallen off when leaning forward, and in more senses than one he had "put his foot in it" and required extra cheek, not less, to compass an exit from the stage.

Such are the drolleries incumbent on a character like Falstaff.

Mr. Tree has his serious moments, however, and none are more serious than his present contemplation of his Dramatic School, which he believes "will appeal not only to the profession of actors, but to all interested in the English theatre, the English language, and English oratory, men whose talents are occupied in public life, in politics, in the pulpit, or at the Bar. Unless a dramatic school can be self-supporting it is not likely to survive. Acting cannot be taught—but many things can—such as voice-production, gesture and deportment, fencing and dancing."

Every one will wish his bold venture success; and if he teaches a few of our "well-known" actors and actresses to speak so that we can follow every word of what they say, which at present we often cannot do, he will confer a vast boon on English playgoers, and doubtless add largely to the receipts of the theatres. It is a brave effort on his part, and he deserves every encouragement.

As this chapter began with a first-night performance, it shall end with first-night thoughts.

Are we not one and all hypercritical on such occasions?

We little realise the awful strain behind the scenes in the working of that vast machinery, the play. Not only is the author anxious, but the actors and actresses are worn out with rehearsals and nervousness: property men, wig-makers, scene-painters, and fly-men are all in a state of extreme tension. The front of the house little realises what a truly awful ordeal a first night is for all concerned, and while it is kind to encourage by clapping, it is cruel to condemn by hissing or booing.

Miss Ellen Terry as Queen Katherine.

Photo by Window & Grove, Baker Street, W.

All behind the footlights do their best, or try so far as nervousness will let them, and surely we in the audience should not expect a perfect or a smooth representation, and should give encouragement whenever possible.

After all, however much the actors may suffer from nervousness and anxiety on a first night, their position is not really so trying as that of the author. If the actor is not a success, it may be "the part does not suit him," or "it is a bad play," there may be the excuse of "want of adequate support," for he is only one of a number; but the poor author has to bear the brunt of everything. If his play fail the whole thing is a *fiasco*. He is blamed by every one. It costs more to put on another play than to change a single actor. The author stands alone to receive abuse or praise; he knows that, not only may failure prove ruin to him, but it may mean loss to actors, actresses, managers, and even the call boy. Therefore the more conscientious he is, the more torture he suffers in his anxiety to learn the public estimation of his work. The criticism may not be judicious, but if favourable it brings grist to the mill of all concerned.

CHAPTER X

OPERA COMIC

How W. S. Gilbert loves a Joke—A Brilliant Companion—Operas Reproduced without an Altered Line—Many Professions—A Lovely Home—Sir Arthur Sullivan's Gift—A Rehearsal of *Pinafore*—Breaking up Crowds—Punctuality—Soldier or no Soldier—*Iolanthe*—Gilbert as an Actor—Gilbert as Audience—The Japanese Anthem—Amusement.

FEW authors are so interesting as their work—they generally reserve their wit or trenchant sarcasm for their books. W. S. Gilbert is an exception to this rule, however; he is as amusing himself as his *Bab Ballads*, and as sarcastic as *H.M.S. Pinafore*. A sparkling librettist, he is likewise a brilliant talker. How he loves a joke, even against himself. How well he tells a funny story, even if he invent it on the spot as "perfectly true."

His mind is so quick, he grasps the stage-setting of a dinner-party at once, and forthwith adapts his drama of the hour to exactly suit his audience.

Like all amusing people, he has his quiet moments, of course; but when Mr. Gilbert is in good form he is inimitable. He talks like his plays, turns everything upside-down with wondrous rapidity, and propounds nonsensical theories in delightful language. He is assuredly the greatest wit of his day, and to him we owe the origin of musical-comedy in its best form.

With a congenial companion Mr. Gilbert is in his element. He is a fine-looking man with white hair and ponderous moustache, and owing to his youthful complexion appears younger than his years. He loves to have young people about him, and is never happier than when surrounded by friends.

In 1901, after an interval of nearly twenty years, his clever comic opera *Iolanthe* was revived at the Savoy with great success. Not one line, not one word of its original text had been altered, yet it took London by storm, just as did *Pinafore* when produced for the second time. How few authors' work will stand so severe a test.

The genesis of *Iolanthe* is referable, like many of Mr. Gilbert's libretti, to one of the *Bab Ballads*. The "primordial atomic globule" from which it traces its descent is a poem called *The Fairy Curate*, in which a clergyman, the son of a fairy, gets into difficulties with his bishop, who catches him in the act of embracing an airily dressed young lady, whom the bishop supposes to be a member of the *corps de ballet*. The bishop, reasonably enough, declines to accept the clergyman's explanation that the young lady is his mother, and difficulties ensue. In the opera, Strephon, who is the son of the fairy Iolanthe, is detected by his *fiancée* Phyllis in the act of embracing *his* mother; Phyllis takes the bishop's view of the situation, and complications arise.

Mr. Gilbert has penned such well-known blank verse dramas as *The Palace of Truth, Pygmalion and Galatea, The Wicked Worlds, Broken Hearts*, besides many serious and humorous plays and comedies—namely, *Dan'l Druce, Engaged, Sweethearts, Comedy and Tragedy*, and some dozen light operas.

It is a well-known fact that almost every comedian wishes to be a tragedian, and *vice versâ*, and Mr. Gilbert is said to have had a great and mighty sorrow all his life. He always wanted to write serious dramas—long, five-act plays full of situations and thought. But no; fate ordained otherwise, when, having for a change started his little barque as a librettist, he had to persevere in penning what he calls "nonsense." The public were right; they knew there was no other W. S. Gilbert; they wanted to be amused, so they continually clamoured for more; and if any one did not realise his genius at the first production, he can hardly fail to do so now, when the author's plays are again presented after a lapse of years, without an altered line, and still make long runs. Some say the art of comedy-writing is dying out, and certainly no second Gilbert seems to be rising among the younger men of the present day, no humourist who can call tears or laughter at will, and send his audience away happy every night. The world owes a debt of gratitude to this gifted scribe, for he has never put an unclean line upon the stage, and yet provokes peals of laughter while shyly giving his little digs at existing evils. His style has justly created a name of its own.

W. S. Gilbert has always had a deep-rooted objection to newspaper interviews, just as he refuses ever to see one of his own plays performed. He attends the last rehearsal, gives the minutest directions up to the final moment, and then usually spends the evening in the green-room or in the wings of the theatre. Very few authors accept fame or success more philosophically than he does. When *Princess Ida* was produced he was sitting in the green-room, where there was an excitable Frenchman, who had supplied the armour used in the piece. The play was going capitally, and the Frenchman exclaimed, in wild excitement, "Mais savez-vous que nous avons là un succès solide?" To which Mr. Gilbert quietly replied, "Yes, your armour seems to be shining brightly."

"Ah!" exclaimed the Frenchman, with a gesture of amazement, "mais vous êtes si calme!"

And this would probably describe the outward appearance of the author on a first night; nevertheless nothing will induce him to go in front even with reproductions.

Mr. Gilbert, who was born in 1836, proudly remarks that he has cheated the doctors and signed a new lease of life on the twenty-one years' principle. During those sixty-eight years he has turned his hand to many trades. After a career at the London University, where he took his B.A. degree, he read for the Royal Artillery, but the Crimean war was coming to an end, and consequently, more officers not being required, he became a clerk in the Privy Council Office, and was subsequently called to the Bar at the Inner Temple. He was also an enthusiastic militiaman, and at one time an occasional contributor to *Punch*, becoming thus an artist as well as a writer. His pictures are well known, for the two or three hundred illustrations in the *Bab Ballads* are all from his clever pencil. Neatly framed they now adorn the billiard-room of his charming country home, and, strange to relate, the originals are not much larger than the reproductions, the work being extremely fine. I have seen him make an excellent sketch in a few minutes at his home on Harrow Weald; but photography has latterly cast its fascinations about him, and he often disappears into some dark chamber for hours at a time, alone with his thoughts and his photographic pigments, for he develops and prints everything himself. The results are charming, more especially his scenic studies.

What a lovely home his is, standing in a hundred and ten acres right on the top of Harrow Weald, with a glorious view over London, Middlesex, Berks, and Bucks. He farms the land himself, and talks of crops and live stock with a glib tongue, although the real enthusiast is his wife, who loves her prize chickens and her roses. Grim's Dyke has an ideal garden, with white pigeons drinking out of shallow Italian bowls upon the lawn, with its wonderful Egyptian tent, its rose-walks and its monkey-house, its lake and its fish. The newly-made lake is so well arranged that it looks quite old with its bulrushes, water-lilies of pink, white, and yellow hue, and its blue forget-me-nots. The Californian trout have proved a great success, and are a source of much sport. Everything is well planned and beautifully kept; no better lawns or neater walks, no more prolific glass houses or vegetable gardens could be found than those at Harrow Weald.

The Gilberts give delightful week-end parties, and the brightest star is generally the host himself.

At one of these recent gatherings, for which Grim's Dyke is famous, some beautiful silver cups and a claret jug were upon the table. They were left by will to Mr. Gilbert by his colleague of so many years, Sir Arthur Sullivan, and are a great pleasure to both the host and hostess of that well-organised country house. I have met many interesting and clever people at Harrow Weald, for the brilliancy of the host and the charm of his wife naturally attract much that is best in this great city. It is a good house for entertaining, the music-room — formerly the studio of F. Goodall, R.A. — being a spacious oak-panelled chamber with a minstrels' gallery, and cathedral windows. Excellent singing is often heard within those walls. Mr. Gilbert declares he is not musical himself; but such is hardly the case, for he on one or two occasions suggested to Sir Arthur Sullivan the style best suited to his words. His ear for time and rhythm is impeccable, but he fully admits he has an imperfect sense of tune.

The Squire of Harrow Weald is seen at his best at rehearsal.

H.M.S. Pinafore was first performed, I believe, in 1878, and about ten years afterwards it was revived in London. Ten years later, that is to say 1899, it was again revived, and one Monday morning when I was leaving Grim's Dyke, Mr. Gilbert, who was coming up to town to attend a rehearsal, asked me if I would care to see it.

"Nothing I should like better," I replied, "for I have always understood that you and Mr. Pinero are the two most perfect stage managers in England."

Mr. W. S. Gilbert.

Photo by Langfier, 23A, Old Bond Street, London, W.

We drove to the stage door of the Savoy, whence down strange and dark stone stairs we made our way to the front of the auditorium itself. We crossed behind the footlights, passing through a small, unpretending iron door into the house, Mr. Gilbert leading the way, to a side box, which at the moment was shrouded in darkness; he soon, however, pushed aside the white calico dust-sheets that hung before it, and after placing chairs for his wife and myself, and hoping we should be comfortable, departed. What a spectre that theatre was! Hanging from gallery to pit were dust-sheets, the stalls all covered up with brown holland wrappers, and gloom and darkness on all things. Verily a peep behind the scenes which, more properly speaking, was before the scenes in this case, is like looking at a private house preparing for a spring cleaning.

Built out over what is ordinarily the orchestra, was a wooden platform large enough to contain a piano brilliantly played by a woman, beside whom sat the conductor of the orchestra, who was naturally the teacher of the chorus, and next to him the ordinary stage manager, with a chair for Mr. Gilbert placed close by. The librettist, however, never sat on that chair. From 11.30 to 1.30—exactly two hours, he walked up and down in front of the stage, directing here, arranging there; one moment he was showing a man how to stand as a sailor, then how to clap his thighs in nautical style, and the next explaining to a woman how to curtsey, or telling a lover how to woo. Never have I seen anything more remarkable. In no sense a musician, Mr. Gilbert could hum any of the airs and show the company the minutest gesticulations at the same time. Be it understood they were already *word* and *music* perfect, and this was the second "stage rehearsal." He never bullied or worried any one, he quietly went up to a person, and in the most insinuating manner said:

"If I were you, I think I should do it like this."

And "this" was always so much better than their own performance that each actor quickly grasped the idea and copied the master. He even danced when necessary, to show them how to get the right number of steps in so as to land them at a certain spot at a certain time, explaining carefully:

"There are eight bars, and you must employ so many steps."

Mr. Gilbert knows every bar, every intonation, every gesture, the hang of every garment, and the tilt of every hat. He has his plans and his ideas, and never alters the situations or even the gestures he has once thought out.

He marched up and down the stage advising an alteration here, an intonation there, all in the kindest way possible, but with so much strength of conviction that all his suggestions were adopted without a moment's hesitation. He never loses his temper, always sees the weak points, and is an absolute master of stage craft. His tact on such occasions is wonderful.

The love and confidence of that company in Mr. Gilbert was really delightful, and I have no hesitation in saying he was the best actor in the whole company whichever part he might happen to undertake. If anything he did not like occurred in the grouping of the chorus he clapped his hands and everybody stopped, when he would call out:

"Gentlemen in threes, ladies in twos," according to a style of his own.

Twenty-five years previously he had been so horrified at chorus and crowd standing round the stage in a ring, that he invented the idea of breaking them up, and thereafter, according to arrangement, when "twos" or "threes" were called out the performers were to group themselves and talk in little clusters, and certainly the effect was more natural.

Mr. Gilbert had no notes of any kind. He brought them with him, but never opened the volume, and yet he knew exactly how everything ought to be done. This was his first rehearsal with the company, who up till then had been in the stage manager's hands and worked according to printed instructions. The scene was a very different affair after the mastermind had set the pawns in their right squares, and made the bishops and knights move according to his will. In two hours they had gone through the first act of *Pinafore*, and he clapped his hands and called for luncheon.

"It is just half-past one," he said; "I am hungry, and I daresay you are hungry, so we will halt for half an hour. I shall be back by five minutes past two—that is five minutes' grace, when"—bowing kindly—"I shall hope to see you again, ladies and gentlemen."

We three lunched at the Savoy next door, and a few minutes before two he rose from the table, ere he had finished his coffee, and said he must go.

"You are in a hurry," I laughingly said.

"Yes," he replied, "I have made it a rule never to be late. The company know I shall be there, so the company will be in their places."

A friend once congratulated him on his punctuality.

"Don't," he said; "I have lost more time by being punctual than by anything else."

One thing in particular struck me as wonderful during the rehearsal. Half a dozen soldiers are supposed to come upon the stage, and at a certain point half a dozen untidily dressed men with guns in their hands marched in. Mr. Gilbert looked at them for a moment, and then he went up to one gallant warrior and said:

"Is that the way you hold your gun?"

"Yes, sir."

"Really! Well, I never saw a soldier with his thumbs down before—in fact, I don't think you are a soldier at all."

"No, sir, I am a volunteer."

Mr. Gilbert turned to the stage manager hastily, and said:

"I told you I wanted soldiers."

"But there is a sergeant," he replied.

"Sergeant," called Mr. Gilbert, "step forward." Which the sergeant did.

"You know your business," the author remarked, watching the man's movements, "but these fellows know nothing. Either bring me real soldiers, or else take these five men and drill them until at least they know how to stand properly before they come near me again."

Later in the proceedings a dozen sailors marched on: he went up to them, asked some questions about how they would man the yard-arm, and on hearing their reply said:

"I see you know your business, you'll do."

As it turned out, they were all Naval Reserve men, so no wonder they knew their business. Still, Mr. Gilbert's universal knowledge of all sorts and conditions of men struck me as wonderful on this and many other occasions. No more perfect stage manager exists, and no one gets more out of his actors and actresses.

At one time *Patience* was being played in the United States by dozens of companies, but that was before the days of copyright, and poor Mr. Gilbert never received a penny from America excepting once when a kindly person sent him a cheque for £100. Had he received copyright fees from the United States his wealth would have been colossal.

When *Iolanthe* was revived in London in 1902 I again attended a "call." An entirely new company began rehearsing exactly ten days before the first night—any one who knows anything of the stage will realise what this means, and that a master-mind was necessary to drill actors and chorus in so short a time—yet the production was a triumph. This was the first occasion on which Sir Arthur Sullivan did not conduct the dress rehearsal or the first night of one of their joint operas. He had died shortly before.

Mr. Gilbert was delighted with the cast, and declared it was quite as good, and in some respects perhaps better, than the original had been. A few of the people had played *principals* in the provinces before; but he would not allow any of their own "business" and remarked quietly:

"In London my plays are produced as I wish them; in the provinces you can do as you like."

And certainly they obeyed him so implicitly that if he had asked them all to stand on their heads in rows, I believe they would have done it smilingly.

When Mr. Gilbert was about thirty-five years old, a *matinée* of *Broken Hearts* was arranged for a charity. The author arrived at the theatre about one o'clock, to find Kyrle Bellew, who was to play the chief part, had fallen through a trap and was badly hurt. There was no understudy—and only an hour intervened before the advertised time of representation.

Good Heavens! what was to be done? The audience had paid their money, which the charity wanted badly, and without the hero the play was impossible.

He good-naturedly and kind-heartedly decided to play the part himself rather than let the entertainment fall through, wired for wig and clothes, and an hour and a half later walked on to the stage as an actor. He knew every line of the play of course, not only the hero's, but all the others', and he had just coached every situation. The papers duly thanked him and considered him a great success. That was his only appearance upon the stage in public.

For twenty-five years he never saw one of his own plays, not caring to sit in front; but once, at a watering-place in the Fatherland where *The Mikado* was being given, some friends persuaded him to see it in German.

"I know what rubbish these comic operas are, and I should feel ashamed to sit and hear them and know they were mine," he modestly remarked.

Nevertheless he went, and was rather amused, feeling no responsibility on his shoulders, and afterwards saw *The Mikado* in England at a revival towards the end of the nineties. He once told me a rather amusing little story about *The Mikado*. A gentleman who had been many years in the English Legation at Yokohama, attended some of the rehearsals, and was most useful in giving hints as to positions and manners in Japan. Mr. Gilbert wanted some effective music for the entrance of the Mikado—nothing Mr. Arthur Sullivan suggested suited—so turning to the gentleman he said:

"Can't you hum the national Japanese anthem?"

"Oh yes," he said cheerily. And he did.

"Capital—it'll just do."

Mr. Sullivan—for he was not then Sir Arthur—made notes, wrote it up, and the thing proved a great success. Some time afterwards a furious letter came from a Japanese, saying an insult had been offered the Mikado of Japan, the air to which that illustrious prince entered the scene instead of being royal was a music hall tune! Whether this is so or not remains a mystery, anyway it is a delightful melody, and most successful to this day.

Mr. Gilbert has been a great traveller—for many years he wintered abroad in India, Japan, Burmah, Egypt, or Greece, and at one time he was the enthusiastic owner of a yacht; but this amusement he has given up because so few of his friends were good sailors, and so he has taken to motoring instead.

Croquet-playing and motoring are the chief amusements of this "retired humourist," as a local cab-driver once described the Squire of Grim's Dyke.

CHAPTER XI

THE FIRST PANTOMIME REHEARSAL

Origin of Pantomime—Drury Lane in Darkness—One Thousand Persons—Rehearsing the Chorus—The Ballet—Dressing-rooms—Children on the Stage—Size of "The Lane"—A Trap-door—The Property-room—Made on the Premises—Wardrobe-woman—Dan Leno at Rehearsal—Herbert Campbell—A Fortnight Later—A Chat with the Principal Girl—Miss Madge Lessing.

EXACTLY nine days before Christmas, 1902, the first rehearsal for the pantomime of *Mother Goose* took place at Drury Lane. It seemed almost incredible that afternoon that such a thing as a "first night," with a crowded house packed full of critics, could witness a proper performance nine days later, one of which, being a Sunday, did not count.

The pantomime is one of England's institutions. It originally came from Italy, but as known to-day is essentially a British production, and little understood anywhere else in the world. For the last three years, however, the Drury Lane pantomime has been moved bodily to New York with considerable success.

What would Christmas in London be without its Drury Lane? What would the holidays be without the clown and harlequin? Young and old enjoy the exquisite absurdity of the nursery rhyme dished up as a Christmas pantomime.

The interior of that vast theatre, Drury Lane, was shrouded in dust-sheets and darkness, the front doors were locked, excepting at the booking office, where tickets were being sold for two and three months ahead, and a long *queue* of people were waiting to engage seats for family parties when the pantomime should be ready.

At the stage door all was bustle; children of all ages and sizes were pushing in and out; carpenters, shifters, supers, ballet girls, chorus, all were there, too busy to speak to any one as they rushed in from their cup of tea at the A.B.C., or stronger drink procured at the "pub" opposite. It was a cold, dreary day outside; but it was colder and drearier within. Those long flights of stone steps, those endless stone passages, struck chill and cheerless as a cellar, for verily the back of a theatre resembles a cellar or prison more than anything I know.

Drury Lane contains a little world. It is reckoned that about one thousand people are paid "back and front" every Friday night. One thousand persons! That is the staff of the pantomime controlled by Mr. Arthur Collins. Fancy that vast organisation, those hundreds of people, endless scenery, and over two thousand dresses superintended by one man, and that a young one.

For many weeks scraps of *Mother Goose* had been rehearsed in drill-halls, schoolrooms, and elsewhere, but never till the day of which I write had the stage been ready for rehearsal. They had worked hard, all those people; for thirteen-and-a-half hours on some days they had already been "at it." Think what thirteen-and-a-half-hours mean. True, no one is wanted continuously, still all must be on the spot. Often there is nowhere to sit down, therefore during those weary hours the performers have to stand — only between-whiles singing or dancing their parts as the case may be.

"I'm that dead tired," exclaimed a girl, "I feel just fit to drop," and she probably expressed the feelings of many of her companions.

The rehearsal of *The Rose of the Riviera*, was going on in the saloon, which a hundred years ago was the fashionable resort of all the fops of the town. Accordingly to the saloon I proceeded where Miss Madge Lessing, neatly dressed in black and looking tired, was singing her solos, and dancing her steps with the chorus.

"It is very hard work," she said. "I have been through this song until I am almost voiceless; and yet I only hum it really, for if we sang out at rehearsal, we should soon be dead."

The saloon was the ordinary *foyer*, but on that occasion, instead of being crowded with idlers smoking and drinking during the *entr'actes*, it was filled with hard-worked ballet girls and small boys who were later to be transformed into dandies. They wore their own clothes. The women's long skirts were held up with safety-pins, to keep them out of the way when dancing, their shirts and blouses were of every hue; on their heads they wore men's hats that did not fit them, as they lacked the wigs they would wear later, and each carried her own umbrella, many of which, when opened, seemed the worse for wear. At the end of the bar was a cottage piano, where the composer played his song for two-and-a-half hours, while it was rehearsed again and again — a small man with a shocking cold conducting the chorus. He is, I am told, quite a celebrity as a stage "producer," and was engaged in that capacity by Mr. George Edwards at the New Gaiety Theatre. How I admired that small man. His energy and enthusiasm were catching, and before he finished he had made those girls do just what he wanted. But oh! how hard he worked, in spite of frequent resort to his pocket-handkerchief and constant fits of sneezing.

"This way, ladies, please" — he repeated over and over, and then proceeded to show them how to step forward on "*Would* — you like a — flower?" and to take off their hats at the last word of the sentence. Again and again they went through their task; but each time they seemed out of line, or out of time, not quick enough or too quick, and back they had to go and begin the whole verse once more. Even then he was not satisfied.

"Again, ladies, please," he called, and again they all did the passage. This sort of thing had been going on since 11 o'clock, the hour of the "call," and it was then 4 p.m. — but the rehearsal was likely to last well into the night and begin again next morning at 11 a.m. This was to continue all day, and pretty well all night for nine days, when, instead of a holiday, the pantomime was really to commence with its two daily performances, and its twelve hours *per diem* attendance at the theatre for nearly four months. Yet there are people who think the stage is all fun and frolic! Little they know about the matter.

Actors are not paid for rehearsals, as we have seen before, and many weeks of weary attendance for the pantomime have to be given gratis, just as they are for legitimate drama. Those beautiful golden fairies, all glitter and gorgeousness, envied by spectators in front, only receive £1 a week on an average for twelve hours' occupation daily, and that merely for a few weeks, after which time many of them earn nothing more till the next pantomime season. It is practically impossible to give an exact idea of salaries: they vary so much. "Ballet girls," when proficient, earn more than any ordinary "chorus" or "super," with the exception of "show girls." Those in the rank of "principals," or "small-part ladies," of course earn more.

Ballet girls begin their profession at eight years of age, and even in their prime can only earn on an average £2 a week.

In the ballet-room an iron bar runs all round the sides of the wall, about four feet from the floor, as in a swimming bath. It is for practice. The girls hold on to the bar, and learn to kick and raise their legs by the hour; with its aid suppleness of movement, flexibility of hip and knee are acquired. Girls spend years of their life learning how to earn that forty shillings a week, and how to keep it when they have earned it; for the ballet girl has to be continually practising, or her limbs would quickly stiffen and her professional career come to an end.

No girl gets her real training at the Lane. All that is done in one of the dancing schools kept by Madame Katti Lanner, Madame Cavalazzi, John D'Auban, or John Tiller. When they are considered sufficiently proficient they get engagements, and are taught certain movements invented by their teachers to suit the particular production of the theatre itself.

The ballet is very grand in the estimation of the pantomime, for supers, male and female, earn considerably less salary than the ballet for about seventy-two hours' attendance at the theatre. Out of their weekly money they have to provide travelling expenses to and from the theatre, which sometimes come heavy, as many of them live a long distance off; they have to pay rent also, and feed as well as clothe themselves, settle for washing, doctor, amusements—everything, in fact. Why, a domestic servant is a millionaire when compared with a chorus or ballet girl, and she is never harassed with constant anxiety as to how she can pay her board, rent, and washing bills. Yet how little the domestic servant realises the comforts—aye luxury—of her position.

The dressing-rooms are small and cheerless. Round the sides run double tables, the top one being used for make-up boxes, the lower for garments. In the middle of the floor is a wooden stand with a double row of pegs upon it, utilised for hanging up dresses. Eight girls share a "dresser" (maid) between them. The atmosphere of the room may be imagined, with flaring gas jets, nine women, and barely room to turn round amid the dresses. The air becomes stifling at times, and there is literally no room to sit down even if the costumes would permit of such luxury, which generally they will not. In this tiny room performers have to wait for their "call," when they rush downstairs, through icy cold passages, to the stage, whence they must return again in time to don the next costume required.

Prior to the production, as we have seen, there are a number of rehearsals, followed for many weeks by two performances a day, consequently the children who are employed cannot go on with their education, and to avoid missing their examinations a school-board mistress has been appointed, who teaches them their lessons during the intervals. These children must be bright scholars, for they are the recipients at the end of the season of several special prizes for diligence, punctuality, and good conduct.

An attempt was recently made to limit the age of children employed on the stage to fourteen, but the outcry raised was so great that it could not be done. For children under eleven a special licence is required.

Miss Ellen Terry said, on the subject of children on the stage: "I am an actress, but first I am a woman, and I love children," and then proceeded to advocate the employment of juveniles upon the stage. She spoke from experience, for she acted as a child herself. "I can put my finger at once on the actors and actresses who were not on the stage as children," she continued. "With all their hard work they can never acquire afterwards that perfect unconsciousness which they learn then so easily. There is no school like the stage for giving equal chances to boys and girls alike."

There seems little doubt about it, the ordinary stage child is the offspring of the very poor, his playground the gutter, his surroundings untidy and unclean, his food and clothing scanty, and such being the case he is better off in every way in a well-organised theatre, where he learns obedience, cleanliness, and punctuality. The sprites and fairies love their plays, and the greatest punishment they can have—indeed, the only one inflicted at Drury Lane—is to be kept off the stage a whole day for naughtiness.

They appear to be much better off in the theatre than they would be at home, although morning school and two performances a day necessitate rather long hours for the small folk. They have a nice classroom, and are given buns and milk after school; but their dressing accommodation is limited. Many of the supers and children have to change as best they can under the stage, for there is not sufficient accommodation for every one in the rooms.

The once famous "Green-room" of Drury Lane has been done away with. It is now a property-room, where geese's heads line the shelves, or golden seats and monster champagne bottles litter the floor.

There have been many changes at Drury Lane. It was rebuilt after the fire in 1809, and reopened in 1812, but vast alterations have been carried out since then. Woburn Place is now part of the stage. Steps formerly led from Russell Street to Vinegar Yard, but they have been swept away and the stage enlarged until it is the biggest in the world. Most ordinary theatres have an opening on the auditorium of about twenty-five feet; Drury Lane measures fifty-two feet from fly to fly, and is even deeper in proportion. The entire stage is a series of lifts, which may be utilised to move the floor up or down. Four tiers, or "flats," can be arranged, and the floor moved laterally so as to form a hill or mound. All this is best seen from the mezzanine stage, namely, that under the real one, where the intricacies of lifts and ropes and rooms for electricians become most bewildering. Here, too, are the trap-doors. For many years they went out of fashion, as did also the ugly masks, but a Fury made his entrance by a trap on Boxing Day, 1902, and this may revive the custom again. The actor steps on a small wooden table in the mezzanine stage, and at a given sign the spring moves and he is shot to the floor above. How I loved and pondered as a child over these wonderful entrances of fairies and devils. And after all there was nothing supernatural about them, only a wooden table and a spring. How much of the glamour vanishes when we look below the surface, which remark applies not only to the stage, but to so many things in life.

Every good story seems to have been born a chestnut. Some one always looks as if he had heard it before. At the risk of arousing that sarcastic smile I will relate the following anecdote, however.

A certain somewhat stout Mephistopheles had to disappear through a trap-door amid red fire, but the trap was small and he was big and stuck halfway. The position was embarrassing, when a voice from the gallery called out:

"Cheer up, guv'nor. Hell's full."

Electricity plays a great part in the production of a pantomime, not only as regards the lighting of the scenes, but also as a motive power for the lifts which are used for the stage. Many new inventions born during the course of a year are utilised when the Christmas festival is put on.

The property-room presents a busy scene before a pantomime, and really it is wonderful what can be produced within its walls. Almost everything is made in *papier mâché*. Elaborate golden chairs and couches, chariots and candelabras, although framed in wood, are first moulded in clay, then covered with *papier mâché*. Two large fires burned in the room, which when I entered was crowded with workmen, and the heat was overpowering. Amid all that miscellaneous property, every one seemed interested in what he was doing, whether making wire frames for poke bonnets, or larger wire frames for geese, or the groundwork of champagne bottles to contain little boys. Each man had a charcoal drawing on brown paper to guide him, and very cleverly many of the drawings were executed. Some of the men were quite sculptors, so admirably did they model masks and figures in *papier mâché*. The more elaborate pieces are prepared outside the theatre, but a great deal of the work for the production is done within old Drury Lane.

What becomes of these extra property-men after the "festive season"? Practically the same staff appear each Christmas only to disappear from "The Lane" for almost another year. Of course there is a large permanent staff of property-men employed, but it is only at Christmas-time that so large an army is required for the gigantic pantomime changes with the transformation scenes.

That nearly everything is made on the premises is in itself a marvel. Of course the grander dresses are obtained from outside; some come from Paris, while others are provided by tradesmen in London. The expense is very great; indeed, it may be roughly reckoned it costs about £20,000 to produce a Drury Lane Pantomime; but then, on the other hand, that sum is generally taken at the doors or by the libraries in advance-booking before the curtain rises on the first night.

An important person at Drury Lane is the wardrobe-woman. She has entire control of thousands of dresses, and keeps a staff continually employed mending and altering, for after each performance something requires attention. She has a little room of her own, mostly table, so far as I could see, on which were piled dresses, poke bonnets, and artists' designs, while round the walls hung more dresses brought in for her inspection. In other odd rooms and corners women sat busily sewing, some trimming headgear, other spangling ribbon. Some were joining seams by machinery, others quilling lace; nothing seemed finished, and yet everything had to be ready in nine days, and that vast pile of chaos reduced to order. It seemed impossible; but the impossible was accomplished.

"Why this hurry?" some one may ask.

"Because the autumn drama was late in finishing, the entire theatre had to be cleared, and although everything was fairly ready outside, nothing could be brought into Drury Lane till a fortnight before Boxing Day. Hence the confusion and hurry."

Large wooden cases of armour, swords and spears, from abroad, were waiting to be unpacked, fitted to each girl, and numbered so that the wearer might know her own.

Among the properties were some articles that looked like round red life-belts, or window sand-bags sewn into rings. These were the belts from which fairies would be suspended. They had leather straps and iron hooks attached, with the aid of which these lovely beings—as seen from the front—disport themselves. What a disillusion! Children think they are real fairies flying through air, and after all they are only ordinary women hanging to red sand-bags, made up like life-belts, and suspended by wire rope. Even those wonderful wings are only worn for a moment. They are slipped into a hole in the bodice of every fairy's back just as she goes upon the stage, and taken out again for safety when the good lady leaves the wings in the double sense. The wands and other larger properties are treated in the same way.

Now for the stage and the rehearsal. We could hear voices singing, accompanied by a piano with many whizzing notes.

The place was dimly lighted. Scene-shifters were busy rehearsing their "sets" at the sides, the electrician was experimenting with illuminations from above; but the actors, heeding none of these matters, went on with their own parts. The orchestra was empty and not boarded over; so that the cottage piano had to stand at one side of the stage, and near it I was given a seat. A T-piece of gas had been fixed above the footlights, so as to enable the prompter to follow his book, and—gently be it spoken—allow some of the actors to read their parts. The star was not there—I looked about for the mirth-provoking Dan Leno, but failed to see him.

Naturally he was the one person I particularly wanted to watch rehearse, for I anticipated much amusement from this wonderful comedian, with his inspiring gift of humour. Where was he?

A sad, unhappy-looking little man, with his MS. in a brown paper cover, was to be seen wandering about the back of the stage. He appeared miserable. One wondered at such a person being there at all, he looked so out of place. He did not seem to know a word of his "book," or, in fact, to belong in any way to the pantomime.

It seemed incredible that this could be one of the performers. He wore a thick top coat with the collar turned up to keep off the draughts, a thick muffler and a billycock hat; really one felt sorry for him, he looked so cold and wretched. I pondered for some time why this sad little gentleman should be on the stage at all.

"Dan, Dan, where are you?" some one called.

"Me? Oh, I'm here," replied the disconsolate-looking person, to my amazement.

"It's your cue."

"Oh, is it? Which cue?" asked the mufflered individual who was about to impersonate mirth.

"Why, so and so— —"

"What page is that?"

"Twenty-three."

Whereupon the great Dan—for it was really Dan himself—proceeded to find number twenty-three, and immediately began reading a lecture to the goose in mock solemn vein, when some one cried:

"No, no, man, that's not it, you are reading page thirteen; we've done that."

"Oh, have we? Thank you. Ah yes, here it is."

"That's my part," exclaimed Herbert Campbell. "Your cue is— —"

"Oh, is it?" and poor bewildered, unhappy-looking Dan made another and happier attempt.

It had often previously occurred to me that Dan Leno gagged his own part to suit himself every night—and really after this rehearsal the supposition seemed founded on fact, for apparently he did not know one word of anything nine days before the production of *Mother Goose*, in which he afterwards made such a brilliant hit.

"Do I say that?" he would inquire, or, "Are you talking to me?"

After such a funny exhibition it seemed really wonderful to consider how excellent and full of humour he always is on the stage; but what a strain it must be, what mental agony, to feel you are utterly unprepared to meet your audience, that you do not know your words, and that only by making a herculean effort can the feat be accomplished.

Herbert Campbell differs from Dan Leno not only in appearance but method. He was almost letter-perfect at that rehearsal, he had studied his "book," and was splendidly funny even while only murmuring his part. He evidently knew exactly what he was going to do, and although he did not trouble to do it, showed by a wave of his hand or a step where he meant business when the time came.

Herbert Campbell's face, like the milkmaid's, is his fortune. That wonderful under lip is full of fun. He has only to protrude it, and open his eyes, and there is the comedian personified. Comedians are born, not made, and the funny part of it is most of them are so truly tragic at heart and sad in themselves.

There is a story I often heard my grandfather, James Muspratt, tell of Liston, the comic actor.

Liston was in Dublin early in the nineteenth century, and nightly his performance provoked roars of laughter. One day a man walked into the consulting-room of a then famous doctor.

"I am very ill," said the patient. "I am suffering from depression."

"Tut, tut," returned the physician, "you must pull yourself together, you must do something to divert your thoughts. You must be cheerful and laugh."

"Good Heavens! I would give a hundred pounds to enjoy a real, honest laugh again, doctor."

"Well, you can easily do that for a few shillings, and I'll tell you how. Go and see Liston to-night, he will make you laugh, I am sure."

"Not he."

"Why not?"

"Because I am Liston."

Collapse of the doctor.

This shows the tragedy of the life of a comic actor. How often we see the amusing, delightful man or woman in society, and little dream how different they are at home. Most of us have two sides to our natures, and most of us are better actors than we realise ourselves, or than our friends give us credit for.

But to return to Drury Lane. Peering backwards across the empty orchestra I saw by the dim light that in the stalls sat, or leaned, women and children. Mr. Collins, who was in the front of the stage, personally attending to every detail, slipped forward.

"Huntsmen and gamekeepers," he cried. Immediately there was a flutter, and in a few minutes these good women—for women were to play the *rôles*—were upon the back of the stage.

"Dogs," he called again. With more noise than the female huntsmen had made, boys got up and began to run about the stage on all fours as "dogs."

They surrounded Dan Leno.

"I shall hit you if you come near me," he cried, pretending to do so with his doubled-up gloves.

The lads laughed.

"Growl," said Mr. Collins—so they turned their laugh into a growl, followed round the stage by Dan, and the performance went on.

It was all very funny—funny, not because of any humour, for that was entirely lacking, but because of the simplicity and hopelessness of every one. Talk about a rehearsal at private theatricals—why, it is no more disturbing than an early stage rehearsal; but the seasoned actor knows how to pull himself out of the tangle, whereas the amateur does not.

About a fortnight after the pantomime began I chanced one afternoon to be at Drury Lane again, and while stopping for a moment in the wings, the great Dan Leno came and stood beside me, waiting for his cue. He was dressed as Mother Goose, and leant against the endless ropes that seemed to frame every stage entrance; some one spoke to him, but he barely answered, he appeared preoccupied. All at once his turn came. On he went, hugging a goose beneath which walked a small boy. Roars of applause greeted his entrance, he said his lines, and a few moments later came out amid laughter and clapping. "This will have cheered him up," thought I—but no. There I left him waiting for his next cue, but I had not gone far before renewed roars of applause from the house told me Dan Leno was again on the stage. What a power to be able to amuse thousands of people every week, to be able to bring mirth and joy into many a heart, to take people out of themselves and make the saddest merry—and Dan can do all this.

The object of my second visit was to have a little chat with Miss Madge Lessing, the "principal girl," who exclaimed as I entered her dressing-room:

"I spend eleven hours in the theatre every day during the run of the pantomime."

After that who can say a pantomime part is a sinecure? Eleven hours every day dressing, singing, dancing, acting, or—more wearisome of all—waiting. No one unaccustomed to the stage can realise the strain of such work, for it is only those who live at such high pressure, who always have to be on the alert for the "call-boy," who know what it is to be kept at constant tension for so many consecutive hours.

Matinée days are bad enough in ordinary theatres, but the pantomime is a long series of *matinée* days extending over three months or more. Of course it is not compulsory to stay in the theatre between the performances; but it is more tiring, for the leading-lady, to dress and go out for a meal than to stay in and have it brought to the dressing-room.

Miss Lessing was particularly fortunate in her room; the best I have ever seen in any theatre. Formerly it was Sir Augustus Harris's office. It was large and lofty, and so near the stage—on a level with which it actually stood—that one could hear what was going on in front. This was convenient in many ways, although it had its drawbacks. Many of our leading theatrical lights have to traverse long flights of stairs between every act; while Miss Lessing was so close to the stage she need not leave her room until it was actually time to step upon the boards.

It was a *matinée* when the pantomime was in full swing that I bearded the lion in her den, and a pretty, dainty little lion I found her. It was a perilous journey to reach her room, but I bravely followed the "dresser" from the stage door. We passed a lilliputian pony about the size of a St. Bernard dog, we bobbed under the heads and tails of horses so closely packed together there was barely room for us to get between. The huntsmen were already mounted, for they were just going on, and I marvelled at the good behaviour of those steeds; they must have known they could not move without doing harm to some one, and so considerately remained still. We squeezed past fairies, our faces tickled by their wings, our dresses caught by their spangles, so closely packed was humanity "behind." There were about two hundred scene-shifters incessantly at work moving "cloths," and "flies," and "drops," and properties of all kinds. Miss Lessing was just coming off the stage, dressed becomingly in white muslin, with a blue Red Riding Hood cape and poppy-trimmed straw hat.

"Come along," she said, "this is my room, and it is fairly quiet here." The first things that strike a stranger are Miss Lessing's wonderful grey Irish eyes and her American accent.

"Both are correct," she laughed. "I'm Irish by extraction, although born in London, and I've lived in America since I was fourteen; so you see there is ground for both your surmises."

Miss Lessing is a Roman Catholic, and was educated at the Convent of the Sacred Heart at Battersea.

"I always wanted to go on the stage as long as ever I can remember," she told me, "and I positively ran away from home and went over to America, where I had a fairly hard time of it. By good luck I managed to get an engagement in a chorus, and it chanced that two weeks later one of the better parts fell vacant owing to a girl's illness, and I got it—and was fortunate enough to keep it, as she was unable to return, and the management were satisfied with me. I had to work very hard, had to take anything and everything offered to me for years. Had to do my work at night and improve my singing and dancing by day; but nothing is accomplished without hard work, is it? And I am glad I went through the grind because it has brought me a certain amount of reward."

One had only to look at Miss Lessing to know she is not easily daunted; those merry eyes and dimpled cheeks do not detract from the firmness of the mouth and the expression of determination round the laughing lips. There was something particularly dainty about the "principal girl" at Drury Lane, and a sense of refinement and grace one does not always associate with pantomime.

"Why, yes," she afterwards added, "I played all over the States, and after nine years was engaged by Mr. Arthur Collins to return to London and appear in the pantomime of *The Sleeping Beauty*. Of course, I felt quite at home in London, although I must own I nearly died of fright the first time I played before an English audience. It seemed like beginning the whole thing over again. Londoners are more exacting than their American cousins; but I must confess, when they like a piece, or an artist, they are most lavish in their applause and approbation."

It was cold, and Miss Lessing pulled a warm shawl over her shoulders and poked the fire. It can be cold even in such a comfortable dressing-room, with the luxury of a fire, for the draughts outside, either on the stage or round it, in such a large theatre are incredible to an ordinary mind. Frequenters of the stalls know the chilly blast that blows upon them when the curtain rises, so they may form some slight idea of what it is like behind the scenes on a cold night.

"After the performance I take off my make-up and have my dinner," laughed Miss Lessing. "I don't think I should enjoy my food if all this mess were left on; at all events I find it a relief to cold-cream it off. One gets a little tired of dinners on a tray for weeks at a time when one is not an invalid; but by the time I've eaten mine, and had a little rest, it is the hour to begin again, for the evening performance is at hand."

"At all events, though, you can read and write between whiles," I remarked.

"That is exactly what one cannot do. I no sooner settle down to a book or letters than some one wants me. It is the constant disturbance, the everlasting interruption, that make two performances a day so trying; but I love the life, even if it be hard, and thoroughly enjoy my pantomime season."

"Have you had many strange adventures in your theatrical life, Miss Lessing?"

"None: mine has been a placid existence on the whole, for," she added, laughing, "I have not even lost diamonds or husbands!"

CHAPTER XII

SIR HENRY IRVING AND STAGE LIGHTING

Sir Henry Irving's Position — Miss Geneviève Ward's Dress — Reforma-
tions in Lighting — The most Costly Play ever Produced — Strong
Individuality — Character Parts — Irving earned his Living at Thir-
teen — Actors and Applause — A Pathetic Story — No Shakespeare
Traditions — Imitation is not Acting — Irving's Appearance — His
Generosity — The First Night of *Dante* — First night of *Faust* — Two
Terriss Stories — Sir Charles Wyndham.

HENRY IRVING is a name which ought to be revered for ever in stageland. He
has done more for the drama than any other actor in any other country. He
has tactfully and gracefully made speeches that have commanded respect. He has
ennobled his profession in many ways.

As Sir Squire Bancroft was the pioneer of "small decorations," so Sir Henry
Irving has been the pioneer of "large details." Artistic effect and magnificent stage
pictures have been his cult; but nothing is too insignificant for his notice.

Miss Geneviève Ward told me that in the play of *Becket* a superb costume was
ordered for her. It cost fifty or sixty guineas, but when she tried it on she felt the
result was disappointing. A little unhappy about the matter she descended to the
stage.

"Great Heavens, Miss Ward! what have you got on?" exclaimed the actor
manager.

"My new dress, sire, may it please you well," was the meek reply, accompanied by a mock curtsey.

"You look a cross between a Newhaven fish-wife and a balloon," he laughed;
"that will never do. It is most unbecoming. As we cannot make you thinner to suit
the dress, we must try and make the dress thinner to suit you."

They chaffed and laughed; but finally it was decided alterations would spoil
the costume — which in its way was faultless — so without any hesitation Henry
Irving relegated it to a "small-part lady," and ordered a new dress for Miss Ward.

Perhaps the greatest reform this actor ever effected was in the matter of stage
lighting. No one previously paid any particular attention to this subject, a red glass
or a blue one achieved all that was thought necessary, until he realised the wonderful effects that might be produced by properly thrown lights, and made a study

of the subject.

It was Henry Irving who first started the idea of changing the scenes in darkness, a custom now so general, not only in Britain but abroad. He first employed varied coloured lights, and laid stress on illumination generally. It was he who first plunged the auditorium into darkness to heighten the stage effects.

"Stage lighting and grouping," said Irving on one occasion, "are of more consequence than the scenery. Without descending to minute realism, the nearer one approaches to the truth the better. The most elaborate scenery I ever had was for *Romeo and Juliet*, but as I was not the man to play *Romeo* the scenery could not make it a success. It never does—it only helps the actor. The whole secret of successful stage management is thoroughness and attention to detail."

To Sir Henry Irving is also due the honour of first employing high-class artists to design dresses, eminent musicians to compose music which he lavishly introduced. It is said that his production of *Henry VIII.*, a sumptuous play, cost £16,000 to mount, but all his great costume plays have cost from £3,000 to £10,000 each.

Sir Henry Irving is famous for his speeches. Few persons know he reads every word of them. Carefully thought out—for he wisely never speaks at random—and type-written, his MS. lies open before him, and being quite accustomed to address an audience, he quietly, calmly, deliberately reads it off with dramatic declamation. His voice has been a subject of comment by many. That characteristic intonation so well known upon the stage is never heard in private life, and even in reading a speech is little noticeable.

If there ever was a case of striking individuality on the stage it is surely to be found in Henry Irving. People often ask if it is a good thing for the exponents of the dramatic profession to possess a strong personality. It is often voiced that it is bad for a part to have the prominent characteristics of the actor noticeable, and yet at the same time there is no doubt about it, it is the men and women of marked character who are successful upon the stage. They may possess great capability for "make-up," they may entirely alter their appearance, they may throw themselves into the part they are playing; but tricks of manner, intonations of voice, and peculiarities of gesture appear again and again, and very often it is this particular personality that the public likes best.

In olden days it was the fashion—if we may judge from last century books—to speak clearly and to "rant" when excited; in modern days it is the fashion to speak indistinctly, and play with "reserved force." The drama has its fancies and its fashions like our dresses or our hats.

No man upon the stage has gone through a more severe mill than Sir Henry Irving. Forty-six years ago he was working in the provinces at a trifling salary on which he had to live. Board, lodging, washing, clothes, even some of his stage costumes, had to come out of that guinea a week. The success he has attained has been arrived at—in addition to his genius and ability—by sheer hard work and conscientious attempts to do his best, consequently at the age of sixty-five he was able to fill a vast theatre like Drury Lane when playing in such a trying part as *Dante*.

Sir Henry Irving.

Photo by Window & Grove, Baker Street, W.

The first years of the actor's life were spent at an office desk. He began to earn his own living as a clerk at thirteen; but during that time he memorised and studied various plays. He learnt fencing, and at the age of nineteen, when he first took to the stage, he was well equipped for his new profession.

For ten years he made little headway, however, and first came into notice as a comedian. In his early days every one thought Irving ought to play "character parts."

"What that phrase means," he remarked later, "I never could understand, for I have a prejudice in the belief that every part should be a character. I always wanted to play the higher drama. Even in my boyhood my desire had been in that direction. When at the Vaudeville Theatre, I recited *Eugene Aram*, simply to get an idea as to whether I could impress an audience with a tragic theme. In my youth I was associated in the public mind with all sorts of bad characters, housebreakers, blacklegs, thieves, and assassins."

And this was the man who was to popularise Shakespeare on the modern English stage—the man to show the world that Shakespeare spelt Fame and Success.

That acting is a fatiguing art Irving denies. He once played Hamlet over two hundred nights in succession, and yet the Dane takes more out of him than any of his characters. Hamlet is the one he loves best, however, just as Ellen Terry's favourite part is Portia.

In Percy Fitzgerald's delightful *Life of Henry Irving* we find the following interesting and characteristic little story:

"Perhaps the most remarkable Christmas dinner at which I have ever been present, was one at which we dined upon underclothing. Do you remember Joe Robins—a nice, genial fellow who played small parts in the provinces? Ah, no! that was before your time. Joe Robins was once in the gentleman's furnishing business in London city. I think he had a wholesale trade, and was doing well. However, he belonged to one of the semi-Bohemian clubs; associated a great deal with actors and journalists, and when an amateur performance was organised for some charitable object, he was cast for the clown in a burlesque called *Guy Fawkes*.

"Perhaps he played the part capitally; perhaps his friends were making game of him when they loaded him with praise; perhaps the papers for which his Bohemian associates wrote went rather too far when they asserted that he was the artistic descendant and successor of Grimaldi. At any rate Joe believed all that was said to and written about him, and when some wit discovered that Grimaldi's name was also Joe, the fate of Joe Robins was sealed. He determined to go upon the stage professionally and become a great actor. Fortunately Joe was able to dispose of his stock and goodwill for a few hundreds, which he invested, so as to give him an income sufficient to prevent the wolf from getting inside his door, in case he did not eclipse Garrick, Kean, and Kemble. He also packed up for himself a liberal supply of his wares, and started in his profession with enough shirts, collars, handkerchiefs, and underclothing to equip him for several years.

"The amateur success of poor Joe was never repeated on the regular stage. He did not make an absolute failure; no manager would trust him with big enough parts for him to fail in; but he drifted down to "general utility," and then out of London, and when I met him he was engaged in a very small way, on a very small salary, at a Manchester theatre.

"His income eked out his salary; Joe, however, was a generous, great-hearted fellow, who liked everybody, and whom everybody liked, and when he had money, he was always glad to spend it upon a friend or give it away to somebody more needy than himself. So piece by piece, as necessity demanded, his princely supply of haberdashery diminished, and at last only a few shirts and underclothes remained to him.

"Christmas came in very bitter weather. Joe had a part in the Christmas pantomime. He dressed with other poor actors, and he saw how thinly some of them were clad when they stripped before him to put on their stage costumes. For one poor fellow in especial his heart ached. In the depth of a very cold winter he was shivering in a suit of very light summer underclothing, and whenever Joe looked at him, the warm flannel under-garments snugly packed away in an extra trunk weighed heavily on his mind. Joe thought the matter over, and determined to give the actors who dressed with him a Christmas dinner. It was literally a dinner upon underclothing, for most of the shirts and drawers which Joe had cherished so long went to the pawnbrokers, or the slop-shop to provide the money for the meal. The guests assembled promptly, for nobody else is ever so hungry as a hungry actor. The dinner was to be served at Joe's lodgings, and before it was placed on the table, Joe beckoned his friend with the gauze underclothing into a bedroom, and pointing to a chair, silently withdrew. On that chair hung a suit of underwear, which had been Joe's pride. It was of a comfortable scarlet colour; it was thick, warm, and heavy; it fitted the poor actor as if it had been manufactured especially to his measure. He put it on, and as the flaming flannels encased his limbs, he felt his heart glowing within him with gratitude to dear Joe Robins.

"That actor never knew—or, if he knew, could never remember—what he had for dinner on that Christmas afternoon. He revelled in the luxury of warm garments. The roast beef was nothing to him in comparison with the comfort of his under-vest: he appreciated the drawers more than the plum-pudding. Proud, happy, warm, and comfortable, he felt little inclination to eat; but sat quietly, and thanked Providence and Joe Robins with all his heart.

"'You seem to enter into that poor actor's feelings very sympathetically.'

"'I have good reason to do so,' replied Mr. Irving, with his sunshiny smile, '*for I was that poor actor!*'"

Irving, like most theatrical folk, has a weakness for applause. It is not surprising that hand-clapping should have an exhilarating effect, or that the volley of air vibrations should set the actor's blood a-tingling. Applause is the breath in the nostrils of every "mummer." On one occasion the great Kean finding his audience apathetic, stopped in the middle of his lines and said:

"Gentlemen, I can't act if you can't applaud."

There is no doubt about it, a sympathetic audience gets far more out of the actor than a half-hearted apathetic one.

"The true value of art," once said Henry Irving, "as applied to the drama can only be determined by public appreciation. It is in this spirit that I have invariably made it my study to present every piece in such a way that the public can rely on getting as full a return for their outlay as it is possible to give. I have great faith in the justice of public discrimination, just as I regard the pit audience of a London theatre as the most critical part of the house.

"Art must advance with the time, and with the advance of other arts there must necessarily be advance in art as applied to the stage. I believe everything that heightens and assists the imagination in a play is good. One should always give the best one can. I have lived long enough to find how short is life and how long is art," he once pithily remarked.

"Have you been guided by tradition in mounting Shakespearian plays?"

"There is no tradition, nor is there anything written down as to the proper way of acting Shakespeare," the great actor replied, and further added: "Imitation is not acting—there is no true acting where individuality does not exist. Actors should act for themselves. I dislike playing a part I have seen acted by any one else, for fear of losing something of my own reading of the character. We all have our own mannerisms; I never yet saw any human being worth considering without them."

There is no doubt that Irving's personality is strong and his appearance striking. He is a tall man—for I suppose he is about six feet high—thin and well knit, with curiously dark and penetrating eyes which are kindly, and have a merry twinkle when amused. The eyebrows are shaggy and protruding, and, oddly enough, remained black after his hair turned grey. He almost always wears eyeglasses, which somehow suit him as they rest comfortably on his aquiline nose. His features are clear-cut and clean-shaven, and the heavy jaw and slightly underhanging chin give strength to his face, which is always pale; the lips are thin and strangely pallid in colouring. Irving, though nearing seventy, has a wonderfully erect carriage, his shoulders are well thrust back and his chest forward, and somehow his movements always denote a man of strength and character. The very dark hair gradually turned grey and is now almost white; it was fine hair, and has always been worn long and thrown well back behind the ears.

There is something about the man which immediately arrests attention; not only his face and his carriage, but his manner and conversation are different from the ordinary. He is the kind of man that any one meeting for the first time would wish to know more about, the kind of man of whom every one would inquire, "Who is he?" if his face were not so well known in the illustrated papers. He could not pass unnoticed anywhere. But after all it is not this personality entirely that has made his fame, for there are people who dislike it as much as others admire it; but as he himself says, any success he has attained is due to the capacity for taking pains.

That Irving's success has been great no one can deny. His reign at the Lyceum was remarkable in every way. He acted Shakespeare's plays until he made them the fashion. He employed great artists, musicians, and a host of smaller fry to give him of their best. He produced wondrous stage pictures—he engaged a good company, and one and all must own he was the greatest actor-manager of the last quarter of the last century. Not only England but the world at large owes him a debt of gratitude. With him mere money-making has been a secondary consideration, and this, coupled with his unfailing generosity, has always kept him comparatively a poor man. No one in distress has ever appealed to him in vain. He has not only given money, but time and sympathy, to those less fortunate than himself, and Henry Irving's list of charitable deeds is endless. But for this he would never have had to leave the Lyceum, a theatre with which his name was associated for so many years.

When Irving opened Drury Lane at Easter, 1903, with *Dante* he had an ovation such as probably no man has ever received from an audience before. It was a pouring wet night; the rain descended in torrents, but the faithful pittites were there to welcome the popular favourite on his return from America. It so chanced that the audience were entering the Opera House next door at the same moment, and this, combined with the rain, which did not allow people to descend from their carriages before they reached the theatre doors, made the traffic chaotic. I only managed to reach my stall a second before the house was plunged in darkness and the curtain rose.

And here let me say how much more agreeable it is to watch the play from a darkened auditorium such as Irving originally instituted than to sit in the glaring illumination still prevalent abroad. When the lights went down, the doors were closed, and half the carriage folk were shut out for the entire first act, thus missing that wondrous ovation. The great actor looked the very impersonation of Dante, and as he bowed, and bowed, and bowed again he grew more and more nervous, to judge by the tremble of his lips and the twitching of his hands. It was indeed a stirring moment and a proud one for the recipient. As the play proceeded the audience found all his old art was there and the magnificent *mise-en-scène* combined to keep up the traditions of the old Lyceum. That vast audience at Drury Lane rose *en masse* to greet him, and literally thundered their applause at the end of the play. The programme is on the following page.

APRIL 30th, 1903.

Theatre Royal  Drury Lane,

LIMITED.

Managing Director	ARTHUR COLLINS.
Business Manager	SIDNEY SMITH.

HENRY IRVING'S SEASON.

Every Evening, at 8.15.

Matinée Every Saturday, at 2.30.

❧ D A N T E ❧

BY

MM. SARDOU & MOREAU.

Rendered into English by LAURENCE IRVING.

Persons in the Play:

Dante		Henry Irving
Cardinal Colonna	*Papal Legate, Resident at Avignon.*	Mr. William Mollison
Nello della Pietra	*(Husband to Pia)*	Mr. Norman McKinnel
Bernardino	*Brother to Francesca da Rimini, betrothed to Gemma*	Mr. Gerald Lawrence
Giotto		Mr. H. B. Stanford
Casella	*Friends to Dante*	Mr. James Hearn
Forese		Mr. Vincent Sternroyd
Bellacqua		Mr. G. Englethorpe
Malatesta	*(Husband to Francesca)*	Mr. Jerold Robertshaw
Corso	*(Nephew to Cardinal Colonna)*	Mr. Charles Dodsworth
Ostasio	*(A Familiar of the Inquisition)*	Mr. Frank Tyars
Ruggieri	*(Archbishop of Pisa)*	Mr. William Lugg
The Grand Inquisitor		Mr. William Farren, Junr.
Paolo	*(Brother to Malatesta)*	Mr. L. Race Dunrobin
Ugolino		Mr. Mark Paton
Lippo	*Swashbucklers*	Mr. John Archer
Conrad		Mr. W. L. Ablett
Enzio	*(Brother to Helen of Swabia)*	Mr. F. D. Daviss
Fadrico		Mr. H. Porter
Merchant		Mr. R. P. Tabb
Merchant		Mr. H. Gaston
Townsman		Mr. T. Reynold
Townsman		Mr. A. Fisher
A Servant		M. J. Ireland
Pia dei Tolomei	*(Wife to Nello della Pietra)*	Miss Lena Ashwell
Gemma	*(Her Daughter)*	
The Abbess of the Convent of Saint Claire		Miss Wallis
Francesca da Rimini		Miss Lilian Eldée

Helen of Swabia	Daughter-in-law to Ugolino	Miss LAURA BURT
Sandra	(Servant to Pia)	Miss ADA MELLON
Picarda		Miss E. BURNAND
Tessa		Miss HILDA AUSTIN
Marozia	Florentine	Miss MAB PAUL
Cilia	Ladies	Miss ADA POTTER
Lucrezia		Miss E. LOCKETT
Julia		Miss MARY FOSTER
Fidelia		Miss DOROTHY ROWE
Maria		Miss MAY HOLLAND
Nun		Miss EMMELINE CARDER
Nun		Miss E. F. DAVIS
Custodian of the Convent of Saint Claire		Miss GRACE HAMPTON
A Townswoman		Miss MABEL REES

Nobles, Guests of the Legate, Pages, Jesters, Nuns, Townsfolk, Artisans, Street Urchins, Catalans, Barbantines, Servants, etc.

Spirits:

The Spirit of Beatrice		Miss NORA LANCASTER
Virgil		Mr. WALTER REYNOLDS
Cain		Mr. F. MURRAY
Charon		Mr. LESLIE PALMER
Cardinal Boc-casini		Mr. F. FAYDENE
Cardinal Orsini		Mr. W. J. YELDHAM
Jacques Molay	(Commander of the Templars)	Mr. J. MIDDLETON

Spirits in the Inferno.

Sir Henry Irving certainly has great magnetic gifts which attract and compel the sympathy of his audience. He always looks picturesque, he avoids stage conventionalities, and acts his part according to his own scholarly instincts. Passion with him is subservient to intellect.

One American critic in summing him up said:

"I do not consider Irving a great actor; but he is the greatest dramatic artist I ever saw."

The version of *Faust* by the late W. G. Wills which modern playgoers know so well was one of the most elaborate and successful productions of the Lyceum days, and amongst the beautiful scenic effects some exquisite visions which appeared in the Prologue at the summons of Mephistopheles will always be remembered. On the first night of the production I am told—for I don't remember the occasion my-self—owing to a temporary break down in the lime-lights, these visions declined to put in an appearance at the bidding of the Fiend. The great actor waved his arm and stamped his foot with no result. Again and again he tried to rouse them from their lethargy, but all to no avail. The visions came not. As soon as the curtain fell Irving strode angrily to the wing, even his stride foreboded ill to all concerned, and the officials trembled at the outburst of righteous wrath which they expected would break forth. The first exclamations of the irate manager had hardly left his lips before they were interrupted by a diminutive "call boy," who rushed forward with uplifted hand, and exclaimed in a high treble key to the great actor-manager fresh from his newest triumph:

"Bear it, bear it bravely! *I* will explain all to-morrow!"

The situation was so ridiculous that there was a general peal of laughter, in which Irving was irresistibly compelled to join.

The last part played at the Lyceum by the veteran actor Tom Mead was that of the old witch who vainly strove to gain the summit of the Brocken, and was always pushed downwards when just reaching the goal. In despair the wretched hag exclaims, "I've been a toiler for ten thousand years, but never, never reached the top." On the first night of *Faust*, the worthy old man was chaffed unmercifully at supper by some of his histrionic friends who insisted that the words he used were, "I've been *an actor* for ten thousand years, but never, never reached the top."

Those who saw the wonderful production of *The Corsican Brothers* at the Lyce-um will remember the exciting duel in the snow by moonlight, between Irving and Terriss. At the last dress rehearsal, which at the Lyceum was almost as important a function as a first night, Terriss noticed that as the combatants moved hither and thither during the fight he seemed to be usually in shadow, while the face of the great actor-manager was brilliantly illuminated. Looking up into the flies, he thus addressed the lime-light man:

"On me also shine forth, thou beauteous moon—there should be no partiality in thy glorious beams."

A friend relates another curious little incident which occurred during the run of *Ravenswood* at the Lyceum. In the last act there was another duel between Wil-liam Terriss and Henry Irving. For the play Terriss wore a heavy moustache which was cleverly contrived in two pieces. Somehow, in the midst of the scuffle, one side of the moustache got caught and came off. This was an awkward predica-ment at a tragic moment, but Terriss had the presence of mind to swerve round before the audience had time to realise the absurdity, and finished the scene with his hair-covered lips on show. When they arrived in the wings Irving was greatly perturbed.

"What on earth do you mean spoiling the act by jumping round like that?" he demanded. "You put me out horribly: it altered the whole scene."

Terriss was convulsed with laughter and could hardly answer; and it was only when Irving had spent his indignation that he discovered his friend was minus half his moustache. This shows how intensely interested actors become in their parts, when one can go through a long scene and never notice his colleague had lost so important an adjunct.

Sir Charles Wyndham is one of the most popular actor-managers upon the stage. He is a flourishing evergreen. Though born in 1841 he never seems to grow any older, and is just as full of dry humour, just as able to deliver a dramatic sermon, just as quick and smart as ever he was.

He began at the very beginning, did Sir Charles, and he is ending at the very end. Though originally intended for the medical profession, he commenced his career as a stock actor in a provincial company, is now a knight, and manager and promoter of several theatres. What more could theatrical heart desire? And he has the distinction of having acted in Berlin in the German tongue.

Wyndham gives an amusing description, it is said, of one of his first appearances on the American stage, when he had determined to transfer his affections from Galen to Thespis. He was naturally extremely nervous, and on his first entrance should have exclaimed:

"I am drunk with ecstasy and success."

With emphasis he said the first three words of the sentence, and then, owing to uncontrollable stage fright, his memory forsook him. After a painful pause he again exclaimed:

"I am drunk." Even then, however, he could not recall the context. He looked hurriedly around, panic seemed to overpower him as he once more repeated:

"I am drunk—"; and, amid a burst of merriment from the audience, he rushed from the stage.

CHAPTER XIII
WHY A NOVELIST BECOMES A DRAMATIST

Novels and Plays—*Little Lord Fauntleroy* and his Origin—Mr. Hall
Caine—Preference for Books to Plays—John Oliver Hobbes—J.
M. Barrie's Diffidence—Anthony Hope—A London Bachelor—A
Pretty Wedding—A Tidy Author—A First Night—Dramatic Crit-
ics—How Notices are Written—The Critics Criticised—Distribu-
tion of Paper—"Stalls Full"—Black Monday—Do Royalty pay for
their Seats?—Wild Pursuit of the Owner of the Royal Box—The
Queen at the Opera.

IT is a surprise to the public that so many novelists are becoming dramatists.

The reason is simple enough: it is the natural evolution of romance. In the
good old days of three-volume novels, works of fiction brought considerable grist
to the mill of both author and publisher; after all it only cost a fraction more to
print and bind a three-volume work which sold at thirty-one shillings and sixpence than it does to-day to produce a book of almost as many words at six shillings.

Then again, half, even a quarter of, a century ago there were not anything like
so many novelists, and those who wrote had naturally less competition; but all this
is changed.

Novels pour forth on every side to-day, and money does not always pour in,
in proportion. One of the first novelists to make a large sum by a play was Mrs.
Hodgson Burnett. She wrote *Little Lord Fauntleroy* about 1885, it proved successful,
and the book contained the element of an actable play. She dramatised the story,
and she has probably made as many thousands of pounds by the play as hundreds
by the book, in spite of its enormous circulation. I believe I am right in saying that
Little Lord Fauntleroy has brought more money to its originator than any other combined novel and play, and the next most lucrative has probably been J. M. Barrie's
Little Minister.

Herein lies a moral lesson. Both are simple as books and plays, and both owe
their success to that very simplicity and charm. They contain no problem, no sex
question, nothing but a little story of human life and interest, and they have succeeded in English-speaking lands, and had almost a wider influence than the more
elaborate physiological work and ideas of Ibsen, Maeterlinck, Sudermann, or Pinero.

For twenty years *Little Lord Fauntleroy* has stirred all hearts, both on the stage and off, in England and America, adored by children and loved by grown-ups.

Being anxious to know how the idea of the play came about, I wrote to Mrs. Burnett, and below is her reply in a most characteristically modest letter:

"NEW YORK,
"November 26th, 1902.

"DEAR MRS. ALEC-TWEEDIE,

"I hope it is as agreeable as it sounds to be 'a-roaming in Spain.' It gives one dreams of finding one's lost castles there. Concerning the play of *Fauntleroy*; after the publication of the book it struck me one day that if a real child could be found who could play *naturally* and ingenuously the leading part, a very unique little drama might be made of the story. I have since found that almost any child can play Fauntleroy, the reason being, I suppose, that only child emotions are concerned in the representation of the character. At that time, however, I did not realise what small persons could do, and by way of proving to myself that it could—or could not—be done with sufficient simplicity and convincingness, I asked my own little boy to pretend for me that he was Fauntleroy making his speech of thanks to the tenants on his birthday. The little boy in question was the one whose ingenuous characteristics had suggested to me the writing of the story, so I thought if it could be done he could do it. He had, of course, not been allowed to suspect that he himself had any personal connection with the character of Cedric. He was greatly interested in saying the speech for me, and he did it with such delightful warm-hearted naturalness that he removed my doubts as to whether a child-actor could say the lines without any air of sophistication—which was of course the point.

Shortly afterwards we went to Italy, and in Florence I began the dramatisation. I had, I think, about completed the first act when I received news from England that a Mr. Seebohm had made a dramatisation and was producing it. I travelled to London at once and consulted my lawyer, Mr. Guadella, who began a suit for me. I felt very strongly on the subject, not only because I was unfairly treated, but because it had been the custom to treat all writers in like manner, and it seemed a good idea to endeavour to find a defence. I was frightened because I could not have afforded to lose and pay costs—but I felt rather fierce, and made up my mind to face the risk. Fortunately Mr. Guadella won the case for me. Mr. Seebohm's version was withdrawn and mine produced with success both in England and America—and, in fact, in various other countries. I never know dates, but I *think* it was produced in London in '88. It has been played ever since, and is played for short engagements on both sides of the Atlantic every year. I have not the least idea how many times it has been given. It is a queer little dear, that story—'plays may come and books may go, but little Fauntleroy stays on for ever.' I am glad I wrote it—I always loved it. I should have loved it if it had not brought me a penny. I am afraid I am not very satisfactory as a recorder of detail of a business nature. I never remember dates or figures. If we were talking together I should doubtless begin to recall incidents. It is the stimulating meanderings of conversation which stir the pools of memory."

Mrs. Hodgson Burnett may indeed be proud of her success, although she writes of it in such a simple, unaffected manner. 'Twas well for her she faced the lawsuit, for ruin scowled on one side while fortune smiled on the other.

No novelist's works have sold more freely than those of Hall Caine and Miss Marie Corelli. Both are highly dramatic in style, but Miss Corelli has not taken to play-writing, preferring the novel as a means of expression.

Hall Caine, on the other hand, has been tempted by the allurements of the stage. When I asked him why he took up literature as a profession, he replied:

"I write a novel because I love the motive, or the story, or the characters, or the scene, or all four, and I dramatise it because I like to see my subject on the stage. If more material considerations sometimes influence me, more spiritual ones are, I trust, not always absent. I don't think the time occupied in writing a book or a play has ever entered into my calculations, nor do I quite know which gives me most trouble."

Continuing the subject, I ventured to ask him whether he thought drama or fiction the higher art.

"I like both the narrative and the dramatic forms of art, but perhaps I think the art of fiction is a higher and better art than the art of a drama, inasmuch as it is more natural, more free, and more various, and yet capable of equal unity. On the other hand, I think the art of the drama is in some respects more difficult, because it is more artificial and more limited, and always hampered by material conditions which concern the stage, the scenery, the actors, and even the audience. I think," he continued, "the novel and the drama have their separate joys for the novelist and dramatist, and also their separate pains and penalties.

"On the whole, I find it difficult to compare things so different, and all I can say for myself is that, notwithstanding my great love of the theatre, I find it so trying in various ways—owing, perhaps, to my limitations—that I do not grudge any one the success he achieves as a dramatist, and I deeply sympathise with the man who fails in that character."

How true that is! By far the most lenient critics are the workers. It is the man who never wrote a book who criticises most severely, the man who never painted a picture who is the hardest to please.

Speaking about the dramatic element of the modern novel, Mr. Caine continued:

"But then the novel, since the days of Scott, has so encroached upon the domain of the drama, and become so dramatic in form that the author who has 'the sense of the theatre' may express himself fairly well without tempting his fate in that most fascinating but often most fatal little world."

Such was Mr. Caine's opinion on the novelist as dramatist.

Hall Caine's personality is too well known to need describing; but his handwriting is a marvel. He gets more into a page than any one I know, unless it be Whistler, Sydney Lee, or Zangwill. Mr. Caine's calligraphy at a little distance looks like Chinese, it is beautifully neat and tidy—but most difficult to read. Like Frankfort Moore, Richard Le Gallienne, and a host of others, he scribbles with a small pad in his hand, or on his knee. Some people prefer writing in queer positions, cramped for room—others, on the contrary, require huge tables and vast space.

"John Oliver Hobbes" is the uneuphonious pseudonym chosen by Pearl Teresa Craigie, another of our novel-dramatists. She has hardly been as successful with her plays as with her brilliant books, and therefore it seems unlikely that she will discard the latter for the former. The world has smiled on Mrs. Craigie, for she was born of rich parents. Although an American she lives in London (Lancaster Gate), and has a charming house in the Isle of Wight. She has only one son, so is more or less independent, can travel about and do as she likes, therefore her thoughtful work and industry are all the more praiseworthy. Ability will out.

Mrs. Craigie is an extremely good-looking woman. She is *petite*, with chestnut hair and eyes; is always dressed in the latest gowns from Paris; has a charming voice; is musical and devoted to chess.

J. M. Barrie, one of the most successful of our novel dramatists, is most reticent about his work. He is a shy, retiring little man with a big brain and a charitable heart; but he dislikes publicity in every form. He seems almost ashamed to own that he writes, and he cannot bear his plays to be discussed—so when he says, "Please excuse me. I have such a distaste for saying or writing anything about my books or plays for publication; if it were not so I should do as you suggest with pleasure," one's hand is tied, and Mr. Barrie's valuable opinion on the novel and the drama is lost.

It was a difficult problem to decide. Naturally the public expect much mention of J. M. Barrie among the playwrights of the day, for had he not four pieces running at London theatres at the same moment? But to make mention means to offend Mr. Barrie and lose a friend.

This famous author creates and writes, but no one must write about him. Whether his simple childhood, passed in a quaint little Scotch village, is the source of this reticence, or whether it is caused by the oppression of the fortune he has accumulated by his plays, no one discourses upon Mr. Barrie except at the risk of earning his grave displeasure. He is probably the most fantastic writer of the day, and most of the accounts of him have been as fantastic as his work. Thus the curtain cannot be lifted, while he smokes and dreams delicately pitiless sentiment behind the scenes so far as this volume is concerned.

"Anthony Hope" is another dramatic novelist. He began his career as a barrister, tried for Parliamentary honours, and failed; took to writing novels and succeeded, and now seems likely to end his days in the forefront of British dramatists.

He was educated at Marlborough, became a scholar of Balliol College, Oxford, where he gained first-class Mods. and first-class Lit. Hum., so he has gone through the educational mill with distinction, and is now inclined to turn aside from novels of pure romance to more psychological studies. This is particularly noticeable in *Quisanté* and *Tristram of Blent*.

The author of *The Prisoner of Zenda* is one of the best-known men in London society. He loves our great city. Mr. Hope is most sociable by nature; not only does he dine out incessantly, but as a bachelor was one of those delightful men who took the trouble to entertain his lady friends. Charming little dinners and luncheons were given by this man of letters, and as he had chambers near one of our largest hotels, he generally took the guests over to his flat after the meal for coffee and cigars. Many can vouch what pleasant evenings those were; the geniality of the host, the frequent beauty of his guests, and the generally brilliant conversation made those bachelor entertainments things to be remembered. His charming sister-in-law often played the *rôle* of hostess for him; she is a Norwegian by birth, and an intimate friend of the Scandinavian writer Björnstjerne-Björnson, whose personality impressed me more than that of any other author I ever met.

The bachelor life has come to an end.

Nearly twenty years ago Anthony Hope began to write novels with red-haired heroines—*The Prisoner of Zenda* is perhaps the best-known of the series. No one could doubt that he admired warm-coloured hair, for auburns and reds appeared in all his books. One fine day an auburn-haired goddess crossed his path. She was young and beautiful, and just the living girl he had described so often in fiction. Anthony Hope, the well-known bachelor of London, was conquered by the American maid. A very short engagement was followed by a beautiful wedding in the summer of 1903, at that quaint old city church, St. Bride's, where his father has been Rector so long. It was a lovely hot day as we drove along the Embankment, through a labyrinth of printing offices and early newspaper carts, to the door of the church. All the bustle and heat of the city outside was forgotten in the cool shade of the handsome old building, decorated for the occasion with stately palms. Never was there a prettier wedding or a more lovely bride, and all the most beautiful women in London seemed to be present.

The bridegroom, who was wearing a red rosebud which blossomed somewhat alarmingly during the ceremony, looked very proud and happy as he led the realisation of twenty years' romance down the aisle.

"Anthony Hope" is not his real name, and yet it is, which may appear paradoxical. He was born a Hawkins, being the second son of the Rev. E. C. Hawkins, and nephew of Mr. Justice Hawkins, now known as Baron Brampton. The child was christened Anthony Hope, and when he took to literature to fill in the gaps in his legal income, he apparently thought it better for the struggling barrister not to be identified with the budding journalist, and consequently dropped the latter part of his name. Thus it was he won his spurs as Anthony Hope, and many people know him by no other title, although he always signs himself Hawkins, and calls himself by that nomenclature in private life. Rather amusing incidents have been the result. People when first introduced seldom realise the connection, and discuss "Lady Ursula," or other books, very frankly with their new acquaintance. Their consequent embarrassment or amusement may be better imagined than described! *Aliases* often lead to awkward moments.

Mr. Anthony Hope.

From a painting by Hugh de T. Glazebrook.

Literary men are not, as a rule, famed for "speechifying," but Mr. Hawkins is an exception. He went to America a few years ago an indifferent orator, and returned a good one. This was the result of a lecturing tour—one of those expeditions of many thousand miles of travel and daily discourse in different towns. Literary men are not generally more orderly at their writing-tables than they are good at delivering a speech, but here again Anthony Hope is an exception. His desk is so neat and precise it reminds one irresistibly of a punctilious old maid (I trust he will forgive the simile?), so methodical are his arrangements. He writes everything with his own hand, and replies to letters almost by return of post, although he is a busy man, for he not only writes for four or five hours a day, but attends endless charity meetings, and takes an energetic part among other things in the working of the Society of Authors, of which he is chairman. He does nothing by halves; everything he undertakes he is sure to see through, being most conscientious in all his work. In many ways Anthony Hope often reminds one of the late Sir Walter Besant, both alike ever ready to help a colleague in distress, ever willing to aid by council or advice those in need, and untiring so far as literary work for themselves, or helping others, is concerned.

Mr. Hawkins is generally calm and collected, but I remember an occasion when he was quite the reverse. It was the first performance of one of his plays, and he stood behind me in a box, well screened from public gaze by the curtain. First he rested on one foot, then on the other, always to the accompaniment of rattling coins. Oh, how he turned those pennies over and over in his pockets, until at last I entreated to be allowed to "hold the bank" until the fall of the curtain.

First nights affect playwrights differently, but although they generally disown it, they seem to suffer tortures, poor creatures.

For an important production there are as many as two or three thousand applications for seats on a "first night," but to a great extent each theatre has its own audience. The critics are of course the most important element. As matters stand they know nothing of what they are going to see, they have not studied or even read the play beforehand, and yet are expected to sum up the whole drama and criticise the acting an hour or two later. The idea is preposterous. If serious dramas are to be considered seriously, time must be given for the purpose, and the premiers must begin a couple of hours earlier, or a dress rehearsal for the critics arranged the night before, just as a "press view" is organised at a picture gallery. As it is, all the critics go in the first night.

That is why the bulk of those in the stalls are men. Some take notes throughout the acts, others jot down pungent lines during the dialogue; but all are working at high pressure, and however clear the slate of their mind may be on entering the theatre, it is well covered with impressions when they leave. From that jumble of ideas they have to unravel the play, criticise the dramatist's work, and make a study of the suitability of the actors to their parts. This unreflecting impression must be quickly put together, for a critic has no time for leisurely philosophic judgments.

The critics, or, rather, "the representatives of the papers," are given their seats;

but the rest of the house pays. Only people of eminence, or personal friends of the management, are permitted the honour of a seat. Their names are on the "first-night list," and if they apply they receive, the outside public rarely getting a chance.

The entrance to a theatre on a first night is an interesting scene. Many of the best-known men and women of London are chatting to friends in the hall; but they never forget their manners, and are always in their places in good time. Between the acts those who are near the end of a row get up and move about; in any case the critics leave their seats, and many of them begin their "copy" during the *entr'acte*. Other men not professionally engaged wander round the boxes and talk to their friends, and a general air of happy expectation pervades the auditorium.

"Stuffed with obesity or anæmia," exclaimed a well-known dramatist when describing the dramatic critics. However that may be the dramatic critic is an important person, and his post no sinecure. It is all very well when first night representations are given on Saturday, because then only the handful of Sunday paper writers have to scramble through their work—but when Wednesday or Thursday is chosen, as sometimes happens, dozens of poor unfortunate men and women have to work far into the night over their column—they have no time to consider the comedy or tragedy from any standpoint beyond the first impression. No doubt a play should make an impression at once, and that is why the drama cannot be criticised in the same way as books. The playwright must make an immediate effect, or he will not make one at all; while the poet or novelist can be contemplated with serenity and commented on at leisure.

There are so many problem plays nowadays, however, that it is often difficult for the critic to make his decision between the close of the theatre at midnight and his arrival at the nearest telegraph office (if he be on a provincial paper), or at the London newspaper office, a quarter of an hour later, when that impression has to be reduced to paper and ink. Only those who have written at this nervous pressure know its terrors. To have a "devil" (the printer's boy) standing at one's elbow waiting for "copy" is horrible—the ink is not dry on the paper as sheet after sheet goes off to the compositor waiting its arrival. By the time the writer reaches his last sentences the first pages are all in type waiting his corrections. At 2 a.m. the notice must be out of his hands for good or ill, because the final "make-up" of the paper necessitates his "copy" filling the exact space allotted to him by the editor, and two hours later that selfsame newspaper, printed and machined, is on its way to the provinces by the "newspaper trains," and on sale in Liverpool, Birmingham, or Sheffield, a few hours only after the latest theatrical criticism has been added to its columns.

The stage is necessarily intimately connected with the press, and a free hand is imperative if the well-reasoned essay, and not merely a reporter's account, is to be of value.

Wise critics refuse to know personally the objects of their criticism, and so avoid many troubles, for many actors are hyper-sensitive by nature. The press is naturally a great factor, but it cannot make or mar a play any more than it can make or mar a book; it can fan the flame, but it cannot make the blaze.

At the O.P. Club Alfred Robbins recently delivered an address on "Dramatic Critics: *Are they any use?*" He pertinently remarked:

"A play is like a cigar—if it is bad no amount of puffing will make it draw; but if good then every one wants a box." He held that the great danger was that the critic should lack pluck to protest against a revolting play on a well-advertised stage, and follow the lead of the applause of programme-sellers in a fashionable house; while making up for it by hunting for faults with a microscope in the case of a young author or manager. The critic should tell not so much how the play affected him as how it affected the audience. Critics were always useful when they were interesting, but not when they tried to instruct.

E. F. Spence, as a critic himself, pointed out that some critics had no words that were not red and yellow, while others wrote entirely in grey. When one man said a play was "not half bad," and another described it as an "unparalleled master-piece," they meant often the same thing. And the readers of each, accustomed to their tone and style, knew what to expect from their words.

Mrs. Kendal thought "criticism would be better after three weeks, when the actor had learnt to know his points." All agreed that the critics of to-day are scrupulously conscientious.

G. Bernard Shaw wrote: "A dramatic criticism is a work of literary art, useful only to the people who enjoy reading dramatic criticisms, and generally more or less hurtful to everybody else concerned."

Clement Shorter's opinion was: "I do not in the least believe in the utility of dramatic critics. The whole sincerity of the game has been spoilt. The hand of the dramatic critic is stayed because the dramatist and the important actor have a wide influence with the proprietors of newspapers."

An anonymous manager wrote: "The few independent critics are of great use, but the critic who turns his attention to play-writing should not be allowed to criticise, for he is never fair to any author's work except his own. It has paid managers to accept plays from critics even if they don't produce them."

Apart from criticism the theatre is in daily touch with the papers, for one of the greatest expenses in connection with a theatre is the "Press Bill." From four to six thousand pounds a year is paid regularly for newspaper advertising, just for those advertisements that appear "under the clock," and in those columns announcing plays, players, and hours.

The distribution of "paper" is a curious custom, some managers prefer to fill their houses by such means, others disdain the practice, especially the Kendals, who are as adverse to "free passes" as they are to dress rehearsals, and who always insist on paying for their own tickets to see their friends act. An empty house is nevertheless dispiriting—dispiriting to the audience and dispiriting to the performers—so a little paper judiciously used may often bolster up a play in momentary danger of collapse.

"Stalls full." "Dress Circle full." "House full." Such notices are often put outside the playhouse during a performance, and in London they generally mean what they say. In the provinces, however, a gentleman arrived at an hotel, and after dinner went off to the theatre as he had no club. He saw the placards, but boldly marched up to the box office in the hope that perchance he might obtain an odd seat somewhere.

"A stall, please."

"Yes, sir, which row?" When he got inside he found the place half empty, in spite of the legend before the doors.

A well-known singer wired for a box in London one night—it being an understood thing that professional people may have seats free if they are not already sold. She prepaid the answer to the telegram as usual. It ran:

"So sorry, no boxes left to-night."

The next day she met a friend at luncheon who had been to that particular theatre the night before. He remarked:

"It was a most depressing performance: the house was half empty, and the actors dull in consequence."

Then the singer told her story, and both had a good laugh over the telegram.

There are certain bad weeks which appear with strict regularity in the theatrical world. Bank-holiday time means empty houses in the West End. Just before Easter or Christmas are always "off" nights. Royal mourning reduces the takings, and one night's London fog half empties the house. Lent does not make anything like so great a difference as formerly; indeed, in some theatres its advent is hardly noticed at all. Saturday always yields the biggest house. Whether this is because Sunday being a day of rest people need not get up so early, or because Saturday is pay day, or because it is either a half or whole holiday, no one knows; but it always produces the largest takings of the week, just as Monday is invariably the fattest booking-day. This may possibly be due to Sunday callers discussing the best performances, and recommending their friends to go to this or that piece. The good booking of Monday is more often than not followed by a bad house on Monday night, which is the "off" day of the week. A play will run successfully for weeks, suddenly Black Monday arrives, and at once down, down, down goes the sale, until the play is taken off; no one can tell why it declines any more than they can predict the success or failure of a play until after its first two or three performances.

It seems to be generally imagined that Royalty do not pay for their seats; but this is a mistake. One fine day a message comes from one of the ticket agents to the theatres to say that the King and Queen, or Prince and Princess of Wales, will go to that theatre on a certain night. Generally a couple of days' notice is given. Consternation often ensues, for it sometimes happens the Royal box has been sold. The purchaser has to be called upon to explain that by Royal command his box is required for the night in question, and will he graciously take it some other evening instead? or he is offered other seats. People are generally charming about the matter and ready to meet the manager at once—but sometimes there are difficulties. Wild pursuit of the owner of the box occasionally occurs; indeed, he sometimes has not been traceable at all, and has even arrived at the theatre, only to be told the situation.

The box is duly paid for by the library; Royalty never accept their seats, and are most punctilious about paying for them.

At the back of the Royal box there is generally a retiring-room, where the gentlemen smoke, and sometimes coffee is served. The King, who is so noted for his cordiality, usually sends for the leading actor and actress during an *entr'acte*, and chats with them for a few minutes in the ante-room; but the Queen rarely leaves her seat. After the death of Queen Victoria it was a long time, a year in fact, before the King went to the theatre at all. After that he visited most of the chief houses in quick succession, but he did not send for the players for at least six months, not, in fact, till the Royal mourning was at an end. His Majesty is probably the warmest and most frequent supporter of the drama in Britain, as the Queen is of the opera.

In olden days Royal visits were treated with much ceremony. Cyril Maude in his excellent book on the Haymarket Theatre tells how old Buckstone was a great favourite with Queen Victoria. The Royal entrance in those days was through the door of "Bucky's" house which adjoined the back of the theatre in Suffolk Street. At the street door the manager waited whenever the Royal box had been commanded. In either hand he carried a massive silver candlestick, and, walking backwards, escorted the Royal party with monstrous pomp to their seats. As soon as he had shown them to their box, however, the amiable comedian had to hurry off to take his place upon the stage.

Nothing of that kind is done nowadays, although the manager generally goes to meet them; but if the manager be the chief actor too, he sends his stage manager just to see that everything is in order—Royal folk like to come and go as unostentatiously as possible.

Many theatres have a private door for Royalty to enter by. As a rule they are punctual, and if not the curtain gives them a few minutes' grace before rising. If they are not in their seats within ten minutes, the play begins, and they just slip quietly into their places.

At the Opera on gala nights it is different—the play waits. When they enter, the band strikes up "God Save the King," and every one stands up. It is a very interesting sight to see the huge mass of humanity at Covent Garden rise together, and see them all stand during the first verse in respect to Royalty. The Queen on ordinary occasions occupies the Royal box on the right facing the stage on the grand tier, and three back from the stage itself, so there are tiers of boxes above and one below; the Queen sits in the corner the farthest from the stage; the King often joins her during the performance, otherwise he sits in the omnibus box below with his men friends. So devoted is Her Majesty to music she sometimes spends three evenings a week at the Opera. She often has a book of the score before her, and follows the music with the greatest interest.

On ordinary operatic nights the Queen dresses very quietly; generally her bodice is cut square back and front with elbow-sleeves, and not off the shoulders as it is at Court. More often than not she wears black with a bunch of pink malmaisons—of course the usual heavy collar composed of many rows of pearls is worn, and generally some hanging chains of pearls. No tiara, but diamond wings or hair combs of that description. In fact, at the Opera our Queen is one of the least conspicuously dressed among the many duchesses and millionairesses who don tiaras and gorgeous gowns. No Opera-house in the world contains so many beautiful women and jewels as may nightly be seen in London.

In front is a number above each box, and at the back of the box is the duplicate number with the name of the person to whom it belongs. They are hired for a season, and cost seven and a half to eight guineas a night on the grand tier. These boxes hold four people, and are usually let for ten or twelve weeks: generally for two nights a weeks to each set of people. Thus the total cost of one of the best boxes for the season is, roughly speaking, from one hundred and fifty, to one hundred and eighty guineas for two nights a week.

At the theatre Queen Alexandra dresses even more simply than at the opera. In winter her gown is often filled in with lace to the neck. She is always a quiet, but a perfect dresser. Never in the fashion, yet always of the fashion, she avoids all exaggerations, moderates her skirts and her sleeves, and yet has just enough of the *dernier cri* about them to make them up to date. She probably never wore a big picture hat in her life, and prefers a small bonnet with strings, to a toque.

Royalty thoroughly enjoy themselves at the play. They laugh and chat between the acts, and no one applauds more enthusiastically than King Edward VII. and his beautiful Queen. They use their opera-glasses freely, nod to their friends, and thoroughly enter into the spirit of the evening's entertainment.

CHAPTER XIV

SCENE-PAINTING AND CHOOSING A PLAY

Novelist—Dramatist—Scene-painter—An Amateur Scenic Artist—
Weedon Grossmith to the Rescue—Mrs. Tree's Children—Mr.
Grossmith's Start on the Stage—A Romantic Marriage—How a
Scene is built up—English and American Theatres Compared—
Choosing a Play—Theatrical Syndicate—Three Hundred and Fif-
teen Plays at the Haymarket.

A NOVELIST describes the surroundings of his story. He paints in words, houses, gardens, dresses, anything and everything to heighten the picture and
show up his characters in a suitable frame.

The dramatist cannot do this verbally; but he does it in fact. He definitely
decides the style of scene necessary for each act, and draws out elaborate plans to
achieve that end. It is the author who interviews the scene-painter, talks matters
over with the costume-artist, the dressmaker, and the upholsterer. It is the author
who generally chooses the cretonnes and the wall-papers—that is to say, the more
important authors invariably do. Mr. Pinero, Mr. W. S. Gilbert, and Captain Robert
Marshall design their own scenes to the minutest detail, but then all three of them
are capable artists and draughtsmen themselves.

Scene-painting seems easy until one knows something about its difficulties. To
speak of a small personal experience—when we got up those theatricals in Harley
Street, mentioned in a previous chapter, my father told me I must paint the scenery, to which I gaily agreed. Having an oil painting on exhibition at the Women
Artists', I felt I could paint scenery without any difficulty.

First of all I bought yards and yards of thick canvas, a sort of sacking. It refused to be joined together by machine, and broke endless needles when the seams
were sewn by hand. It appeared to me at the time as if oakum-picking could not
blister fingers more severely. After all my trouble, when finished and stretched
along a wall in the store-room in the basement, with the sky part doubled over the
ceiling (as the little room was not high enough to manage it otherwise), the surface
was so rough that paint refused to lie upon it.

I had purchased endless packets of blue and chrome, vermilion and sienna,
umber and sap-green; but somehow the result was awful, and the only promising thing was the design in black chalk made from a sketch taken on Hampstead
Heath. Sticks of charcoal broke and refused to draw; but common black chalk at

last succeeded. I struggled bravely, but the paint resolutely refused to adhere to the canvas, and stuck instead to every part of my person.

Mr. Weedon Grossmith.

Photo by Hall, New York.

At last some wiseacre suggested whitewashing the canvas, and, after sundry boilings of smelly size, the coachman and I made pails of whitewash and proceeded to get a groundwork. Alas! the brushes when full of the mixture proved too heavy for me to lift, and the unfortunate coachman had to do most of that monotonous field of white.

So far so good. Now came "the part," as the gallant jehu was pleased to call it.

It took a long time to get into the way of painting it at all. The window had to be shut, the solitary gas-jet lighted, endless lamps unearthed to give more illumination while I struggled with smelling pots.

Oh, the mess! The floor was bespattered, and the paint being mixed with size, those spots remain as indelible as Rizzio's blood at Holyrood. Then the paint-smeared sky—my sky—left marks on the ceiling—my father's ceiling—and my own dress was spoilt. Then up rose Mother in indignation, and promptly produced an old white garment—which shall be nameless, although it was decorated with little frills—and this I donned as a sort of overall. With arms aching from heavy brushes, and feet tired from standing on a ladder, with a nose well daubed with yellow paint, on, on I worked.

In the midst of my labours "Mr. Grossmith" was suddenly announced, and there below me stood Weedon Grossmith convulsed with laughter. At that time he was an artist and had pictures "on the line" at the Royal Academy. His studio was a few doors from us in Harley Street.

"Don't laugh, you horrid man," I exclaimed; "just come and help."

He took a little gentle persuading, but finally gave in, and being provided with another white garment he began to assist, and he and I finally finished that wondrous scene-painting together.

After a long vista of years Mrs. Beerbohm Tree—who, it will be remembered, also acted with us in Harley Street—and Weedon Grossmith—who helped me paint the scenery for our little performance—were playing the two leading parts together at Drury Lane in Cecil Raleigh's *Flood Tide*.

The two little daughters of the Trees, aged six and eight respectively, were taken by their father one afternoon to see their mother play at the Lane. They sat with him in a box, and enjoyed the performance immensely.

"Well, do you like it better than *Richard II.*?" asked Tree.

There was a pause. Each small maiden looked at the other, ere replying:

"It isn't quite the same, but we like it just as much."

When they reached home they were asked by a friend which of the two plays they really liked best.

"Oh, mother's," for naturally the melodrama had appealed to their juvenile minds, "but we did not like to tell father so, because we thought it might hurt his feelings."

The part that delighted them most at Drury Lane was the descent of the rain, that wonderful rain which had caused so much excitement, and which was composed of four tons of rice and spangles thrown from above, and verily gave the effect of a shower of water.

But to return to Weedon Grossmith. Whether he found art didn't pay at the studio in Harley Street, or whether he was asked to paint more ugly old ladies than pretty young ones, I do not know; but he gave up the house, and went off to America for a trip. So he said at the time, but the trip meant that he had accepted an engagement on the stage. He made an instantaneous hit. When he returned to England, sure of his position, as he thought, he found instead that he had a very rough time of it, and it was not until he played with Sir Henry Irving in *Robert Macaire* that he made a London success. Later he "struck oil" in Arthur Law's play, *The New Boy* under his own management.

Round the *The New Boy* circled a romance. Miss May Palfrey, who had been at school with me, was the daughter of an eminent physician who formerly lived in Brook Street. She had gone upon the stage after her father's death, and was engaged to play the girl's part. The "engagement" begun in the theatre ended, as in the case of Forbes Robertson, in matrimony, and the day after *The New Boy* went out, the new girl entered Weedon Grossmith's home as his wife.

Success has followed success, and they now live in a delightful house in Bedford Square, surrounded by quaint old furniture, Adams' mantelpieces, overmantels, and all the artistic things the actor appreciates. A dear little girl adds brightness to the home life of Mr. and Mrs. Weedon Grossmith.

Artist, author, actor, manager, are all terms that may be applied to Weedon Grossmith, but might not scene-painter be added after his invaluable aid in the Harley Street store-room with paints and size?

So much for the amateur side of the business: now for the real.

The first thing a scenic artist does is to make a complete sketch of a scene. This, when approved, he has "built up" as a little model, a miniature theatre, in fact, such as children love to play with. It is usually about three feet square, exactly like a box, and every part is designed to scale with a perfection of detail rarely observed outside an architect's office.

One of the most historic painting-rooms was that of Sir Henry Irving at the Lyceum, for there some of the most elaborate stage settings ever produced were constructed, inspired by the able hand of Mr. Hawes Craven.

A scene-painter's workshop is a large affair. It is very high, and below the floor is another chamber equally lofty, for the "flats," or large canvases, have to be screwed up or down for the artist to be able to get at his work. They cannot be rolled wet, so the entire "flat" has to ascend or descend at will.

To make the matter clear, a scene on the stage, such as a house or a bridge, is known as a "carpenter's scene." The large canvases at the back are called "flats," or "painters' cloths." "Wings" are unknown to most people, but really mean the side-pieces of the scene which protrude on the stage. The "borders" are the bits of sky or ceiling which hang suspended from above, and a "valarium" is a whole roof as used in classical productions.

A scene-painter's palette is a strange affair; it is like a large wooden tray fixed to a table, and that table is on wheels; along one side of the tray are divisions like stalls in a stable, each division containing the different coloured paints, while in front is a flat piece on which the powders can be mixed. The thing that strikes one most is the amount of exercise the scenic artist takes. He is constantly stepping back to look at what he has done, for he copies on a large scale the minute sketch he has previously worked out in detail. Assistants generally begin the work and lay the paint on; but all the finishing touches are done by the master, who superintends the whole thing being properly worked out from his model.

The most elaborate scenery in the world is to be found in London, and Sir Henry Irving, as mentioned before, was the first to study detail and effect so closely. Even in America, where many things are so extravagant, the stage settings are quite poor compared with those of London.

Theatres in England and America differ in many ways. The only thing I found cheaper in the United States than at home was a theatre stall, which in New York cost eight shillings instead of ten and sixpence. They are also ahead of us inasmuch as they book their cheaper seats, which must be an enormous advantage to those unfortunate people who can always be seen—especially on first nights—wet or fine, hot or cold, standing in rows outside a London pit door.

There is no comparison between the gaiety of the scene of a London theatre and that of New York. Long may our present style last. In London every man wears evening dress in the boxes, stalls, and generally in the dress circle, and practically every woman is in evening costume, at all events without her hat. Those who do not care to dress, wisely go to the cheaper seats. This is not so across the Atlantic. It is quite the exception for the male sex to wear dress clothes; they even accompany ladies to the stalls in tweeds, probably the same tweeds they have worn all day at their office "down town," and it is not the fashion for women to wear evening dress either. What we should call a garden-party gown is *de rigueur*, although a lace neck and sleeves are gradually creeping into fashion. Little toques are much worn, but if the hat be big, it is at once taken off and disposed of in the owner's lap. Being an American she is accustomed to nursing her hat by the hour, and does not seem to mind the extra discomfort, in spite of fan, opera-glass, and other etceteras.

The result of all this is that the auditorium is in no way so smart as that of a London theatre. The origin of the simplicity of costume in the States of course lies in the fact that fewer people in proportion have private carriages, cabs are a prohibitive price, and every one travels in a five cents (2½*d.*) car. The car system is wonderful, if a little agitating at first to a stranger, as the numbers of the streets— for they rarely have names in New York—are not always so distinctly marked as they might be. It is far more comfortable, however, to get into one's carriage, a hansom, or even a dear old ramshackle shilling "growler" at one's own door, than to have to walk to the nearest car "stop" and find a succession of electric trams full when you arrive there, especially if the night happens to be wet. The journey is cheap enough when one does get inside, but payment of five cents does not necessarily ensure a seat, so the greater part of one's life in New York is spent hanging on to the strap of a street car.

"Look lively," shouts the conductor, almost before one has time to look at all, and either life has to be risked, or the traveller gets left behind altogether.

Not only travelling in cars, but many things in the States cost twopence half-penny. It seems a sort of tariff, that five cents, or nickle, as it is called. One has to pay five cents for a morning or evening paper, five cents to get one's boots blacked, and even in the hotels they only allow a darkie to perform that operation as a sort of favour.

It is a universal custom in the States to eat candies during a performance at the theatre, but when do Americans refrain from eating candies—one dare not say "chewing-gum," for we are told that no self-respecting American ever chews gum nowadays!

The theatres I visited in New York, Chicago, Philadelphia, New Orleans, and even in far-away San Antonio, Texas, were all comfortable, well warmed, well ventilated, and excellently managed, but the audience were certainly not so smart as our own, not even at the Opera House at New York, where the performers are the same as in London, and the whole thing excellently done, and where it is the fashion to wear evening dress in the boxes. Even there one misses the beauty of our aristocracy, and the glitter of their tiaras.

Choosing a play is no easy matter. Hundreds of things have to be considered. Will it please the public? Will it suit the company? If Miss So-and-So be on a yearly engagement and there is no part for her, can the theatre afford out of the weekly profits of the house to pay her a large salary merely as an understudy? What will the piece cost to mount? What will the dramatist expect to be paid? This latter amount varies as greatly as the royalties paid to authors on books.

As nearly every manager has a literary adviser behind his back, so almost every actor-manager has a syndicate in the background. Theatrical syndicates are strange institutions. They have only come into vogue since 1880, and are taken up by commercial gentlemen as a speculation. When gambling ceases to attract on the Stock Exchange, the theatre is an exciting outlet.

The actor-manager consequently is not the "sole lessee" in the sense of being the only responsible person. He generally has two or three backers, men possessed of large incomes who are glad to risk a few thousand pounds for the pleasure of a stall on a first night, or an occasional theatrical supper. Sometimes the syndicate does extremely well: at others ill; but that does not matter—the rich man has had his fun, the actor his work, the critic his sneer, and so the matter ends.

The actor-manager draws his salary like any other member of the company; but should the play prove a success his profits vary according to arrangement.

If, on the other hand, the venture turn out a failure, in the case of the few legitimate actor-managers—if one may use the term—he loses all the outgoing expenses. Few men can stand that. Ten thousand pounds have been lost through a bad first night, for although some condemned plays have worked their way to success, or, at least, paid their expenses, that is the exception and by no means the rule.

Many affirm there should be no actor-managers: the responsibility is too great;

but then no man is sure of getting the part he likes unless he manages to secure it for himself.

Every well-known manager receives two or three hundred plays per annum. Cyril Maude told me that three hundred and fifteen dramas were left at the Haymarket Theatre in 1903, and that he and Frederick Harrison had actually read, or anyway looked through, every one of them. They enter each in a book, and put comments against them.

"The good writing is Harrison's," he remarked, "and the bad scribble mine"; but that was so like Mr. Maude's modesty.

After that it can hardly be said there is any lack of ambition in England to write for the stage. The extraordinary thing is that only about three per cent. of these comedies, tragedies, burlesques, or farces are worth even a second thought. Many are written without the smallest conception of the requirements of the theatre, while some are indescribably bad, not worth the paper and ink wasted on their production.

It may readily be understood that every manager cannot himself read all the MSS. sent him for consideration, neither is the actor-manager able to see himself neatly fitted by the parts written "especially for him." Under these circumstances it has become necessary of late years at some theatres to employ a literary adviser, as mentioned on the former page. All publishing-houses have their literary advisers, and woe betide the man who condemns a book which afterwards achieves a great success, or accepts one that proves a dismal failure! So likewise the play reader.

Baskets full of dramatic efforts are emptied by degrees, and the few promising productions they contain are duly handed over to the manager for his final opinion.

In spite of the enormous number of plays submitted yearly, every manager complains of the dearth of suitable ones.

CHAPTER XV

THEATRICAL DRESSING-ROOMS

A Star's Dressing-room—Long Flights of Stairs—Miss Ward at the Haymarket—A Wimple—An Awkward Predicament—How an Actress Dresses—Herbert Waring—An Actress's Dressing-table—A Girl's Photographs of Herself—A Grease-paint Box—Eyelashes—White Hands—Mrs. Langtry's Dressing-room—Clara Morris on Make-up—Mrs. Tree as Author—"Resting"—Mary Anderson on the Stage—An Author's Opinion—Actors in Society.

AFTER ascending long flights of stone stairs, traversing dreary passages with whitewashed walls, and doors on either side marked one, two, or three, we tap for admission to a dressing-room.

Where is the fairy pathway? where the beauty?—ah! where? That long white corridor resembles some passage in a prison, and the little chambers leading off it are not very different in appearance from well-kept convict cells, yet this is the home of our actors or actresses for many hours each day.

In some country theatres the dressing-rooms are still disgraceful, and the sanitary arrangements worse.

Even in London it is only the "stars" who have an apartment to themselves. At such an excellently conducted theatre as the Haymarket, Miss Winifred Emery has to mount long flights between every act. Suppose she has to change her costume four times in the play, she must ascend those stone stairs five times in the course of each evening, or, in other words, walk up two hundred and fifty steps in addition to the fatigue of acting and the worry of quick changing, while on *matinée* days this exertion is doubled. She is a leading lady; she has a charming little room when she reaches it, and the excitement, the applause, and the pay of a striking part to cheer her—but think of the sufferers who have the stairs without the redeeming features. An actress once told me she walked, or ran, up eight hundred steps every night during her performance.

While speaking of dressing-rooms I recall a visit I paid to Miss Geneviève Ward at the Haymarket during the run of *Caste* (1902). It was a *matinée*, and, wanting to ask that delightful woman and great actress a question, I ventured to the stage door and sent up my card.

"Miss Ward is on the stage; but I will give it to her when she comes off in four minutes," said the stage-door-keeper.

Accordingly I waited near his room.

The allotted time went by—it is known in a theatre exactly how long each scene will take—and at the expiration of the four minutes Miss Ward's dresser came to bid me follow her up to the lady's room. The dresser was a nice, complacent-looking woman, *l'âge ordinaire*, as the French would say, arrayed in a black dress and big white apron.

Miss Ward had ascended before us, and was already seated on her little sofa.

"Delighted to see you, my dear," she exclaimed. "I have three-quarters of an hour's wait, so I hope you will stay to cheer me up."

How lovely she looked. Her own white hair was covered by a still whiter front wig, while added colour had given youth to her face, and the darkened eyelids made those wondrous grey orbs of hers even more striking.

"Why, you look about thirty-five," I exclaimed, "and a veritable *grande dame!*"

"It is all the wimple," she said.

"And what may that be?"

"Why, this little velvet string arrangement from my bonnet, with the bow under my chin; when you get old, my dear, you must wear a wimple too; it holds back those double, treble, a nd quadruple chins that are so annoying, and restores youth—*me voilà.*"

Miss Ward was first initiated into the mysteries and joys of a wimple when about to play in *Becket* at the Lyceum.

While we chatted she took up her knitting—being as untiring in that line as Mrs. Kendal. Miss Ward was busy making bonnets for hospital children, and during all those long hours she waited in her dressing-room, this indefatigable woman knitted for the poor. After about half an hour her dresser returned and said:

"It is time for you to dress, madame."

"Shall I leave?" I asked.

"Certainly not—there is plenty of room for us all;" and in a moment the knitting was put aside, and her elaborate blue silk garment taken off and hung on a peg between white sheets. Rapidly Miss Ward transformed herself into a sorrowing mother—a black skirt, a long black coat and bonnet were placed in readiness, when lo, the dresser, having turned everything over, exclaimed:

"I cannot see your black bodice."

Miss Ward looked perturbed.

"I do believe I have left it at home—I went back in it last night, if you remember, because I was lazy; and forgot all about it. Never mind, no one will see the bodice is missing when I put on my cloak, if I fasten it tight up, and I must just melt inside its folds."

But when the cloak was fastened there still appeared a decidedly *décolleté* neck. Time was pressing, the "call boy" might arrive at any moment. Miss Ward seized a black silk stocking, which she twirled round her neck, secured it with a jet brooch, powdered her face to make it look more doleful, and was ready in her garb of woe ere the boy knocked.

Then we went down together.

These theatrical dressers become wonderfully expert. I have seen an actress come off the stage after a big scene quite exhausted, and yet only have a few minutes before the next act. She stood in the middle of her dressing-room while we talked, and at once her attendant set to work. The great lady remained like a block. Quickly the dresser undid her neck-band, and unhooked the bodice after removing the lace, took away the folded waistband, slipped off the skirt, and in a twinkling the long ball dress was over the actress's head and being fastened behind. Her arms were slipped into the low bodice, and while she arranged the jewels or her corsage the dresser was doing her up at the back. Down sat the actress in a chair placed for her, and while she rouged more strongly to suit the gaiety of the scene, the dresser was putting feathers and ornaments into her hair, pinning a couple of little curls to her wig to hang down her neck, and just as they both finished this rapid transformation the call boy rapped.

Off went my friend.

"I shall be back in seven minutes," she exclaimed, "so do wait, as I have fourteen minutes' pause then."

The dresser caught up her train and her cloak, and followed the great lady to the wings, where I saw her arranging the actress's dress before she went on, and waiting to slip on the cloak and gloves which she was supposed in the play to come off and fetch.

A good dresser is a treasure, and that is why most people prefer their own to those provided at the theatres.

Apropos of knowing exactly how long an actor is on the stage, I may mention that Herbert Waring once invited me to tea in his dressing-room.

"At what time?" I naturally asked.

"I'll inquire from my dresser," was his reply. "I really don't know when I have my longest 'wait.'"

Accordingly a telegram arrived next day, which said "tea 4.25," so at 4.25 I presented myself at the stage door, where Mr. Waring's man was waiting to receive me.

Others joined us. A tin tray was spread with a clean towel; as usual, the theatrical china did not match, and the spoons and the seats were insufficient, but the tea and cakes were delicious, and the rough-and-tumble means of serving them in a star's dressing-room only in keeping with the usual arrangements of austere simplicity behind the scenes.

"What was the most amusing thing that ever happened to you on the stage?"

Mr. Waring looked perplexed.

"I haven't the slightest idea. Nothing amusing ever happens; it is the same routine day, alas, after day, the same dressing, undressing, acting, finishing, going gleefully home, and returning next day to begin exactly the same thing over again. I must be a very dull dog, but I cannot ferret out anything 'amusing' from the back annals of a long theatrical career," and up he jumped to slip on his powdered wig—which he had removed to cool his head—and away he ran to entertain his audience.

Mr. Waring's amusing experiences, or lack of them, seem very usual in theatrical life. What a delightful man he is, and what a gentleman in all his dealings. He is always loved by the companies with whom he acts, and never makes a failure with his parts.

The most important thing in an actress's dressing-room is her table—verily a curious sight. It is generally very large, more often than not it is composed of plain deal, daintily dressed up in muslin flouncings over pink or blue calico. There seems to be a particular fashion in this line, probably because the muslin frills can go to the wash—a necessary proviso for anything connected with the theatre. In the middle usually reposes a large looking-glass, and as one particular table is in my mind's eye, I will describe it, as it is typical of many, and belonged to a beautiful comic-opera actress.

The looking-glass was ornamented with little muslin frills and tucks, tied with dainty satin bows, on to which were pinned a series of the actress's own photographs. These cabinet portraits formed a perfect garniture, they represented the lady in every conceivable part she had ever played, and were tied together with tiny scarlet ribbons, the foot of one being fixed to the head of the next. The large mirror over the fireplace—for she was a star and had a fireplace—was similarly ornamented, so was the cheval glass, and above the chimneypiece was a complete screen composed of another set of her own photographs from another piece. These had to stand up, so the little red bows which fixed them went from side to side, by which means they stood along the board zig-zag fashion, like a miniature screen, without tumbling down. She was not in the least egotistical, it was simply the craze for photographs, which all theatrical folk seem to have, carried a little further than usual, and in her own dressing-room she essayed to have her own photographs galore. As she was very pretty and many of the costumes charming, she showed her good taste.

In front of the looking-glass was a large pincushion stuffed with a multiplication of pins of every shape and size, endless hat-pins, safety-pins, and little brooches, in fact, a supply sufficient to pin everything on to her person that exigency might require. There were large pots of powder, flat tablets of rouge, hares' feet, for putting on the rouge, fine black pencils for darkening eyes, blue chalk pencils for lining the lids, wonderful cherry-red arrangements for painting Cupid's lips, for even people with large mouths can by deft artistic treatment be made to appear to have small ones. There were bottles of white liquid for hands and neck, because it is more important, of course, to paint the hands than the face, otherwise they are apt to look appallingly red or dirty behind the footlights.

There were two barber's blocks on which stood the wigs for the respective acts, since it is much quicker and less trouble to put on a wig than adjust one's hair, and probably no one, except Mrs. Kendal, has ever gone through an entire theatrical career and only twice donned a wig.

Of course there were endless powders as well as perfumes of every sort and kind. There were hand-mirrors and three-fold mirrors, and electric light that could be moved about, for it is important to look well from all sides when trotting about the stage.

Theatrical dressing-rooms are so small that the dressing-table is their chief feature, and if there be room for a sofa or arm-chair, they are accounted luxurious.

All the costumes, as a rule, are hung against the wall, which is first covered with a calico sheet, then each dress is hung on its own peg, over which other calico sheets fall. This does not crush them, keeps all clean, and avoids creases; nevertheless, the most brilliant theatrical costumes look like a series of melancholy ghosts when not in use.

One of the actress's most important possessions is the grease paint-box, which in tin, separated into compartments for paints, costs about ten and sixpence. Into these little compartments she puts vaseline, coco butter, Nuceline, and Massine for cleaning the skin. For the face has to be washed, so to speak, with grease, preparatory to being made up.

A fair woman first lays on a layer of grease paint of a cream ground. On to that she puts light carmine on her cheeks, and follows the lines of her own colour as much as she can. Some people have colour high up on the cheek-bones, others low down, and it is as well to follow this natural tint if possible.

She blue-pencils round her eyes to enhance their size, gets the blue well into the corners and down a little at the outside edges to enlarge those orbs. Then she powders her face all over to get rid of that look of grease which is so distressing, and soften down the general make-up, and then proceeds to darken her eyelashes and eyebrows.

One little actress told me she always wound a piece of cotton round a hairpin, on to which she put a blob of cosmetic, heated it in the gas or candle, and when it was melted, blinked her eyelashes up and down upon it so that they might take on the black without getting it in hard lumps, but as a level surface. She put a little red blob in the corner of her eyes to give brightness, and a red line in the nostrils to do away with the black cavern-like appearance caused by the strong lights of the stage.

"I never make up the lips full size," she said, "or else they look enormous from the front. I put on very bright little 'Cupid's bow' middles, which gives all the effect that is necessary. After I have powdered my face and practically finished it, I just dust on a little dry rouge with a hare's foot to get the exact amount of colour I wish for each act. Grease paints are absolutely necessary to get the make-up to stay on one's face, but they have to be well powdered down or they will wear greasy."

"I always think the hands are so important," I remarked.

"Oh yes," she replied. "Of course, for common parts, such as servants, one leaves one's hands to look red, for the footlights always make them look a dirty red, but for aristocratic ladies we have to whiten our hands, arms, and neck, and I make a mixture of my own of glycerine and chalk, because it is so much cheaper than buying it ready-made.

"Sometimes it takes me an hour to make up my face. You see, a large nose can be modified; and a small nose can be made bigger by rouging it up the sides and leaving a strong white line down the middle. It is wonderful how one can alter one's face with paint, though I think it is better to make up too little than too much."

Thus it will be seen an hour is quite a usual length of time for an actress to sit in front of her dressing-table preparatory to the performance.

Mrs. Langtry's dressing-room at the Imperial Theatre may be mentioned. An enormous mirror is fastened against one wall, and round it, in the shape of a Norman arch, are three rows of electric lights giving different colour effects. The plain glass is to dress by in the ordinary way; pink tones give sunset and evening effect; while the third is a curious smoked arrangement to simulate moonlight or dawn. Dresses can be chosen and the face painted accordingly to suit the stage colouring of the scene. The lights turn on above, below, or at the sides, so the effect can be studied from every point of view.

While on the subject of making up, a piece of advice from the great actor Jefferson to the wonderful American actress, Clara Morris, is of interest:

"Be guided as far as possible by Nature. When you make up your face, you get powder on your eyelashes. Nature made them dark, so you are free to touch the lashes themselves with ink or pomade, but you should not paint a great band about your eye, with a long line added at the corner to rob it of expression. And now as to the beauty this lining is supposed to bring, some night when you have time I want you to try a little experiment. Make up your face carefully, darken your brows and the lashes of *one eye*; as to the other eye, you must load the lashes with black pomade, then draw a black line beneath the eye, and a broad line on its upper lid, and a final line out from the corner. The result will be an added lustre to the make-up eye and a seeming gain in brilliancy; but now, watching your reflection all the time, move slowly backwards from the glass, and an odd thing will happen; that made-up eye will gradually grow smaller and will gradually look like a black hole, absolutely without expression."

Clara Morris followed Jefferson's counsel and never blued or blacked her eyes again.

I once paid an interesting visit to a dressing-room: it came about in this wise.

In 1898 the jubilee of Queen's College, in Harley Street, was celebrated. It was founded fifty years previously as *the first college open to women*. A booklet in commemoration of the event was got up, and many old girls were persuaded to relate their experiences. Among them were Miss Sophia Jex Blake, M.D., Miss Dorothea

Beale (of Cheltenham), Miss Adeline Sargent, the novelist, Miss Louisa Twining, whose work on pauperism and workhouses is well known, Miss Mary Wardell, the founder of the Convalescent Home, etc. Mrs. Tree agreed to write an article on the stage as a profession for women. At the last moment, when all the other contributions had gone to press, hers was not amongst them. It was a *matinée* day, and as editor I went down to Her Majesty's, and bearded the delinquent in her dressing-room. She was nearly ready for the performance, in the midst of her profession, so to speak; but realising the necessity of doing the work at once or not at all, she seized some half-sheets of paper, and between her appearances on the stage jotted down an excellent article. It was clever, to the point, and full of learning. It appeared a few days later, and some critic was unkind enough to say "her husband or some other man had written it for her." I refute the charge; for I myself saw it hastily sketched in with a pencil at odd moments on odd scraps of paper.

Mrs. Tree is a woman who would have succeeded in many walks of life, for she is enthusiastic and thorough, a combination which triumphantly surmounts difficulties. She has a strong personality. In the old Queen's College days she used to wear long æsthetic gowns and hair cut short. Bunches of flowers generally adorned her waist, offerings from admiring young students, whom she guided through the intricacies of Latin or mathematics.

The Beerbohm Trees have a charming old-fashioned house at Chiswick, and three daughters of various and diverse ages, for the eldest is grown up while the youngest is quite small. Both parents are devoted to reading and fond of society, but their life is one long rush. Books from authors line their shelves, etchings and sketches from artists cover their walls; both have great taste with a keen appreciation of genius. Few people realise what an unusually clever couple the Beerbohm Trees are, or how versatile are their talents. They fly backwards and forwards to the theatre in motor-cars, and pretend they like it in spite of midnight wind and rain.

Theatrical work means too much work or none. It is a great strain to play eight times a week, to dress eight times at each performance, as in a Drury Lane drama, and to rehearse a new play or give a *matinée* performance as well, and yet this has to be done when the work is there, for what one refuses, dozens, aye dozens, are waiting eagerly to take. Far more actors and actresses are "resting" every evening than are employed in theatres, poor souls.

"*Resting!*" That word is a nightmare to men and women on the stage. It means dismissal, it means weary waiting—often actual want—yet it is called "resting." It spells days of unrest—days of dreary anxiety and longing, days when the unfortunate actor is too proud to beg for work, too proud even to own temporary defeat—which nevertheless is there.

A long run of luck, the enjoyment of many months, perhaps years, when all looked bright and sunny, when money was plentiful and success seemed assured, suddenly stops. There is no suitable part available, new blood is wanted in the theatre, and the older hands must go. Then comes that cruelly enforced "rest," and, alas! more often than not, nothing has been laid by for the rainy day, when £10 a week ceases even to reach 10*s*. Expenses cannot easily be curtailed. Home and family are there, the actor hopes every week for new work, he refuses to retrench, but lives on that miserable farce "keeping up appearances," which, although sometimes good policy, frequently spells ruin in the end.

Mrs. Beerbohm Tree.

Photo by Bassano, 25, Old Bond Street, W.

Some of the best actors and actresses of the day are forced into this unfortunate position; indeed, they suffer more than the smaller fry—for each theatre requires only one or two stars in its firmament. Theatrical folk are sometimes inclined to be foolish and refuse to play a small part for small pay, because they think it beneath their dignity, so they prefer to starve on their mistaken grandeur, which is, alas! nothing more nor less than unhappy pride.

Clara Morris, one of America's best-known actresses, shows the possible horrors, almost starvation, of an actress's early years in her delightful volume, *Life on the Stage*.

She nearly died from want of food, and after years and years of work all over the States made her first appearance as "leading lady" at Daly's Theatre in New York at a salary of thirty-five dollars a week, starting with only two dollars (eight shillings) in her pocket.

Her first triumph she discussed with her mother and her dog over a supper of bread and cheese. She had attained success—but even then it was months and months, almost years, before she earned enough money either to live in comfort or be warmly clothed.

The beautiful Mary Anderson, in her introduction to the volume, says:

"I trust this work will help to stem the tide of girls who so blindly rush into a profession of which they are ignorant, for which they are unfitted, and in which dangers unnumbered lurk on all sides. If with Clara Morris's power and charm so much had to be suffered, what is—what must be—the lot of so many mediocrities who pass through the same fires to receive no reward in the end?"

Every one who knows the stage, knows what weary suffering is endured daily by would-be actors who are "resting"; and as they grow older that "resting" process comes more often, for, as one of the greatest dramatists of the day said to me lately:

"The stage is only for the young and beautiful, they can claim positions and salaries which experience and talent are unable to keep. By the time youth has thoroughly learnt its art it is no longer physically attractive, and is relegated to the shelf."

"That seems very hard."

"Ah, but it is true. At the best the theatrical is a poor profession, and ends soon. Believe me, it is only good for handsome young men and lovely girls. When the bloom of youth has gone, good acting does not command the salary given to beautiful inexperience."

"How cruelly sad!"

"Perhaps—but truth is often sad. When a girl comes to me and says she has had an offer of marriage, but she doesn't want to give up her Art, I reply:

"'Marry the man before your Art gives you up.'"

This was severe, but I have often thought over the subject since, and seen how true were the words of that man "who knew."

Half a century ago only a few favoured professionals were admitted into the sacred circle called Society, and then only on rare occasions, but all that is now changed: actors and actresses are the fashion, and may be found everywhere and anywhere. Their position is remarkable, and they appear to enjoy society as much as society enjoys them. They are *fêted* and feasted, the world worships at their feet. In London the position of an actor or actress of talent is a brilliant one socially.

CHAPTER XVI

HOW DOES A MAN GET ON THE STAGE?

A Voice Trial—How it is Done—Anxious Faces—Singing into Cimmerian Darkness—A Call to Rehearsal—The Ecstasy of an Engagement—Proof Copy; Private—Arrival of the Principals—Chorus on the Stage—Rehearsing Twelve Hours a Day for Nine Weeks without Pay.

"HOW does a man get on the stage?" is a question so continually asked that the mode of procedure, at any rate for comic opera, may prove of interest.

After application the would-be actor-singer, if lucky, receives a card, saying there will be a "voice trial" for some forthcoming musical comedy at the theatre on such a date at two o'clock. Managements that have a number of touring companies arrange voice trials regularly once a week, but others organise them only when necessary.

Let us take a case of Special Trial for some new production. There are usually so many persons anxious to procure employment, that three days are devoted to these trials from two till seven o'clock.

Upon receiving a card the would-be artist proceeds to his destination in a state of wild excitement and overpowering nervousness at a quarter to two, having in the greenness of inexperience arranged to meet a friend at three o'clock, expecting by then to be able to tell him he has been engaged.

On arriving at the corner of the street the youth is surprised to see a seething mass of struggling humanity striving to get near the stage door; something like a gallery entrance on a first night. At this spectacle his nervousness increases, for he has a vague fear that some of these voices and dramatic powers may be better than his own. During the wait outside, people recognise and hail friends whom they have played with in other companies on tour, or met on the concert platform, or perhaps known in a London theatre. Every one tries to look jaunty and gay, none would care to acknowledge the cruel anxiety they are enduring, or own how much depends on an engagement.

After half an hour, or probably an hour's wait, the keen young man reaches the stage door, and finally gets into the passage. In his eagerness he fancies he sees space in that passage to slip past a number of people who are waiting round the door-keeper's room, and congratulates himself on his smartness in circumventing them. Somehow he contrives to get through, and finally runs gaily down a flight of stairs, to find himself—not on the stage, as he had hoped, but underneath it. A piano and voice are heard overhead. Quickly retracing his steps he mounts higher and higher in his anxiety to be an early performer, tries passage after passage, to find nothing but dressing-rooms, until he arrives breathless at the top of the building opposite two large apartments relegated later to the chorus. Utterly bewildered by the intricacies of the theatre, and a sound of music which he cannot locate, the poor novice is almost in despair of reaching the stage at all. One more effort, and a man who looks like a carpenter remarks:

"These 'ere is the flies, sir: there's the stage," and he points down below over some strange scaffolding.

The singer looks. Lo, there are fifty or sixty people on the stage.

"And those people?"

"All trying for a job, sir; but, bless yer 'eart, not one in twenty will get anything."

This sounds cheerless to the stage beginner, whose only recommendation is a good, well-trained voice.

With directions from the carpenter he wends his way down again, not with the same elastic step with which he bounded up the stairs. "Bless yer 'eart, not one in twenty will get anything" was not a pleasant piece of news.

Ah, here is a glass door, through which—oh joy! he sees the stage at last. He is about to enter gaily when he is stopped by a theatre official who demands his "form."

"Form? What form? I have none."

"Go back to the stage door, sign your name and address there, and fill in the printed form you will get there," says this gentleman in stentorian tones that cause the poor youth to tremble while he inquires:

"Where *is* the stage door?"

"Up those stairs, first to the right, and second to the left."

Back he goes, and after another wait, during which he notes many others filling in forms one by one and asking endless questions, he gets the book, signs his name, and receives a form in which he enters *name, voice, previous experience, height,* and *age*. There is also a column headed *"Remarks,"* which the would-be actor feels inclined to fill with superlative adjectives, but is informed that "the stage manager fills in this column himself."

At last he is on the stage, and after all the ladies have sung and some of the men, his name is called and he steps breezily down to the footlights. Ere he reaches them, however, some one to his left says:

"Where is your music?" and some one else to his right:

"Where is your form?"

He hands the form to a person seated at a table, and turning round sees a very ancient upright piano, where he gives his music to the accompanist. Then comes a trying moment. The youth has specially chosen a song with a long introduction so as to allow time to compose himself. But that introduction is omitted, for the accompanist in a most inconsiderate manner starts two bars from the end of it and says:

"Now then, please, if you're ready."

The singer gets through half a verse, when he is suddenly stopped by:

"Sing a scale, please."

He sings an octave, and is about to exhibit his beautiful tenor notes, when he is again interrupted by the question:

"How low can you go?"

He climbs down, and with some difficulty manages an A.

"Is that as deep as you can get?"

"Yes, but I'm a tenor. Shall I sing my high notes?"

A voice from the front calls out, "Your name."

All this is abruptly disconcerting, and the lad peers into Cimmerian darkness. In the stalls he sees two ghost-like figures, as "in a glass dimly." These are the manager and the composer of the new piece, while a few rows behind, two or three more spirits may be noted flitting restlessly about in the light thrown from the stage.

"Mr. A— —" again says that voice from the front.

"Yes, sir."

"Did you say you were a tenor?"

"Yes."

"Ah, I'm afraid we've just chosen the last one wanted. We had a voice trial yesterday, you know." And the tone sounded a dismissal.

"May I not sing the last verse of my song?" the young fellow almost gasps.

"If you like." He does like, and the two figures in front lean over in conversation; but he thinks he detects a friendly nod.

"Have we your address?" asks one of them.

"Yes, sir, I left it at the stage door."

"Thank you; we'll communicate with you should we require your services." The tenor is about to murmur his thanks, when another voice from the side of the stage calls, "Mr. Jones, please," and he hurries off, hearing the same questions from the two attendant spirits, "Where is your form?" "Where is your music?" addressed to the new-comer.

Just as he reaches the door he hears Mr. Jones stopped after three bars with "Thank you, that will do. Mr. Smith, please."

This is balm to his soul; after all, he was not hurried off so quickly, and he passes out into the light of day with the "Where is your form?" "Where is your music?" "Bless yer 'eart, not one in twenty will get anything," still ringing in his ears. And so to tea with what appetite he may bring at a quarter to seven instead of three o'clock as arranged.

Ten weary days pass—he receives no letter, hears nothing. He has almost given up all hope of that small but certain income, when a type-written missive arrives:

"Kindly attend rehearsal at the —— Theatre on Tuesday next at twelve o'clock."

The words swim before his eyes. Can it be true? Can he be among the successful ones after all? He is so excited he is scarcely able to eat or sleep, waiting for Tuesday to come. It does come at last, and he sets out for the theatre, thinking he will not betray further ignorance, and arrives fashionably late at a quarter to one. This time he sees no signs of life at the stage door.

"Of course, now that I belong to the theatre, I must go in through the front of the house, not at the side entrance," he says to himself. Round, therefore, he goes to the front, where some one sitting in the box office asks:

"What can I do for you?"

"Nothing, thanks; I am going to rehearsal."

"You're late. The chorus have started nearly an hour."

Good chance here to make an impression.

"Chorus? I'm a principal." This is not quite true at the moment, but may be in a year or two.

"Principal? Then you're too early, sir! Principals won't be called for another three weeks."

The tenor slinks out and goes round to the stage door again, where "You're very late, sir," is the door-keeper's greeting. "I should advise you to hurry up, they started some time ago. You'll find them up in the saloon. On to the stage, straight through to the front of the house, and up to the back of the circle."

He goes down on the stage, where he finds the same old piano going, and some one sitting in the stalls, watching a girl in a blouse and flaming red petticoat, who is dancing, whilst three or four other girls in various coloured petticoats, none wearing skirts, are waiting their turn. In the distance he hears sounds of singing, which make the most unpleasant discord with the dance tune on the stage. The accompanist points to an iron door at the side, passing through which the youth finds himself outside another door leading to the stalls, and, guided by his ear, finally reaches the saloon. He enters unobserved to find it filled with some forty girls and men, standing or sitting about, and singing from printed copies of something. Sitting down he looks over his neighbour's shoulder, and notices that each copy has printed on it "Proof copy. Private." After half an hour the stage manager, who has been standing near the piano, says:

"Thank you, ladies and gentlemen, that will do: back in an hour, please. Is Mr. A— — here? And Mr. A— — replies "Yes," and is told to wait, and asked why he did not answer to his name before.

"I was a little late, I fear."

"Don't be late again, or I shall have to fine you."

Off he goes to luncheon, and returns with the rest, who after a further three hours' work are dismissed for the day.

This goes on for six hours a day, during a fortnight, when the chorus is joined by eight more ladies and gentlemen styled "Small-part people," who, however, consider themselves very great people all the same.

Next the young man is told that in two days every one must be able to sing without music, as rehearsals will commence on the stage. In due course comes the first rehearsal on the stage, and after a couple of days *Position*, *Gestures*, and *Business* are all taken up in turn.

The saloon is then used by the principals, who have now turned up, and in the intervals of rest the chorus can hear sounds of music floating toward them.

In another week the principals join the company on the stage, and are told their places, while all principals read from their parts at first, such being the etiquette even if they know their lines. Books are soon discarded, however, and rehearsals grow rapidly longer, while everything shows signs of active progress towards production. Scenery and properties begin to be on view, and every one is sent to be measured for costumes, wigs, and boots. Then comes the first orchestral rehearsal, and finally, a week before the production, night rehearsals start in addition to day, so that people positively live in the theatre from 11.30 in the morning till 11.30 at night or later. Apart from all the general rehearsals there are extra rehearsals before or after these, for the dances.

There are generally two or three semi-dress rehearsals, followed by the full-dress rehearsal on Friday afternoon at two o'clock, or sometimes seven in the evening, when all the reserved seats are filled with friends of the management or company, various professionals connected in any way with the stage, and a number of artists and journalists, making sketches for the papers. At the end of each act the curtain is rung up and flash-light photographs taken of the effective situation and the *finale*, and so at last the curtain rises on the first night. Nine weeks' rehearsal were given for a comic opera lately, and no one was paid for his or her services during all that time. It only ran for six weeks, when the salaries ceased.

In comic opera there are such constant changes, of dialogue, songs, and alterations, that the company have a general rehearsal at least once a fortnight on the average, right through the run of a piece, and there is always an entire understudying company ready to go on at any moment.

CHAPTER XVII

A GIRL IN THE PROVINCES

Why Women go on the Stage—How to prevent it—Miss Florence
St. John—Provincial Company—Theatrical Basket—A Fit-up
Tour—A Theatre Tour—Répertoire Tour—Strange Landladies—
Bills—The Longed-for Joint—Second-hand Clothes—Buying
a Part—Why Men Deteriorate—Oceans of Tea—E. S. Willard—
Why he Prefers America—A Hunt for Rooms—A Kindly Clergy-
man—A Drunken Landlady—How the Dog Saved an Awkward
Predicament.

IT is continually being asked: Why do women crowd the stage?

The answer is a simple one—because men fail to provide for them. If every
man, willing and able to maintain a wife, married, there would still be over a
million women left. Many women besides these "superfluous" ones will never
marry—many husbands will die, and leave their widows penniless, and therefore
several millions of women in Great Britain must work to live. Their parents bring
them into the world, but they do not always give them the means of livelihood.

Marriage with love is entering a heaven with one's eyes shut, but marriage
without love is entering hell with them open.

What then?

Women must work until men learn to protect and provide for, not only their
wives, but their mothers, daughters, and sisters. All men should respect the woman toiler who prefers work to starvation, as all must deplore the necessity that
forces her into such a position. Women of gentle blood are the greatest sufferers;
brought up in luxury, they are often thrust on the world to starve through no fault
of their own what ever. The middle-class father should also be obliged to make
some provision by insurance for every baby girl, which will enable her to live, and
give her at least the necessities of life, so that she may not be driven to sell herself
to a husband, or die of starvation. The sons can work for themselves, and might
have a less expensive up-bringing, so that the daughters may be provided for by
insurance, if the tragedies of womanhood now enacted on every side are to cease.

It is no good for young men to shriek at the invasion of the labour market by
women: the young men must deny themselves a little and provide for their wom-
en folk if it is to be otherwise. It is no good grinding down the wages of women
workers, for that does harm to men and women alike, and only benefits the em-

ployer. Women must work as things are, and women do work in spite of physical drawbacks, in spite of political handicap, in spite—too often—of lack of sound education. The unfortunate part is that women work for less pay than men, under far harder conditions, and the very men who abuse them for competing on their own ground, are the men who do not raise a hand to make provision for their own women folk, or try in any way to help the present disastrous condition of affairs.

Men can stop this overcrowding of every profession by women if they really try, and until they do so they should cease to resent a state of affairs which they themselves have brought about.

Luckily there is hardly any trade or profession closed to women to-day. They cannot be soldiers, sailors, firemen, policemen, barristers, judges, or clergymen in England, but they can be nearly everything else. Even now, in these so-called enlightened days, men often leave what money they have to their sons and let chance look after their daughters. They leave their daughters four alternatives—to starve, to live on the bitter bread of charity, to marry, or to work. Independent means is a heritage that seldom falls to the lot of women. There are too many women on the stage as there are too many women everywhere else; but on the stage as in authorship, women are at least fairly treated as regards salary, and can earn, and do earn, just as much as men.

The provinces are the school of actors and actresses, so let us now turn to a provincial company, for after all the really hard work of theatrical life is most severely felt in the provinces. A pathetic little account of early struggles appeared lately from the pen of Miss Florence St. John. At fourteen years of age she sang with a Diorama along the South coast, and a few months after she married. Her parents were so angry they would have nothing more to do with her, and not long afterwards her husband's health failed and he died. Sheer want pursued her during those years.

"My efforts to secure work seemed almost hopeless."

That is the *crux* of so many theatrical lives. Those eight words so often appear—and yet there are sanguine people who imagine employment can always be obtained on the stage for the mere asking, which is not so; but let us now follow the fortunes of a lucky one.

After a play has been sufficiently coached in London, at the last rehearsal a "call" is put up on the board, which says:

"*Train call*. All artistes are to be at — — Station at — — o'clock on such and such a date. Train arrives at A — — at — — o'clock."

When the actors reach the station they find compartments engaged for them, it being seldom necessary nowadays to charter a private train. Those compartments are labelled in large lettering with the name of the play for which they have been secured. The party travel third class, the manager as a rule reserving first-class compartments for himself and the stars. Generally the others go in twos and twos according to their rank in the theatre, that is to say, the first and second lady travel together, the third and fourth, and so on. Often the men play cards during the whole journey; generally the women knit, read, or enliven the hours of weary travel by making tea and talk!

At each of the stations where the train pauses people look into the carriages in a most unblushing manner, taking a good stare at the theatrical folk, as if they were wild beasts at the Zoo instead of human beings. Sometimes also they make personal and uncomplimentary remarks, such as:

"Well, she ain't pretty a bit," or, "My! don't she look different hoff and hon!"

Each actress has two supplies of luggage, one of which, namely, a "*theatrical basket*," contains her stage dresses, and the other the personal belongings which she will require at her lodgings. As a rule, ere leaving London she is given two sets of labels to place on her effects, so that the baggage-man may know where to take her trunks and save her all further trouble.

Naturally theatrical folk must travel on Sunday. On a "Fit-Up" tour, when they arrive at the station of the town in which they are to play, each woman collects her own private property, and those who can afford the expense drive off in a cab, while the others—by far the more numerous—deposit it in the "Left Luggage Office." After securing a room, the tired traveller returns to the station and employs a porter to deliver her belongings.

Sometimes a girl experiences great difficulty in finding a suitable temporary abode, for, although in large towns a list of lodgings can be procured, in smaller places no such help is available, and she may have to trudge from street to street to obtain a decent room at a cheap rate. By the time what is wanted is found, she generally feels so weary she is only too thankful to share whatever the landlady may chance to have in the way of food, instead of going out and procuring the same for herself.

On a "Theatre Tour" the members of a company nearly always engage their rooms beforehand and order dinner in advance, because they can go to recognised theatrical lodgings, a list of which may be procured by applying to the Actors' Association, an excellent institution which helps and protects theatrical folk in many ways. When rooms can be arranged beforehand, life becomes easier; but this is not always possible, and then poor wandering mummers meet with disagreeable experiences, such as finding themselves in undesirable lodgings, or at the tender mercy of a landlady who is too fond of intoxicants. A liberal use of insect powder is necessary in smaller towns.

A girl friend who decided to go on the stage has given me some valuable information gathered during six or seven years' experience of provincial theatrical life. Hers are the experiences of the novice, and bear out Mrs. Kendal's advice in an earlier chapter. She was not quite dependent on her profession, having small means, but for which she says she must have starved many a time during her noviciate.

"One comes across various types of landladies," she explained, "but they are nearly always good-natured, otherwise they would never put up with the erratic hours for meals, and the late return of their lodgers. Some of them have been actresses themselves in the olden days, but, having married, they desire to 'lead a respectable life,' by which remark they wish one to understand that the would-be lodger is not considered 'respectable' so long as she remains in the theatrical profession.

"They are sometimes very amusing, at others the reminiscences of their own experiences prove a little trying; but after all, even such folk are better than the type of lodging-house-keeper who has come down in the world, and is always referring to her 'better days.' A great many of these people do not appear ever to have had better days. Now and then, however, one finds a genuine case and receives every possible attention, being made happy with flowers—a real luxury when on tour—nice table linen, fresh towels, all things done in a civilised manner, and oh dear! what a joy it is to come across such a home."

"Are the rooms, then, generally very bare?" I asked.

"One never finds any luxuries. As a rule one has to be content with horse-hair-covered chairs and sofas, woollen antimacassars, wax or bead flowers under glass cases, often with the addition of a stuffed parrot brought home by some fa-vourite sailor son. But simplicity does not matter at all so long as the lodgings do not smell stuffy. The bedroom furniture generally consists of the barest necessar-ies, and if one's couch have springs or a soft mattress it proves indeed a delightful surprise.

"There is a terrible type of landlady who rushes one for a large bill just at the last moment. As a rule the account should be brought up on Saturday night and settled, but this sort of woman generally manages to put off producing hers until the last moment on Sunday morning, when one's luggage is probably on its way to the station. Then she brings forth a document which takes all the joy out of life, and sends the unhappy lodger off without a penny in her pocket. Arguing is not of the slightest use, and if one happens to be a woman, as in my case, she has to pay what is demanded rather than risk a scene."

My friend's experiences were so practical I asked her many questions, in reply to some of which she continued:

"I have always managed to share expenses with some one I knew, which ar-rangement, besides being less lonely, reduced the cost considerably; but even then there is a terrible sameness about one's food. An egg for breakfast is very general, as some 'ladies' even object to cooking a rasher of bacon. Jam and other delicacies are beyond our means. Everlasting chop or steak with potatoes for dinner. One never sees a joint; it is not possible unless a slice can be begged from the landlady, in which case one often has to pay dearly for the luxury.

"We generally have supper after we return from the theatre, from which we often have to walk home a mile or more after changing. Many landladies refuse to cook anything hot at night, in which case tinned tongue or potted meat suffice; but a hot meal, though consisting only of a little piece of fish or poached eggs, is such a joy when one comes home tired and worn out, that it is worth a struggle to try to obtain.

"The least a bill ever comes to in a week is fifteen shillings, and that after studying economy in every way possible. Even though two of us lived together I never succeeded in reducing my share below that."

"What is the usual day?"

"One has breakfast as a rule between ten and eleven—earlier, of course, if a rehearsal has been called for eleven, in which case ten minutes' grace is given for the difference in local clocks; any one late after that time gets sharply reprimanded by the management. After rehearsal on tour a walk till two or three, a little shopping, dinner 4.30, a rest, a cup of tea at 6.30, after which meal one again proceeds to the theatre, home about 11.30, supper and bed. Week in, week out it is pretty much the same.

"For the first four years I only earned a guinea a week, and as it was necessary for me to find all my own costumes for the different parts in the companies in which I played, I had to visit second-hand shops and buy ladies' cast-off ball dresses and things of that sort, although cheap materials and my sewing machine managed to supply me with day garments. It is extraordinary what wonderful effects one can get over the footlights with a dress which by daylight looks absolutely filthy and tawdry, provided it be well cut; that is why it is advisable to buy good second-hand clothes when possible.

"In my own theatre basket I have fourteen complete costumes, and with these I can go on any ordinary tour. I travelled for some time with a girl who, though well-born, had out of her miserable guinea a week to help members of her family at home. She was an excellent needlewoman, and used to send her sewing-machine with her basket to the theatre, where she sat nearly all day making clothes or cutting them out for other members of the company. By these means she earned a few extra shillings a week, which helped towards the expenses of her kinsfolk. She was a nice girl, but delicate, and I always felt she ought to have had all the fresh air possible instead of bending over a sewing-machine in a stuffy little dressing-room.

"Of course it is necessary for us to take great care of our private clothes, and in order to save them I generally keep an old skirt for trudging backwards and forwards through the dust and dirt, and for rehearsals, since at some of the ill-kept provincial theatres a good gown would be ruined in a few days; added to which, one often gets soaked on the way to and from the theatre, for we can rarely afford cabs, and even if we could, on a wet night the audience take all available vehicles, so that by the time the performers are ready to leave, not one is to be procured."

Perhaps it may be well to say a little more concerning the theatre basket. It looks like a large washing basket, but being made of wicker-work is light. It is lined inside with mackintosh, and bears the name of the company to which it belongs on the outside. It is taken to the theatre on Sunday when the party arrives in the town, and as a rule each actress goes first thing on Monday morning for rehearsal and to unpack. The ordinary provincial company usually comprises about five men and five women, but in important dramas there are many more, and sometimes a dozen women and girls will have to dress in one room.

Of course the principal actresses select the best dressing-rooms, and each chooses according to her rank. Round the wall of the room a table is fastened, such a table as one might find in a dairy, under which the dress baskets stand. Those who can afford it, provide their own looking-glass and toilet-cover to put over their scrap of table, also sheets to cover the dirty walls, ere hanging up their skirts; but as every one cannot afford to pay for the washing of such luxuries, many have to dispense with them.

Mrs. Patrick Campbell.

From a painting by Hugh de T. Glazebrook.

There is seldom a green-room in the provinces, so as a rule the actresses sit upon their own baskets during the waits; and as in many theatres there are no fireplaces in these little dressing-rooms, and not always artificial heat, there they remain huddled in shawls waiting their "call."

"The most interesting form of company," said my friend, "is the 'Répertoire,' for that will probably give three different pieces a week, which is much more lively than performing in the same play every night for months.

"If any one falls out of the cast through illness or any other reason, and a new man or woman join the company, a fortnight is required for rehearsals, and during that fortnight we unfortunate players have to give our gratuitous services every day for some hours."

On asking her whether she thought it wise for a girl to choose the stage as a profession, she shook her head sadly.

"I do not think a woman should ever choose the stage as a profession if she have any person depending upon her, for it is practically impossible to live on one's precarious earnings. It is only the lucky few who can ever hope to make a regular income, and certainly in the provinces very few of us do even that. Many managers like to engage husbands and wives for their company, as this means a joint salary and a saving in consequence. These married couples do not generally get on well, and certainly fail to impress one with the bliss of professional wedded life."

"What are the chances of success?" I inquired.

"The chances of getting on at all on the stage are small in these days, when advancement means one must either have influence at headquarters, or be able to bring grist to the manager's mill. It is heart-breaking for those who feel they could succeed if they were but given a chance, to see less talented but more influential sisters pushed into positions. One gradually loses all hope of true merit finding its own reward, while it is no uncommon thing for a girl to pay down £20 to be allowed to play a certain part. She may be utterly unfitted for the *rôle*, but £20 is not to be scoffed at, and she is therefore pitchforked into it to succeed or fail. In most cases she fails, and cannot get another engagement unless she produces a second £20.

"No, I do not consider the stage a good profession for a girl, simply because there is no authority over her, and few people take enough interest in the young creature to even warn her of the peril. In the theatrical profession, and especially on tour, the sexes meet on an equal footing. No chivalry need be expected, and is certainly rarely received, because when one is vouchsafed any little attention or politeness, such as one would naturally claim in society or take for granted in daily intercourse, it is merely because the man has some natural instinct which causes him to be polite in spite of adverse circumstances.

"The majority of men upon the stage to-day are so-called gentlemen, but there is something in the life which does not conduce to keep them up to the standard from which they start. They become careless in their manners, dress, and conversation, and keep their best side for the audience. As a rule they are kind-hearted and willing to help women, but men upon the stage get 'petty.' I do not know whether it is the effect of the paint, the powder, and the clothes, or the fact of their doing nothing all day, but they certainly deteriorate; one sees the decadence month by month. They begin by being keen on sport, for instance, but gradually they find even moving their bicycles about an expense and leave them behind. They have nowhere to go, are not even temporary members of clubs, so gradually get into the habit of staying in bed till twelve or even two o'clock for lack of something to interest them, and finish the rest of the day in a 'gin crawl,' which simply means sitting in public-houses drinking and smoking.

"Unfortunately this love of drink sometimes increases, and as alcohol can be readily procured by the dresser, men and women too, feeling exhausted, often take things which had better be avoided. You see their meals are not sufficiently substantial—how can they be on the salary paid? Girls live on small rations of bread, butter, and oceans of tea, and the men on endless sausage rolls and mugs of beer."

This reminds me of a little chat I had with E. S. Willard. On the fiftieth night of that excellent play *The Cardinal*, by Louis N. Parker, at the St. James's Theatre, a mutual friend came to ask me to pay a visit behind the stage to the great Mr. Willard.

We arrived in Mr. Alexander's sitting-room described elsewhere, at the end of the third act, and a moment later the rustling silk of the Cardinal's robe was heard in the passage.

"I'm afraid this is unkind of me," I said: "after that great scene you deserve a 'whisky and soda' instead of a woman and talk."

"Not at all," said this splendid-looking ecclesiastic, seating himself gaily. "I never take anything of that sort till my work is done."

"But you must be fearfully exhausted after such a big scene?"

"No. It is the eighth performance this week, and the second to-day; but I'm not really tired, and love my work, although I do enjoy my Sunday's rest."

Mr. Willard looks handsomer off the stage than on. His strong face seems to have a kindlier smile, his manner to be even more courtly, and I was particularly struck with the fact that he wore little or no make-up.

"You are an Englishman," I said, "and yet you have deserted your native land for America?"

"Not so. I'm English, of course, though I love America," was the reply. "Seven years ago I went across the Atlantic and was successful, then I had a terrible illness which lasted three years. When I was better I did not dare start afresh in England and risk failure, so I began again in the States, where I was sure of the dollars. They have been so kind to me over there that I do not now like to leave them. You see America is so enormous, the constant influx of emigrants so great, one can go on playing the same piece for years and years, as Jefferson is still doing in *Rip van Winkle*. Here new plays are constantly wanted, and even if an actor is an old favourite he cannot drag a poor play to success. Management in London has become a risky matter. Expenses are enormous, and a few failures mean ruin."

Alas! at that moment the wretched little bell which heralds a new act rang forth, and I barely had time to reach the box before Mr. Willard was once more upon the stage, continuing his masterly performance. He is an actor of strong personality, and can ill be spared from England's shores.

But to return to the provinces, and the experiences of the pretty little actress.

"The familiarity which necessarily exists between the sexes," continued she, "both in acting together at night, and rehearsing together by day, is in itself a danger to some girls who are unfortunate enough to be thrown into close companionship with unprincipled men, and have not sufficient worldly wisdom or instinct to guard against their advances.

"The idea of the stage door being besieged by admirers is far from true in the provinces. With musical comedies of rather a low order there may be a certain amount of hanging about after the performance, but in the case of an ordinary company this rarely happens. The real danger in the provinces does not come from outside.

"Life on tour for a single man is anything but agreeable. He has no one to look after his clothes, for, needless to say, no landlady will do that, and therefore both his theatre outfit and his private garments are always getting torn and worn. As a rule, however, there are capable women in the company who are willing to sew on buttons, mend, or darn, and if it were not for their good nature, many men would find themselves in sorry plight."

She was an intelligent, clever girl, and I asked her how she got on the stage.

"After having been trained under a well-known manager for six months and paying him thirty guineas for his services, I was offered an engagement in one of his companies then starting for a 'Fit-Up' tour through Scotland at a £1 week, payable in two instalments, namely, 10s. on Wednesday and 10s. on Saturday. Fortunately, being a costume play, dresses were provided, but I had to buy tights, grease-paint, sandals, and various ornaments, give two weeks' rehearsals in London free, play for three nights and live for three days in Scotland before I received even the first ten shillings.

"Happily I was the proud possessor of small means, and shared my rooms and everything with a girl friend who had trained at the same time as myself, consequently we managed with great care to make both ends meet; but it was hard work for us even with my little extra money, and what girls do who have to live entirely on their pay, and put by something for the time when they are out of an engagement, a time which often comes, I do not pretend to know.

"A 'Fit-Up' tour is admittedly the most expensive kind of work for actors, because it means that three nights is the longest period one ever remains in any town, most of the time being booked for 'one-night places' only. On this particular tour of sixteen weeks there were no less than sixty 'one-night places,' and my total salary amounted to £16.

"It may sound ridiculous to travel with a dog, but mine proved of the greatest use to me on more than one occasion. Our first hunt was always for rooms; the term sounds grand, for the 'rooms' generally consisted of one chamber with a bed sunk into the wall, as they are to-day at a great public school like Harrow. To get to this abode we sometimes had to pass through the family apartments, a most embarrassing proceeding, as the members had generally retired to rest before our return from the theatre; but still, 'beggars cannot be choosers,' and in some ways we often felt ourselves in that position.

"Supposing we arrived at a one-night place, we would sally forth and buy

¼   lb. tea,

¼   lb. butter,

1   small loaf,

½   lb. steak or chop for dinner,

2   eggs for breakfast.

"The landlady's charge as a rule for two lodgers sharing expenses varied from 2*s.* 6*d.* to 3*s.* for a single night, or 5*s.* for three nights, so that the one-night business was terribly extravagant.

"Being our first tour we were greatly interested by the novelty of everything; it was this novelty and excitement which carried us through. We really needed to be sharp and quick, for in that particular play we had to change our apparel no less than six times. We were Roman ladies, slaves, and Christians intermittently during the evening, being among those massacred in the second act, and resuscitated to be eaten by lions at the end of the play; therefore, while the audience were moved to tears picturing us being devoured by roaring beasts, we were ourselves roaring in the wings in imitation of those bloodthirsty animals.

"A 'Fit-Up' carries all its own scenery, and nearly always goes to small towns which have no theatre, only a Town Hall or Corn Exchange, while the dressing-rooms, especially in the latter, are often extremely funny, being like little stalls in a stable, where we sometimes found corn on the floor, and could look over at each other like horses in their stalls.

"The 'Fit-Up' takes its own carpenter, who generally plays two or three parts during the evening. He has to make the stage fit the scenery or *vice versâ*, and get everything into working order for the evening performance.

"On one occasion we arrived at a little town in Scotland and started off on our usual hunt for rooms. We were growing tired and depressed; time was creeping on, and if we did not obtain a meal and rooms soon, we knew we should have to go to the theatre hungry, and spend that night in the wings. Matters were really getting desperate when we met two other members of the company in similar plight. One of them was boldly courageous, however, and when we saw a clergyman coming towards us, suggested she should ask him if he knew of any likely place. She did so, and he very kindly told her to mention his name at an inn where he was sure they would, if possible, put her and her friend up, but he added,

'There is only one room.' This, of course, did not help my friend and myself, so after the two had started off we stood wondering what was to become of us.

"'Can you not tell us of any other place?' we asked. No, he could not, but at this moment a lady appeared on the scene who asked what we wanted. We explained the difficulty of our situation, and she pondered and thought, but intimated there was no lodging she could recommend, whereupon we proceeded disconsolately on our way, not in the least knowing what we were to do.

"A moment or two afterwards we heard some one running behind. It was the clergyman. Taking off his hat and almost breathless, he exclaimed, 'My wife wishes to speak to you,' and lo and behold that dear wife hurried after him to say she felt so sorry for the position in which we were placed that she would be very glad if my friend and I would give her the pleasure of our company and stay at her house for the night.

"We went. She sent from the vicarage to the station for our belongings, and we could not have been more kindly treated if we had been her dearest friends. She had a fire lighted in our bedroom, and there were lovely flowers on the table when we returned from the theatre. They took us for a charming expedition to some old ruins on the following morning, invited friends to meet us at luncheon, and although they did not go to the theatre themselves at night, they sat up for us and had a delightful little supper prepared against our return.

"I shall never forget the great kindness they showed us. I am sure there are very few people who would be tempted to proffer such courtesy and hospitality to two wandering actresses; and yet if they only knew how warmly their goodness was appreciated and how beneficent its influence proved, they would feel well repaid.

"In the afternoon when it was time to leave, rain was pouring down, but that fact did not deter the clergyman from accompanying us to the station, carrying an umbrella in one hand and a bag in the other, while his little son followed with a great bunch of flowers.

"As if to take us down after such luxurious quarters, we fell upon evil days at the very next town, where we were told it was difficult to get accommodation at all, and therefore made up our minds to take the first we met. It did not look inviting, but the woman said that by the time we had done our shopping she would have everything clean and straight. We bought our little necessaries, and as the door was opened by a small boy handed them in to him, saying we were going for a walk but would be back in less than an hour for tea. On our return we were admitted, but saw no signs of tea, so rang the bell. No one came. We waited ten minutes and rang again. A pause. Suddenly the door was burst open and in reeled the landlady, who banged down a jug of boiling water on the table and departed. We gazed at each other in utter consternation, feeling very much frightened, for we both realised she was drunk.

"We rang again after a time, but as no one attempted to answer our summons, and it being impossible to make a meal off hot water, I crept forth to reconnoitre. There was not a soul to be seen, not even the little boy, but I ventured into the kitchen to try if I could not find the bread, butter, and tea, so that we might prepare something to eat for ourselves. While so engaged a sonorous sound made me turn round, and there upon the floor with her head resting upon a chair in the corner of the room lay our landlady, dead drunk. It was an appalling sight. We gathered our things together as quickly as we could and determined to leave, put a shilling on the table to appease the good woman's wrath when she awoke, and were glad to shake the dust of her home from our feet.

"Not far off was a Temperance Hotel, the sight of which after our recent experience we hailed with delight, and where we engaged a bedroom, to which we repaired, when our evening's work was finished.

"My dog, who always lay at the foot of my bed, woke us in the middle of the night by his low growls. He seemed much perturbed, so we lay and listened. The cause of his anxiety soon became clear; *some one was trying to turn the handle of the door*, while the voices of two men could be heard distinctly, one of which said:

"'Only two actresses, go on,' and then the door handle turned again and his friend was pushed in. It was all dark, but at that moment my dog's growls and barks became so furious and angry as he sprang from the bed that the man precipitately departed, and we were left in peace, although too nervous to sleep.

"Of course we complained next morning, but equally of course the landlady knew nothing about the matter. These were our best and worst experiences during my first tour."

CHAPTER XVIII

PERILS OF THE STAGE

Easy to Make a Reputation—Difficult to Keep One—The Theatrical
Agent—The Butler's Letter—Mrs. Siddons' Warning—Theatri-
cal Aspirants—The Bogus Manager—The Actress of the Police
Court—Ten Years of Success—Temptations—Late Hours—An
Actress's Advertisement—A Wicked Agreement—Rules Behind
the Scenes—Edward Terry—Success a Bubble.

MANKIND curses bad luck, but seldom blesses good fate. It is comparatively
easy to make a reputation once given a start by kindly fate; but extremely
difficult to maintain one in any walk of life, and this applies particularly to the
stage.

Happening to meet a very pretty girl who had made quite a hit in the provinces and was longing for a London engagement, I asked her what her experience of
theatrical agents had been.

"Perfectly horrible," she replied, "and heart-breaking into the bargain. For
three whole months I have been daily to a certain office, and in all this weary time
I have only had five interviews with the manager."

"Is it so difficult to get work?"

"It is almost impossible. When I arrive, the little stuffy office is more or less
crowded; there are women seeking engagements for the music halls, fat, common,
vulgar women who laugh loud and make coarse jokes; there are sickly young men
who want to play lovers' parts on the legitimate stage, and who, according to the
actors' habit, never take their hats off. It is a strange fact that actors invariably
rehearse in hats or caps, and sit in them on all occasions like Jews in synagogues.

"There are children who come alone and wait about daily for an engagement,
children who have been employed in the pantomime, and whose parents are more
or less dependent on their gains, and there is one girl, she is between thirteen and
fourteen, whom I have met there every day for weeks and weeks. Seventy-four
days after the pantomime closed she was still without work, and I watched that
child get thinner and paler time by time as she told me with tears in her eyes she
was the sole support of a sick mother.

"When I go there, the gentleman who has the office makes me shrivel up.

"'Do you specialise?' he asks, peeping over the edge of his gold-rimmed spectacles. He jots down my replies on a sheet of paper. 'Character or juvenile parts?' he inquires. 'What salary? Whom have you played with?' And having made these and other inquiries he looks through a series of books, turns over the pages, says, 'I am sorry I have nothing for you to-day, you might look in again to-morrow.' And this same farce or tragedy is repeated every time."

"But is it worth while going?" I asked.

"Hardly; one wears out one's shoe-leather and one's temper; and yet after all the theatrical agent is practically my only chance of an engagement. This man is all right, he is not a bogus agent, but he simply has a hundred applicants for every single post he has to fill."

She went back day after day, and week after week, and each time the same scene was enacted, but no engagement came of it. Finally, brought to the verge of starvation, she had to accept work again in the provinces, and so desert an invalid father. She happened to be a lady, but of course many applicants for histrionic fame ought to be kitchen-maids or laundry-maids: they have no qualifications whatever to any higher walk of life.

Below is an original letter showing the kind of person who wants to go on the stage. It was sent to one of our best-known actresses when she was starring with her own company.

"... CASTLE
"*Oct 19th 1897*

"DEAR MADAM

"i writ you this few lins to see if you would have a opening for me as i would be an Actor on the Stage for my hole thought and life is on the stage and when i have any time you will always feind me readin at some play i make a nice female as i have a very soft voice Dear Madam i hop you will not refuse me i have got no frends alive to keep me back and every one tells me that you would make the best teacher that i could get Dear lady i again ask you not to refuse me i will go on what ever termes you think best i have been up at the theatre 4 times seeing you i enclose my Card to let you see it plese to send it back again and i enclose 12 stamps to you to telegraf by return if you would like to see me or if you would like to come down to the Castle to see me No more at present

"but remans your
"Obedient servant
"PETER W — —."

This was a letter from a man with aspirations, and below is a letter from Mrs. Siddons. If this actress, whose position was probably the grandest and greatest of any woman on the stage, can express such sentiments, what must be the experiences of less successful players?

"Mrs. Siddons presents her compliments to Miss Goldsmith,

& takes the liberty to inform her, that altho' herself she has enjoyed all the advantages arising from holding the first situation
in the drama, yet that those advantages have been so counterbal-
anced by anxiety & mortification, that she long ago resolved never
to be accessory to bringing any one into so precarious & so ardu-
ous a profession."

The deterrent words of Mrs. Siddons had little effect in her day, just as the
deterrent words of those at the top of the profession have little effect now. Consequently, not only does the honest agent flourish, but the bogus agent and bogus
manager grow rich on the credulity of young men and women.

Speaking of the bogus manager, Sir Henry Irving observed:

"The actor's art is thought to be so easy—in fact, many people deny it is an
art at all—and so many writers persistently assert no preparation is needed for
a career upon the stage, that it is little wonder deluded people only find out too
late that acting, as Voltaire said, is one of the most rare and difficult of arts. The
allurements, too, held forth by unscrupulous persons, who draw money from foolish folk under the pretence of obtaining lucrative engagements for them, help to
swell very greatly the list of unfortunate dupes. I hope that these matters may in
time claim the attention of serious-minded persons, for the increasing number of
theatrical applicants for charity, young persons, too, is little less than alarming."

This remark of Sir Henry's is hardly surprising when below is a specimen
application received by the manager of a London suburban theatre from a female
farm servant in Essex:

"DEER SUR,—I works hon a farm but wants to turn actin.
Would lik ingagement for the pantomin in hany ways which you
think I be fit for. I sings in the church coir and plais the melodion.
I wants to change my work for the stage, has am sik of farm wark,
eas last tater liftin nigh finished me."

Another was written in an almost illegible hand which ran:

"HONOURED SIR,—i wants to go on the staige i am a servent
and my marster sais i am a good smart made so i wod like to play
act mades parts untill i can do laidies i doant mind wages for a bit
as i like your acting i'd like to act in your theter so i am going to
call soon."

Truly the assurance of people is amazing; to imagine they can enter the theatrical profession without even common education is absurd. Only lately another stage-struck servant appeared in the courts. Although an honest girl, she was
tempted to steal from her mistress to pay £3 7s. to an agent for a problematical
theatrical engagement. She is only one of many.

One day a woman stood before a manager. She had been so persistent for days
in her desire to see him, and appeared so remarkable, that the stage door-keeper at
last inquired if he might admit her.

"Please, sir, I wants to be an actress," she began, on entering the manager's room.

"Do you? And what qualifications have you?"

"I'm a cook."

"That, my good woman, will hardly help you on the stage."

"And I've been to the the-a-ters with my young man—I'm keeping company with 'im ye know, and——"

"Well, well."

"And 'e and I thinks you ain't got the right tone of hactress for them parts. Now I'm a real cook I am, and I don't wear them immoral 'igh 'eels, and tiny waists, I dresses respectable I do, and I'd just give the right style to the piece. My pal—she's a parlourmaid she is—could do duchesses and them like—she's the air she 'as—but I ain't ambitious, I'd just like to be what I am, and show people 'ow a real cook should be played—Lor' bless ye, sir, I don't cook in diamond rings."

That manager did not engage the lady; but he learnt a lesson in realism which resulted in Miss FitzClair being asked to dispense with her rings on the stage that night.

With a parting nod the "lady" said as she left the door:

"Your young man don't make love proper neither, you should just see 'ow 'Arry makes love you should, he'd make you all sit up, I know, he does it that beautiful he do—your man's a arf-'arted bloke 'e is, seems afraid of the gal, perhaps it's 'er 'igh 'eels and diamonds 'e's afraid of, eh?"

The lady took herself off.

These are only a few instances to show how all sorts and conditions of people are stage-struck. That delightful man Sir Walter Besant lay down an excellent rule for young authors, "Never pay to produce a book"—it spells ruin to the aspirant. The same may be said of the stage. *Never part with money to get on the stage.* It may be advisable to accept a little if one cannot get much; but never, never to pay for a footing. Services will be accepted while given free or paid for, and dispensed with when the time comes for payment to be received.

Among the many temptations of stage life is drink. The actor feels a little below par, he has a great scene before him, and while waiting in his dressing-room for the "call boy" he flies to a glass of whiskey or champagne. He gets through the trying ordeal, comes off the boards excited and streaming at every pore, flings himself into a chair, and during the time his dresser is dragging him out of his clothes, or rubbing him down, yields to the temptation of another glass. Many of our actors are most abstemious, though more than one prominent star has been known to mumble incoherently on the stage.

Matinée days are always a strain for every one in the theatre, and there are people foolish enough to think a little stimulant will enable them to get through, not knowing a continuance of forced strength spells damnation.

Yes. The stage is surrounded by temptations. Morally, extravagantly, and alcoholically the webs of excess are ready to engulf the unwary, and therefore, when people keep straight, run fair, and save their pennies, they are to be congratulated, and deserve the approbation of mankind. He who has never been tempted, is not a hero in comparison with the man who has turned aside from the enticing wiles of sin.

There is a certain class of woman who continually appears in the police courts, described as an "actress." She is always "smartly dressed," and is generally up before the magistrate or judge for being "drunk and disorderly"—suing her husband or some one else for maintenance—or claiming to have some grievance for a breach of promise or lost jewellery.

These "ladies" often describe themselves as actresses: and perhaps they sometimes are; but if so they are no honour to their profession. There is another stamp of woman who becomes an actress by persuading some weak man to run a theatre for her. Sympathy between men and women is often dangerous. She generally ends by ruining him, and he in running away from her. These bogus actresses, with their motor cars and diamonds, are more dangerous and certainly more attractive than the bogus manager. They are the vultures who suck young men's blood. They are the flashy, showy women who attract silly servant-girls with the idea the stage spells wealth and success; but they are the scourge of the profession.

Good and charming women are to be found upon the stage. Virtue usually triumphs; they are happy in their home life, devoted to their children, sympathetic to their friends, and generous almost to a fault. The leading actresses are, generally speaking, not only the best exponents of their art, but the best women too. The flash and dash come to the police courts, and end their days in the workhouse.

The stage at best means very, very hard work, and theatrical success is only fleeting in most cases. It must be seized upon when caught and treated as a fickle jade, because money and popularity both take wings and fly away sooner than expected. In all professions men and women quickly reach their zenith, and if they are clever may hold that position for ten years. After that decline is inevitable and more rapid than the ascent has been.

If a reputation is to be made, it is generally achieved by either man or woman before the age of forty. By fifty the summit of fame is reached, and the downward grade begun. One can observe this again and again in every profession.

A great actor, doctor, lawyer, writer, or painter has ten years of success, and if he does not provide for his future during those ten years, 'tis sad for him. As the tide turns on the shore, so the tide turns on the careers of men and women alike.

Public life is not necessarily bad. In the first place, it is only the man with strong individuality who can ever attain publicity. He must be above the ordinary ruck and gamut, or he will never receive public recognition. If, therefore, he is stronger than his brother, he should be stronger also to resist temptation, to disdain self-love or vainglory. The moment his life becomes public he is under the microscope, and should remember his influence is great for good or ill. Popular praise is pleasant, but after all it means little; one's own conscience is the thing, that alone tells whether we have given of our best or reached our ideal. The true artist is never satisfied, therefore the true artist never suffers from a swelled head; it is the minor fry who enjoy that ailment.

The temptations behind the footlights are enormous. It is useless denying the fact. One may love the stage, and count many actors and actresses among one's friends; but one cannot help seeing that theatrical life is beset by dangers and pit-falls.

Young men and women alike are run after and fawned upon by foolish people of both sexes. Morally this is bad. Actors are flattered and worshipped as though they were little gods. This in itself tends to evoke egotism. The gorgeous apparel of the theatre makes men and women extravagant in their dress; the constant go-ing backwards and forwards in all weathers inclines them to think they must save time or themselves by driving; the fear of catching cold makes them indulge in cabs and carriages they cannot afford, and extravagance becomes their besetting sin. Every one wants to look more prosperous than his neighbour, every recipient of forty shillings a week wishes the world to think his salary is forty pounds.

Apart from pay, the life is exacting. The leaders of the profession seldom sup out: they are tired after the evening's work, and know that burning the candle at both ends means early extinction, but the Tottie Veres and Gladys Fitz-Glynes are always ready to be entertained.

The following advertisement appeared one day in a leading London paper:

> "STAGE.—I am nearly eighteen, tall, fair, good-looking, have a little money, and wish to adopt the stage as a profession. Engage-ment wanted."

What was the result? Piles of letters, containing all sorts of offers to help Miss A—— to her doom. A certain gentleman wrote from a well-known fashionable club, the letter being marked *Private*, saying: "I should like if possible to assist you in your desire to go on the stage, but I am not professional myself in any way. This is purely a matter in which I might be happy to take an interest and assist, if you think proper to communicate with me by letter, stating exactly the circumstances, and when I can have an interview with you on the subject." This letter might be ca-pable of many interpretations. The gentleman might, of course, have been purely philanthropic in his motives; we will give him the benefit of the doubt.

Others were yet more strange and suggestive of peril for the girl of eighteen.

What might have been the end of all this? Supposing Miss A—— had granted an interview to No. 1. Supposing further he had advanced the money for the nov-ice to buy an engagement, what might have proved her fate? She would have been in his clutches—young, inexperienced, powerless, in the hands of a man who, if really philanthropic, could easily have found persons needing interest and assis-tance among his own immediate surroundings, instead of going wide afield to dispense his charity and selecting for the purpose an unknown girl of eighteen who innocently stated she was good-looking.

Miss Geneviève Ward, a woman who has climbed to the top of her profession, allows me to tell the following little story about herself as a warning to others, for it was only her own genius—a very rare gift—which dragged her to the front.

Mr. George Grossmith.

By permission of W. Boughton & Sons, Photographers, Lowestoft.

When she first came to England, with a name already well established in America, expecting an immediate engagement, she could not get work at all. She applied to the best-known theatrical agents in London. Day after day she went there, she a woman in her prime and at the top of her profession, and yet she was unable to obtain work.

"Tragedy is dead, Miss Ward," exclaimed Mr. B— —. "Young women with fine physical developments are what we want."

It was not talent, not experience, that were required according to this well-known agent, but legs and arms—a poor standard, truly, for the drama of the country.

However, at last there came a day, after many weary months of waiting, when some one was wanted to play tragedy at Manchester. It was only a twelve weeks' engagement, and the pay but £8 a week. It was a ridiculous sum for one in Miss Ward's position to accept, but she was worn out with anxiety, and determined not to go back to America and own herself vanquished; therefore she accepted the offer, paid the agent heavily, and went to Manchester, where she played for twelve weeks as arranged. Before many nights had passed, however, she had signed a further engagement at double the pay. Her chance in England had come and she had won.

If such delay, such misery, such anxiety can befall those whose position is already established, and whose talents are known, what must await the novice?

"I suppose I have kept more girls off the stage than any living woman," said Miss Ward. "Short, ugly, fat, common, hopeless girls come to me to ask my advice. There is not one in twenty who has the slightest chance, not the very slightest chance, of success. Servants come, dressmakers, wives of military men, daughters of bishops and titled folk. The mania seems to spread from high to low, and yet hardly one of them has a voice, figure, carriage, or anything suitable for the stage, even setting dramatic talent aside."

"What do you say to them?"

"Tell them right out. I think it is kinder to them, and more generous to the drama. 'Mind you,' I say, 'I am telling you this for your own good; if I consulted personal profit I should take you as a pupil and fill my pocket with your guineas; but you are hopeless, nothing could possibly make you succeed with such a temperament, or voice, or size, or whatever it may be, so you had better turn your attention at once to some other occupation.'"

I have known several cases in which Miss Ward has been most kind by helping real talent gratuitously; many of the women on the stage to-day owe their position to her timely aid.

"Warn girls," she continued, "when asked for a bonus, *never*, NEVER to give one."

It is no uncommon thing for a bogus agent to ask for a £10 bonus, and promise to secure an engagement at £1 a week. That engagement is never procured, or, if it be, lasts only during rehearsals—which are not paid for—or for a couple of weeks, after which the girl is told she does not suit the part, and dismissed. Thus the matter ends so far as a triumphal stage entry is concerned.

It may be well here to give an actual case of bonus as an example.

A wretched girl signed an agreement to the following effect. She was to pay £20 down to the agent as a fee, to provide her own dresses and travelling expenses, and to play the first four months without any salary at all. At the expiration of that time she was to receive 10s. a week for six months, with an increase of £1 a week for the following year.

On this munificent *want* of salary the girl was expected to pay rent, dress well for the stage, have good food so as to be able to fulfil her engagements properly, attend endless rehearsals, and withal consider herself fortunate in obtaining a hearing at all. She broke the engagement on excellent advice, and the agent wisely did not take action against her, as he at first threatened to do.

In the sixties Edward Terry essayed the stage. Seeing an advertisement, the future comedian offered his services at a salary of 15s. a week.

Above the door was announced in grand style:

"Madame Castaglione's Dramatic Company, taking advantage of the closing of the Theatres Royal Covent Garden, Drury Lane, Lyceum, etc., will appear at Christchurch for six nights only."

It was an extraordinary company, in which several parts were acted by one person during the same evening. There was only one play-book, from which every actor copied out his own part, no one was ever paid, and general chaos reigned. Edward Terry had fallen into the hands of one of the most notorious bogus managers of his time. His next engagement was more lucrative. He was always sure of playing eighteen parts a week, and sometimes received 20s. in return. Matters are better now; but strange stories of early struggle crop up occasionally, and the bogus manager-agent, in spite of the Actors' Association and the Benevolent Fund, still exists.

Edward Terry had to fight hard in order to attain a position, and thoroughly deserves all the success that has fallen to his lot; but all stage aspirants are not Edward Terrys, and then their plight in the hands of the bogus agent is sad indeed, especially in the provinces where he flourishes.

Those who know the stage only from the front of the house little realise the strict regulations enforced behind the scenes in our first-class London theatres, the discipline of which is almost as severe as that of a Government office. Each theatre has its code of rules and regulations, which generally number about twenty, but are sometimes so lengthy they are embodied in a handbook. These rules and regulations have to be signed by every one, from principal to super, and run somewhat in this wise:

"The hair of the face must be shaven if required by the exigencies of the play represented."

"All engagements to be regarded as exclusive, and no artiste shall appear at any other theatre or hall without the consent in writing of the manager or his representative."

"All artistes engaged are to play any part or parts for which they may be cast, and to understudy if required."

"In the event of the theatre being closed through riot, fire, public calamity, royal demise, epidemic, or illness of principal, no salary shall be claimed during such closing."

A clause in a comic opera agreement ran:

"No salary will be payable for any nights or days on which the artiste may not perform, whether absenting himself by permission, or through illness, or any other unavoidable cause, and should the artiste be absent for more than twelve consecutive performances under any circumstances whatever, this engagement may be cancelled by the manager without any notice whatsoever."

Thus it will be seen an engagement even when obtained hangs on a slender thread, and twelve days' illness, although an understudy may step in to take the part, threatens dismissal for the unfortunate sufferer.

Of course culpable negligence of the rules may be punished by instant dismissal, but for ordinary offences fines are levied, in proportion to the salary of the offender. Sometimes a fine is sixpence, sometimes a guinea, but an ordinary one is half a crown "for talking behind the scenes during a performance." Some people are always being fined.

In the case of legitimate drama the actor is not permitted to "build up" his part at his own sweet will; in comic opera, however, "gagging" and "business" have often gone far to make success.

The upholder of law and order behind the scenes is the stage manager. If power gives happiness he should be happy, but his position is such a delicate one, and tact so essential, that it is often difficult for him to be friendly with every one and yet a strict and impartial disciplinarian.

Life is a strange affair. We all try to be alike in our youth, and individual in our middle age. As we grow up we endeavour to shake ourselves out of that jelly-mould shape into which school education forces us, although we sometimes mistake eccentricity for individuality. Just as much real joy comes to the woman who has darned a stocking neatly or served a good dinner, as is vouchsafed by public praise; just as much pleasure is felt by the man who has helped a friend, or steered a successful bargain. In the well-doing is the satisfaction, not in indiscriminate and ofttimes over-eulogistic applause.

Stage aspirants soon learn those glorious press notices count for naught, and they cease to bring a flutter to the heart.

Success is but a bubble. It glistens and attracts the world as the soap globe glistens and attracts the child. It is something to strive for, something to catch, something to run after and grasp securely; yet, after all, what is it? It is but a shimmer—the bubble bursts in the child's hand, the glistening particles are nothing, the ball once gained is gone. Is not success the same? We long for, we strive to attain our goal, and then find nothing but emptiness.

If we are not satisfied with ourselves, if we know our best work has not yet been attained, that we have not reached our own high standard, worldly success has merely pricked the bubble of ambition, that bubble we had thought meant so much and which really is so little. People are a queer riddle. One might liken them to flowers. There are the beautiful roses, the stately lilies, the prickly thorns and clinging creepers; there are the weeds and poisonous garbage. Society is the same. People represent flowers. Some live long and do evil, some live a short while and do good, sweetening all around them by the beauty of their minds. Our friends are like the blooms in a bouquet, our enemies like the weeds in our path.

What diversified people we like. This woman excites our admiration because she is beautiful, that one because she is clever, yon lady is sympathetic, and the trend of the mind of the fourth stimulates our own. They are absolutely dissimilar, that quartette, we like them all, and yet they have no points in common. It does us good to be with some people, they have an ennobling, refining, or softening effect upon us—it does us harm to be with others.

And so we are all many people in one. We adapt ourselves to our friends as we adapt our clothes to the weather. We expand in their sunshine and frizzle up in their sarcasm. We are all actors. All our life is merely human drama, and imperceptibly to ourselves we play many parts, and yet imagine during that long vista of years and circumstances we are always the same.

We act—you and I—but we act ourselves, and the professional player acts some one else; but that is the only difference, and it is less than most folk imagine.

Love of the stage is the fascination of the mysterious, which is the most insidious of all fascinations.

CHAPTER XIX

"CHORUS GIRL NUMBER II. ON THE LEFT"

A FANTASY FOUNDED ON FACT

Plain but Fascinating — The Swell in the Stalls — Overtures — Persistence — Introduction at Last — Her Story — His Kindness — Happiness crept in — Love — An Ecstasy of Joy — His Story — A Rude Awakening — The Result of Deception — The Injustice of Silence — Back to Town — Illness — Sleep.

THE curtain had just risen; the orchestra was playing the music of the famous operetta *Penso*, when a man in the prime of life in a handsome fur coat entered the stalls. He was alone. Having paid for his programme and taken off his furs, he quietly sat down to survey the scene.

The chorus was upon the stage; sweeping his glasses from end to end of the line of girls upon the boards, his eyes suddenly lighted upon the second girl on the left. She was not beautiful. She had a pretty figure, and a most expressive face; but her features were irregular and her mouth was large. Far more lovely girls stood in that row, many taller, with finely chiselled features and elegant figures, but only that girl — *Number II. on the Left* — caught and riveted his attention. He looked and looked again. What charm did she possess, he wondered, which seemed to draw him towards her? She was singing, and making little curtsies like the others in time to the music: she was waving her arms with those automatic gesticulations the chorus learn; she was smiling, and yet behind it all he seemed to see an unutterable sadness in the depths of her dark grey eyes. The girl fascinated him; he listened not to the music of *Penso*, he hardly looked at any one else; so long as *Number II. on the Left* remained upon the stage his entire thoughts were with her. She enchained, she almost seemed to hypnotise him, and yet she seldom looked his way. During the *entr'acte* Allan Murray went outside to try and discover the name of *Number II. on the Left*. No one, however, was able to tell him, or if they were, they would not.

Disappointed he returned to his seat in time for the second act. She had changed her dress, and the new one was perhaps less becoming than the first.

"She is not pretty," he kept repeating to himself, "but she is young. She is neither a great singer nor a dancer, but she is a gentlewoman."

So great was the fascination she had exerted over the man of the world, that he returned the next night to a seat in the stalls, and as he gazed upon the operetta he felt more than ever convinced that there was some great tragedy lying hidden behind the smiling face of *Number II. on the Left*. He desired to unravel it.

A short time before Christmas, being absolutely determined to find out who she was, he succeeded in worming the information from some one behind the scenes. Her real name was Sarah Hopper—could anything be more hideous?—her professional one Alwyn FitzClare—could anything be more euphonious? He went off to his club after one of the performances was over, and wrote her a note. Days went by and he received no answer. Then he purchased some beautiful flowers and sent them to the stage door for Miss Alwyn FitzClare with his compliments. Still no answer; but in the meantime he had been back to the theatre, and had been even more struck than before with the appearance of the girl, and felt sorry for the look of distress he thought he saw lurking behind her smiles.

It was now two days before Christmas, and writing her a note begging her not to take it amiss from a stranger, who wished her a very pleasant Christmas, he enclosed two five-pound notes, hoping she would drink his health and remember she had given great pleasure to one of her audience.

Christmas morning brought him back the two notes with a formal stiff little letter, saying that Miss FitzClare begged to return her thanks and was quite unable to accept gifts from a stranger.

For weeks and weeks he occupied a stall at the theatre, whenever he had an off-night. He continued to write little notes to Miss Alwyn FitzClare, but never received any reply. However, at last he ventured to beg that she would grant him an interview. If she would only tell him where she came from, or give him an inkling of her position, he would find some means to obtain a formal introduction. She answered this letter not quite so stiffly as the former one containing the bank-notes, and stated that she came from Ipswich. Time passed; he succeeded in gaining an introduction, and sent it formally to *Number II. on the Left*. At the same time he invited her to lunch with him at a famous restaurant. She accepted; she came out of curiosity, she ultimately vowed, although in spite of the introduction, and in spite of the months of persuasion on his part, she felt doubtful as to the wisdom of doing so.

The girl who had looked plain but interesting upon the stage, appeared before him in a neat blue serge costume, well fitting and undecorated, and struck Mr. Murray as very much better looking, and smarter altogether in the capacity of a private person than she did in the chorus. "A gentlewoman" was writ big all over her. No one could look at her a second time and not feel that she was well born.

"Do you know," she said, "I often have funny letters from people on the other side of the footlights; but yours is the only one I ever answered in my life. Tell me why you have been so persistent?"

"Because of the trouble in your face," he answered.

"In mine? But I am always laughing on the stage—that is part of the duty of the chorus."

"Yes," he replied, "you laugh outwardly; but you cry inwardly. It was your sad expression which first attracted my attention."

He was very sympathetic and very kind, and gradually she told him her story. Her father had been a solicitor of good birth. He had a large practice, but dying suddenly left a family of nine children, all under the age of twenty, practically unprovided for, for the small amount for which his life was insured soon dwindled away in meeting the funeral expenses and settling outstanding bills.

"I was not clever enough to become a governess," she said, "I had not been educated for a secretary—in fact, I had no talent of any sort or kind except the ability to sing a little. Luck and hard work brought me the chance of being able to earn a guinea a week on the stage, out of which I manage to live and send home a shilling or so to help mother and the children."

It was a tragic little story—one of many which a great metropolis can unfold, where men bring children into the world without giving a thought to their future, and leave them to be dragged up on the bitter bread of charity, or to work in that starvation-mill which so many well-born gentlewomen grind year after year.

The rich gentleman and *Number II. on the Left* became warm friends. Months went by and they often met. She lunched with him sometimes; they spent an occasional Sunday on the river, and she wrote to him, and he to her, on the days when they did not meet. She was very proud; she would accept none of his presents, she would not take money, and was always most circumspect in her behaviour. Gradually that sad look melted away from her eyes, and a certain beauty took its place. He was kind to her, and by degrees, little by little, the interest aroused by her mournful expression deepened—as it disappeared—into love. She, on her side, looked upon him as a true friend, practically the only disinterested friend she had in London; and so time wore on, bringing happiness to both: neither paused to think. Her life was a happy one. She grew not to mind her work at the theatre, or the sewing she did for the children at home, sitting hour by hour alone in her little attic lodging, looking forward to those pleasant Sunday trips which brought a new joy into her existence. His companionship and friendship were very precious to this lonely girl in London.

One glorious hot July Sunday which they spent near Marlow-on-Thames seemed to Sarah Hopper the happiest day of her life. She loved him, and she knew it. He loved her; and had often told her so; but more than that had never passed between them. It was nearly two years since they first met, during which time the only bright hours in the life of *Number II. on the Left* had been those spent in Allan Murray's company. His kindness never changed. His consideration for her seemed to Alwyn delightful.

On that sunny afternoon they pulled up under the willows for tea, which she made from a little basket they always took with them. They were sitting chatting pleasantly, watching the water-flies buzzing on the stream, throwing an occasional bit of cake to a swan, and thoroughly enjoying that delightful sense of laziness which comes upon most of us at the close of a hot day, when seated beneath the shady trees that overhang the river.

He took her hand, and played with it absently for a while.

"Little girl," he said at last, "this cannot go on. I love you, and you know it;

you love me, and I know that too; but do you love me sufficiently to give yourself to me?"

"I don't think I could love you any more," she replied, "however hard I tried, for you have been my good angel for two happy years, you have been the one bright star of hope, the one pleasant thing in my life. I love you, *I love you*, I LOVE YOU," she murmured, as she leaned forward and laid her cheek upon his hand. He felt her warm breath thrill through him.

"I know it, dear," he said, and a sad pained look crossed his face; "but what I want to know is, do you care for me sufficiently?"

"I hardly understand," she answered, frightened she knew not why.

"Will you give me the right to keep you in luxury and protect you from harm?"

She looked up anxiously, there was something in his words and something in his tone she did not comprehend. His face was averted, but she saw how pale and haggard he looked.

"What do you mean?" she questioned, turning sick with an inexplicable dread.

"Could you give up the stage, the world for me? Instead of being your friend I would be your slave."

She seemed to be in a dream; his words sounded strange, his halting speech, his ashen hue denoted evil.

"Tell me what you mean," she cried.

"Dearest," he murmured, and then words seemed to fail him.

"But?" and she looked him through and through, a terrible suspicion entering her soul, "but — —"

"But," he replied, turning away from her, "you can never be my wife."

"Great God!" exclaimed the girl. "This from the one friend I thought I had on earth, from the one man I had learned to love and respect. Not your wife?" she repeated. "Am I losing my senses or are you?"

"You cannot be my wife," he reiterated desperately.

"So you think 1 am not good enough?" she gasped almost hysterically. "It is true I am only *Number II. on the Left*, and yet I was born a lady. I am your equal in social standing, and no breath of scandal has ever soiled my name. You have made love to me for two years, you have vowed you love me, and now, when you know my whole heart is given to you, you turn round and coolly say, 'You are not good enough to be my wife.'"

"My darling," he said, taking her hand and squeezing her fingers until the blood seemed to stand still within them, "this is torture to me."

"And what do you suppose it is to me?" she retorted. "It is not only torture but insult. You have brought me to this. I loved you so intensely and trusted you so implicitly, I never paused to think. I have lived like a blind fool in the present, happy when with you, dreaming of you when away, drifting on, on, in wild Elysium, hoping—yes, hoping, I suppose—that some day I might be your wife, or if not that, at any rate that I could still continue to respect myself and respect you. To think that you, you, whom I trusted so much, should insult me like this," and she buried her face in her hands and sobbed.

"My darling, I cannot marry," he replied. "It is not your position, it is not the stage, it is nothing to do with you that makes me say so. Had it been possible I should have asked you to be my wife a year ago or more, but, little girl, dearest love, how can I tell you?" and almost choking with emotion he added, *I am a married man.*"

She left his side and staggered to the other end of the boat, where, throwing herself upon the cushions, she wept as if her heart would break.

"Have I deserved this," she cried, "that you in smiling guise should come to me as an emblem of happiness? You have stolen my love from me, and oh, your poor, poor, wretched wife!"

She was a good, honest, womanly girl, and even in her own anguish of heart did not forget she was not the only sufferer from such treachery.

In a torrent of words he told her how he had married when a student at the 'Varsity—married beneath him—how his life had ever since been misery. How the pretty girl-bride had developed into a vulgar woman, how for years she and her still commoner family had dogged his footsteps, how he had paid and paid to be rid of her, how his whole existence had been ruined by the indiscretion of his youth, and the wiles of the designing landlady's daughter, how he had never felt respect and love for woman until he had met her, *Number II. on the Left.*

It was a tragic moment in both their lives. He felt the awful sin he had committed in not telling her from the first that he could never marry. He felt the injustice of it all, the punishment for his own folly that had fallen upon him, and she, poor soul, not only realised the shock to her ideal, but the horrible barrier that had risen between them.

*   *   *   *   *

They travelled up to town together, both silent—each feeling that all the world was changed. They parted at Victoria—she would not let him see her home.

The idol of two years was rudely shattered, the happy dreams of life had suddenly turned to miserable reality.

He returned to his chambers, where he cursed himself, and cursed his luck, as he walked up and down his rooms all night, and realised the root of the misery lay in the deception he had practised. He, whose life had been ruined by the deception of a designing, low-class minx, had himself in his turn committed the selfsame sin of misrepresentation. The thought was maddening; his remorse intense. But alack! the past cannot be recalled, and the curse that had followed him for many years he had, alas! cast over a sinless girl.

Sarah Hopper returned to her cheap little lodging at Islington, for after two years' hard work her salary was still only 30s. a week, and throwing herself into an arm-chair, she sat and thought. Her head throbbed as if it would burst, her eyes seemed on fire as she reviewed the whole story from every possible side. She had been a blind fool; she had trusted in a man she believed a good man, the web of fate had entangled her, and this—this was the end. She could never see him again.

By morning she was in a high state of fever, and when the landlady came to her later in the day she was so alarmed at her appearance she sent at once for the doctor. The doctor came.

"Mental shock," he said.

Days went by and in wild delirium the little chorus girl lay upon her bed in the lodging, till one night when the landlady had fallen asleep the broken-hearted girl managed to scramble up, and getting a piece of paper and an envelope wrote:

"You have killed me, but for the sake of the honest love of those two years, I forgive you all."

She addressed it in a firm hand to Alan Murray, and crawling back into bed fell asleep.

A few hours later the landlady awoke; all was silent in the room—so silent, in fact, that she began to wonder. The wild raving had ceased, the restless head was no longer tossing about on the pillow. Drawing back the muslin curtains to let the light of early morning—that soft gentle light of a summer's day—pour into the room, she went across to the bed.

The kindly old woman bent over the broken-hearted girl to find her sleeping peacefully—the sleep of death.

Lector House believes that a society develops through a two-fold approach of continuous learning and adaptation, which is derived from the study of classic literary works spread across the historic timeline of literature records. Therefore, we aim at reviving, repairing and redeveloping all those inaccessible or damaged but historically as well as culturally important literature across subjects so that the future generations may have an opportunity to study and learn from past works to embark upon a journey of creating a better future.

This book is a result of an effort made by Lector House towards making a contribution to the preservation and repair of original ancient works which might hold historical significance to the approach of continuous learning across subjects.

HAPPY READING & LEARNING!

LECTOR HOUSE LLP
E-MAIL: lectorpublishing@gmail.com